Paperback Cellulloid: Elmore Leonard on Film

Writers-on-Film 2022

By: Andy Rohmer
Cover art: Maria Ramos
Editing, layout and marketing: Ana Ramos

Copyright © 2023 Eduardo Ramos

LIBRARY OF CONGRESS CATALOG IN PUBLICATION DATA
Rohmer, Andy
Paperback Cellulloid: Elmore Leonard on Film
Registration # TXu 002351387
ISBN: 9798366227971

Writers-on-Film Bodrum Lisbon London New York

PAPERBACK CELLULOID
Elmore Leonard on film

Andy Rohmer

Contents

Introduction	1

Part I: The Writer	**6**
Biographical Sketch	7
Literary Work	16
Working methods	16
Influences	17
Themes	21
Style	26
Periodization	29
Position in American literature	30

Part II: The Films	**33**
3:10 to Yuma (1957)	34
3:10 to Yuma (2007)	41
Border Shootout (1990)	46
The Tall T (1957)	51
Last Stand at Saber River (1997)	58
Hombre (1967)	62
The Big Bounce (1969)	69
The Big Bounce (2004)	74
The Moonshine War (1970)	78
Valdez is Coming (1971)	85
Joe Kidd (1972)	90

Mr. Majestyk (1974)	96
The Ambassador (1984)	102
Fifty-Two Pickup (1986)	107
Life of Crime (2013)	113
High Noon Part II - The Return of Will Kane (1980)	118
Gold Coast (1997)	122
Split Images (1992)	126
Cat Chaser (1989)	132
Stick (1985)	138
Glitz (1988)	146
The Rosary Murders (1987)	152
Desperado (1987)	157
Touch (1997)	161
Freaky Deaky (2012)	170
Killshot (2008)	176
Get Shorty (1995)	183
Jackie Brown (1997)	191
Pronto (1997)	201
Out of Sight (1998)	206
Be Cool (1998)	217
Conclusion	224
Sources and Bibliography	227

Introduction

The reason why I wrote this book is I thought it would be fun. But in order to blacken a few more lines I'll expand: it resulted from a lifelong love of film, a comparatively recent discovery of Elmore Leonard's work, and a curiosity in ascertaining to what extent the film adaptations of his novels or original screenplays would lend themselves to orthodox auteur analysis, an admittedly severely outdated critical approach to film which nevertheless still runs strongly in my veins.

The menu was mouthwatering: Elmore Leonard wrote 45 novels, 9 of which Westerns, 3 of which "historical",[1] the remaining 33 being an admixture of crime thriller, caper and/or police procedural – the author was never enthusiastic about shoehorning his work into accepted genres – he is most renowned for. He further wrote 9 screenplays, 4 adapted from his novels, 1 which served as basis for a novel published after the film's release and a further 4 which were written directly for the screen and were never published in book format. Additionally, 2 of his early 50s Western short stories were also adapted to the screen, 1 of them twice.

All in all, 31 films were made from books (23), scripts (5) or short stories (3) written by Elmore Leonard. His writing career spanned more than 60 years, from 1951, when he published his first Western short story (*Trail of the Apache*) to 2012, the year before his death, when he published his last novel (*Raylan*). The film adaptations

---

[1] *The Moonshine War* (1969) takes place during Prohibition, *Cuba Libre* (1998) immediately before the Spanish-American War of 1898, and *Up in Honey's Room* (2007) during World War II.

thereof span, to date,[2] from 1957, when the 2 short stories were first adapted to the screen (*The Tall T*, by Budd Boetticher, and *3.10 to Yuma*, by Delmer Daves), to 2013 (*Life of Crime*, by Daniel Schechter, and adaptation of the 1978 novel *The Switch*). 25 films were produced for the big screen and 6 for TV. With the exception of Delmer Daves' *3.10 to Yuma*, all were shot in colour. A few were major productions directed by major directors (Quentin Tarantino), some were minor or average productions directed by major directors (Bud Boetticher, Richard Fleischer) some others, mostly for TV, routine fare directed by illustrious unknowns. The rest falls somewhere in between.

Few writers, and possibly none of the stature of Elmore Leonard, had so much of their output adapted to the screen. From the 1960's on he admitted he often wrote with an eye on film rights, and from the late 70's onwards the vast majority of his work was filmed, including most of his novels from the 50's to the mid-70's. After the turn of the century the fashion faded, and only 4 films were produced since then, all based on novels written before 2000. Is there unity to this eclecticism? That's what I intend to find out. Two notes on methodology: (1) it is chronologically reverse-auteurish, meaning the films will be covered by order of the publication of the novels, which, with the exception of the 4 unpublished screenplays, were very often produced years or decades after the books they are based on, meaning that the sequence of the book will flash back and forward from the 1950s to the 2010s in consideration of bibliographical order, a

---

[2] At the time of writing, several further adaptations of Leonard's work are in consideration or preproduction: *Bandits*, the film rights of which were bought by Bruce Willis in 1988 and which has been announced on and off since 2015, *Forty Lashes Less One*, hyped to be in preproduction by Quentin Tarantino since 2015. *The Trespassers*, based on a posthumously published short story written in 1958, to be directed by Anna Chazelle, seems at this stage to be the one closer to materializing.

table illustrating this being attached hereunder; (2) this book does not address the 5 Elmore Leonard novels adapted to TV series. Incidentally, 3 of these were also adapted to film: *Get Shorty* (Barry Sonnenfeld, 1995), *Pronto* (Jim McBride, 1997), and *Out of Sight* (Steven Soderbergh, 1998). The other two are *Riding the Rap* (1995) and *Rayland*, which, together with *Pronto* and several earlier short stories, were bungled together in the TV Western series *Justified*, which ran 6 seasons from 2010 to 2016.

List of Elmore Leonard literary works and film adaptations, by order of publication (screenplays excepted)

Year	Novel/short story/screenplay	Film adaptation
1953	*Three-Ten to Yuma*	1957 - *Three-Ten to Yuma* 2010 - *Three-Ten to Yuma*
1954	*The Law at Randado*	1990 – *Border Shootout*
1955	The Captives	1957 – *The Tall T*
1959	*Last Stand at Saber River*	1997 – *Last Stand at Saber River*
1961	*Hombre*	1967 – *Hombre*
1969	*The Big Bounce*	1969 – *The Big Bounce* 2004 – *The Big Bounce*

Year	Novel/short story/screenplay	Film adaptation
	The Moonshine War	1970 – *The Moonshine War*
1970	*Valdez Is Coming*	1971 – *Valdez Is Coming*
1972	*Joe Kidd*	1972 – *Joe Kidd*
1974	*Mr. Majestyk*	1974 – *Mr. Majestyk*
1974	*Fifty-Two Pickup*	1984 – The Ambassador 1986 – *52 Pick-Up*
1976	*The Switch*	2013 – *Life of Crime*
1980	*High Noon, Part II*	1980 - *High Noon, Part II*
1980	*Gold Coast*	1997 – *Gold Coast*
1981	*Split Images*	1992 – *Split Images*
1982	*Cat Chaser*	1989 – *Cat Chaser*
1983	*Stick*	1985 – *Stick*
1985	*Glitz*	1988 – *Glitz*
1987	*The Rosary Murders*	1987 - *The Rosary Murders*

Year	Novel/short story/screenplay	Film adaptation
	Desperado	1987 – *Desperado*
	Touch	1997 – *Touch*
1988	*Freaky Deaky*	2012 – *Freaky Deaky*
1989	*Killshot*	2008 – *Killshot*
1990	*Get Shorty*	1995 – *Get Shorty*
1992	*Rum Punch*	1997 – *Jackie Brown*
1993	*Pronto*	1997 – *Pronto*
1996	*Out of Sight*	1998 – *Out of Sight*
1999	*Be Cool*	2005 – *Be Cool*

Part I:
The Writer

Biographical Sketch

Elmore Leonard was born in New Orleans, Louisiana, on 11 October 1925, the second child of Flora Amelia (née Rive), of Alsatian origin, and Elmore John Leonard Sr, Irish-American. His big sister, Margaret, was 6 years his senior.[3] Because his father worked as a site locator for General Motors, the family moved several times, to Dallas, Oklahoma City and Memphis, before finally settling in Detroit in 1934. Although Leonard left New Orleans at a very young age, the city left a lasting impression on him, portrayed vividly in novels like *La Brava* (1983) and *Bandits* (1987).[4]

In Detroit, Leonard enrolled in the Blessed Sacrament catholic school,[5] where he showed the first signs of his literary and "secondary" cinematic calls: he loved to watch movies and tell their stories to his classmates,[6] and wrote a school play inspired by Erich Maria Remarque's *All Quiet on the Western Front*, serialized at the time in a Detroit newspaper in the wake of the success of the eponymous film adaptation directed by Lewis Milestone, which had won the Oscar for the best film in 1930.

Throughout high school, Leonard spent much of his free time playing baseball and football. Writing, other than for schoolwork, took second stage. It was during this period a classmate gave him his nickname, "Dutch", after the Washington Senators baseball team player Emil "Dutch" Leonard, who pitched for the team from 1938 to 1946 and

---

[3] Paul Challen, *Get Dutch! A Biography of Elmore Leonard*, ECW Press, Toronto, 2000, p.19.
[4] James E Devlin, *Elmore Leonard*, Twayne Publishers, New York, 1999, p.4.
[5] Devlin, op. et loc. cit.
[6] Challen, op. cit. p.8.

got the nickname due to his Flemish heritage. Elmore Leonard wore it with pride, literally: he had it tattooed.[7]

He graduated from the University of Detroit Jesuit High School in 1943 and joined the Navy, serving for three years in the South Pacific. It was during this period that Leonard developed his enthusiasm for beer, later to progress to wine and whisky.[8] After the end of World War II Leonard returned to Detroit, enrolling at the University of Detroit in 1946, and started to pursue writing more seriously, entering his work in short story contests and submitting it to magazines for publication. In 1947 is father opened his own GM dealership in Las Cruces, New Mexico. Leonard Sr's intentions were that junior would eventually join him in the car sales business, a prospect which at the time did not displease the future writer, but when his father died in 1948, GM decided against this option, decision which might be the origin of one of the most remarkable American literary careers of the 20th and early 21st Centuries.[9]

In 1949 he married Beverly Clare Cline, with whom he would have five children — two daughters and three sons — and around the same year he got a job as a copy writer with the Campbell-Ewald Advertising Agency, a position he kept for several years, reportedly excelling at ads for Chevrolet trucks.[10] His writing was much appreciated for its freshness and inspiration but sometimes felt to be too forward.[11]

---

[7] Done in Seattle, cost 1$. Cf. 'The Sound of Young America: Elmore Leonard', Jesse Thorn, 3rd July 2007, Maximum Fun, https://maximumfun.org/episodes/bullseye-with-jesse-thorn/podcast-tsoya-elmore-leonard/ (accessed 3 August 2021).
[8] Devlin, op. cit. p.5.
[9] Challen, op. cit. p.27.; Charles Rzekpa, Being Cool: The Work of Elmore Leonard, Johns Hopkins University Press, Baltimer, 2003, p.45.
[10] David Geherin, Elmore Leonard, Continuum, New York, 1989, p.3.
[11] Geherin, op. et loc. cit.

Elmore Leonard graduated in 1950 with a bachelor's degree in English and Philosophy. He received his first break in the fiction market during the 1950s, regularly publishing pulp Western novels and short stories.[12] He decided to try the genre because he liked western films but also because he found the average writing quality of the material published easy to compete with.[13] He had his first success in 1951, when *Argosy* published the short story *Trail of the Apache*, for which he got 1000$,[14] a welcome financial supplement for a 25 year old father of one with another on the way who made 275$ a week in an advertising company.[15] To make matters better, he was subsequently approached by New York literary agent Margaret Harper,[16] who subsequently represented Leonard until her death in 1966 and with whom he maintained a vivid correspondence (including a piece of advice not to quit his day job until he hit big time)[17] someone might wish to compile and publish sometime.[18] During the 1950s and early 1960s, he continued writing Westerns, publishing 5 novels and more than 30 short stories. He wrote his first novel, *The Bounty Hunters*, in 1953, sold for 3,000$, followed by four other Westerns.[19] During this period he also published over 20 short stories in all the major coeval Western pulp magazines, such as *Argosy* or *Gunsmoke*.

---

[12] Which, according to one secondary source (available at *Life Between Frames*, http://lifebetweenframes.blogspot.com/2016/05/why-dont-you-come-to-your-senses.html (accessed 5th January 2022), initially sold for 2 cents a word.
[13] Devlin, op. cit. p.7.
[14] Jesse Thorn, loc. cit.
[15] Geherin, op. cit. p.5.
[16] Challen, op. cit. p.30.
[17] Jesse Thorn, loc. cit. Also, Devlin, op. et loc. cit.
[18] Challen, op. et loc. cit.; Devlin, op. cit. p.9.
[19] Devlin, op. cit. p.10.

1957 was a watershed year for Elmore Leonard, as two major films based on his short stories were released: *The Tall T* (Budd Boetticher) and *3.10 to Yuma* (Delmer Daves) the latter – and in my view by far the lesser - being selected in 2012 by the US Library of Congress for the National Film Registry as being "culturally, historically or aesthetically" significant. In 1961 he published *Hombre*, the last and best of his early Westerns, and in a leap of faith disregarded Margaret Harper's advice and quit his job at Campbell-Ewing to become a full time writer.[20]

Unfortunately, this decision coincided with the sudden and steep fall of popularity of the Western, both on screen and in print, and *Hombre*, although his best, took more than 2 years to sell, forcing Leonard to go freelance and establish his own small ad agency, which supported him until Fox bought the film rights for the novel in 1965 for 10.000$. The following year Margaret Harper died and Leonard found a new agent in the person of H L Swanson, who represented the likes of Fitzgerald and Faulkner in their dealings with Hollywood. Upon reading the first works Leonard sent him, Swanson reportedly asked: "did you really write this?" and, receiving and affirmative reply, proclaimed: "kiddo, I am going to make you rich", a pledge he subsequently fulfilled.[21]

1969 marked the beginning of the end of the lean period and a major turning point for Leonard's writing career, after an 8 year publishing hiatus: after 2 years, 84 rejections and a title change, H N Swanson finally sold *The Big Bounce*, Leonard's first crime novel, for 50.000$, to Gold Medal Books.[22] Equally importantly, this was Leonard's first

---

[20] Cashing in his 11.500$ profit-sharing plan, which he subsequently put that against the mortgage of a house (Jesse Thorn, loc. cit.).
[21] Quotations of this exchange are profuse. See Devlin, op. cit., p.13; Geherin, op. cit., p 9.
[22] Challen, op. cit. p.61.

novel – and one of very few, as the table in the previous chapter shows – to be adapted to the screen immediately upon publication. From now on, Leonard would be a well-to-do caper writer/screenwriter, with a solid reputation in the publishing and film businesses, if still a relative unknown to the general public.

In 1972 Leonard sold his first screenplay, Joe Kidd, to Clint Eastwood. His professional success, however, was offset by personal and health problems. His drinking got worse, to the point of being hospitalized for vomiting blood and being arrested several times for DUI.[23] In 1974 he left Beverly, moved to a separate apartment, and wrote Fifty-Two Pickup," which established his writing direction for the next 20 plus years",[24] catching the attention of the New York Times, a clear sign that the literary critical establishment had begun to take him seriously.[25] The novel also inaugurated the Detroit phase of Leonard's crime fiction, being the first of what his biographer Charles Rzepka calls "the Motor City Five", a series of five crime novels set in the city, still Leonard's home town, written between 1974 and 1980.[26]

In 1977 Leonard quit drinking "exactly at 9.00 AM January 24 1977", stopped attending daily mass, joined the AA and divorced Beverly.[27] Four biographies, two monographies, two TV documentaries and several in-depth interviews notwithstanding, the reason behind Leonard's estrangement from his wife of 24 years and mother of five children remains obscure. Also this year, Hombre was

---

[23] Leonard would later claimed drinking had become a routine rather than a means of escape or an addiction, cf. Challen, op. cit. p.67.
[24] Devlin, op. cit., p.15
[25] New York Times Book Review, 4 April 1976, p.34. Quoted in Geherin, op. cit., p.14, footnote 26.
[26] Rzepka, op. cit. p.92.
[27] Geherin, op. cit., p.129.

named one of the twenty-five best western novels of all time (#24) by Western Writers of America.

In 1979 Leonard married Joan Shepard, whom he had met during his separation from Beverly, and who was to become a significant influence in his life and work, including concerning his awareness of gender issues.[28] In the same year he was interviewed for the *Monthly Detroit* by journalist and long-time fan Greg Sutter, who was to become his lifelong associate as researcher and location scout.[29] Despite his growing literary reputation, Leonard still lived mostly off screenplays, doing hack jobs for indifferent fare like *High Noon II* (1980), for which CBS paid him 50.000$.[30]

Literarily, after the Detroit phase came the Florida phase, started in 1980 with *Gold Coast*. The change of setting didn't entail a change of style or subject matter and even most of the early characters of this phase were Detroiters. *LaBrava*, a Floridian novel published in 1983, received the Edgar Award, and was the occasion for a *New York Times* review which "promoted" Leonard from mystery writer to novelist [31]. His next book, *Glitz*, an Atlantic City gambling story published in 1985, spent 16 weeks on *The New York Times* Bestseller list (Leonard remained there practically permanently until his death). The same year he received the Michigan Foundation of the Arts Award.[32]

---

[28] Challen, op. cit. p.82.
[29] Challen, op. et loc. cit. See also Geherin, *The Sense of Place in Elmore Leonard's Crime Fiction*. Rzepka, op. (ed) cit. p.51.
[30] Geherin, op. cit., p.14.
[31] *The Edgars,* http://theedgars.com/awards/ (accessed 3 August 2021).
[32] *Michigan News*, 2000, https://news.umich.edu/elmore-leonard-to-speak-dec-17-at-winter-commencement/ (accessed 3 August 2021).

The novels that followed were all best sellers, and by now Leonard's advance on a book was 1-1,5M$.[33] Compounding his commercial and critical success, Leonard's reputation was branching out to *Rolling Stone*,[34] *Heavy Metal*[35] and even *Playgirl*, which in 1987 selected him as one of the ten sexiest men of the year. Characteristically, upon being informed of the distinction, Leonard quipped he wondered what year was that.[36] In the same year he published two novels, the last time he would be this productive: *Bandits* and the very uncharacteristically spiritual *Touch*. Baffled at success so lately earned, he mused "these days, I could sell my letters to my mother".[37] Accolades and honours kept coming: in 1991 he received the International Association of Crime Writers' Hammett Prize, the first of its kind, for *Maximum Bob*, and in 1992 the Mystery Writers of America Grand Master Award, which is to the Edgar Award roughly what the Lifetime Achievement Oscar is to the standard Oscar.[38]

As sometimes happens, grief struck Leonard at the height of his artistic and commercial success. Joan died of cancer in January 1993. The available literature omits details on the effect the loss of his partner and most trusted advisor of two decades had on him. What is known is that later that same year he met Christine Kent, 23 years his junior, who worked in a gardening company he had hired to take care of their garden after Joan died. In June he asked

---

[33] Challen, op. cit., p.131.
[34] Geherin, op. cit., p.16.
[35] *Heavy Metal*, January 1984, P 4, quoted in Geherin, op. cit, p 141 footnote 39.
[36] Geherin, op. et loc. cit.
[37] Ben Yagoda, 'Elmore Leonard's Rogues' Gallery' *New York Times Magazine*, 30 December 1984, p. 22. Quoted in Geherin, op. cit. p.17 footnote 37.
[38] http://www.crimewritersna.org/hammett/past.html

her for a date, the first time he had done so in some 45 years.[39] They married on the 19th of August.

Leonard spent the next two decades with Catherine in their home in the affluent Detroit suburb of Bloomfield Hills. These years were awash with success and acknowledgement. Along the nascent scholarly attention the footnotes to this chapter document, he continued to write books at a rate of almost one a year, almost always with critical and commercial success. 1995 witnessed the film adaptation of *Get Shorty* (1991) which triggered the cinematic wave of adaptations that consecrated Leonard's pop icon status. 18 of the 31 films based on his work were produced thereafter. Asked if it wasn't frustrating to hit the real big time only at the age of 70 after 45 of working at writing, Leonard gave a typical Leonardian reply: "No, because it's a fact".[40]

In 1996 he received an honorary doctorate at the Atlantic University of Florida.[41] In 2000 the University of Michigan did the same,[42] followed by the University of Detroit Mercy in 2007.[43] But not all the awards he received in his later years were *honoris causa*. In 2008 he received the F. Scott Fitzgerald Literary Award, previously bestowed on

---

[39] Challen, op. cit. p.141.
[40] Challen, op. cit. p.132. But when inquired on this point in an interview he considered less laconically: "(...) I've always done very well. It never occurred to me during all those years that I wasn't successful". *UPI Arts and Entertainment* 23 January 1987, quoted in Geherin, op. cit. p. 17 footnote 4.
[41] Honorary Doctorate Recipients, *Florida Atlantic University*, https://www.fau.edu/president/awards/honorary-doctorates/ (accessed 3 August 2021).
[42] 'Elmore Leonard to speak Dec. 17 at winter commencement' November 16 2000, *Michigan News*, https://news.umich.edu/elmore-leonard-to-speak-dec-17-at-winter-commencement/ (accessed 12 August 2021).
[43] 'Leonard, Elmore "Dutch"', 2007, *Detroit Mercy*, https://libraries.udmercy.edu/archives/special-collections/index.php?record_id=327&collectionCode=honors_hon (accessed 12 August 2021).

Joyce Carol Oates, Norman Mailer, EL Doctorow and John Updike, among others.[44] In 2009, the Owen Sister Lifetime achievement award of the Western Writers of America, repeating the double whammy he had on the Edgar 17 years before.[45] In 2012 he was awarded the National Book Awards Medal for Distinguished Contribution, also bestowed on Toni Morrison and Saul Bellow, to name but Nobel Laureates.

That same year, Elmore Leonard and Christine Kent divorced, for reasons unknown. On July 29, 2013 Leonard suffered a stroke and on August 20 he died at home of stroke complications, less than two months shy of his 88th birthday.

---

[44] 'The History', *F. Scott Fitzgerald Literary Festival*, https://www.fscottfestival.org/ourhistory (accessed 12 August 2021).
[45] 'The Owen Wister Award', *Western Writers*, https://westernwriters.org/the-owen-wister-award/ (accessed 12 August 2021).

Literary Work
Working methods

A professional and commercially oriented writer, Elmore Leonard never saw himself as an artist, or at least never admitted as much.[46] Between the early 50's and 1961, he tried to reconcile ad agency work with writing, which he did every morning from 5 to 7, not allowing himself to have coffee before he wrote at least two pages.[47] At 7 he would leave home to attend daily mass before going to work.[48] After starting to work full time he kept a strict 9.30 AM to 6.00 PM writing schedule, which he relaxed only in his 70s.

Elmore Leonard composed longhand and rewrote until he thought he reached the final product, subsequently typing his own manuscript. At this stage, changes to the text were generally minor. During his years with Joan, at the end of the day he would sometimes read manuscripts to her and she would comment uninhibitedly, comments Leonard often took into account.[49]

Although Leonard wrote with film rights as more than an afterthought, he always kept the industry at a respectful

---

[46] "My purpose is to entertain and tell a story", cf. Geherin, op cit, p.135 footnote 27. Brings to mind Hitchcock, who also claimed he didn't see himself "particularly" as an artist, oblivious or indifferent to Malraux's "art and industry" maxim. This attitude might be generally attributable to the "commercial versus artistic" antithetic mindset dominant in the US, perhaps to this day.

[47] Challen, op. cit. p.33; Geherin, op cit p.76; Rzepka, op. cit. p.22. Not sure, personally, this rule necessarily propitiates quality writing, but the published result strongly vouches against me.

[48] Guilio Sedato, *Una commedia americana – Temi, innovazioni e religione nell'opera di Elmore Leonard*, Mimesis, Milan, 2018, p.141. Other Leonard scholars also allude to this, but Segato is the only one to have written an entire book on the religion connection. Although both his parents were catholic, neither was nearly as devout as Leonard, who seems to have bucked his generation's general trend toward secularization.

[49] Geherin, op. cit. p.18. See also Geherin, *The Sense of Place in Elmore Leonard's Crime Fiction*, Rzepka op. (ed) cit. p.52.

distance, often flying from Detroit to LA in the morning for meetings with producers and the like and returning to Detroit late the same evening. In an interview to *American Film* in December 1984 he explained: "Limos are seductive. They make you feel important and the next thing you know you're taking yourself too seriously".[50]

The employment of Gregg Sutter as full-time researcher and location scout satisfied Leonard's obsession with accurate detail and with the minutiae of the things he wrote about, be they Native American ethnography, police procedure or weapons, which are often described in detail in his novels,[51] although the author himself never owned one.[52] In his mid-70s Leonard was asked by Challen why he still kept such an assiduous and presumably taxing publishing rate, to which Leonard replied: "Because it's the most fun thing I can think of doing".[53]

Influences

The first major influence on Elmore Leonard's fiction were the Western films he saw in his childhood and puberty, in particular those featuring Gary Cooper, an avowed favourite, whose screen characters were the model for Leonard's Western protagonists. As previously mentioned, Leonard started his literary career with Western novels, a genre he himself was not in the habit of reading, because he thought, rightly in retrospect, it would be easy to beat the competition. Influence by, or even awareness of, writers such as Louis L'Amour was simply absent.[54] Revealingly, in

---

[50] Geherin, op. cit. p.43, footnote 4
[51] Geherin, op. cit. p.80; Devlin, op. cit. p.115.
[52] Devlin, op. cit. p.35.
[53] Challen, op. cit. p.158.
[54] Sedato, op. cit. p.19 passim.

light of Leonard's later scriptwriting, other films, foremost, as alluded to above, *All Quiet on the Western Front*, were also early major influences.[55]

James Devlin, Guilio Sedato and to a lesser extent Rzepka devote some space to the influence of James Fenimore Cooper on Leonard's work.[56] Never having read Cooper I will not comment, except to state that these three scholars themselves leave the impression that this putative influence was more in the general nature of Cooper's importance for the development of Western fiction and in the creation of the American Frontier myth, thus framing Leonard's Western output as much as anyone else's, rather than constituting a direct thematic or stylistic ascendancy.

Universally acknowledged, including by the author himself, is the influence of Ernest Hemingway, in particular *For Whom the Bell Tolls*.[57] Rzepka specifically points out to the "Hemingway code" as a model for the ethics of Leonard protagonists and Sedato, to me more perceptively, points out to the element of irony and humour present in Leonard's work but all but absent in Hemingway (in fairness I must disclose it's been over 40 years since I read *For Whom the Bell Tolls*, and have otherwise not read much Hemingway lately).

Other relevant influences, not nearly as reputedly strong as Hemingway's but which resonate more with me personally, are John Steinbeck,[58] for the unmistakable

---

[55] 'The Elmore Leonard Interviews', *CrimeCulture*, https://www.crimeculture.com/?page_id=3435 (accessed 28 September 2021).

[56] Devlin, op. cit. p.33 passim; Rzepka op. cit. p.65, 165; Sedato op. et loc cit. Sedato actually chooses the same title as Devlin to expand his thesis: "*From Cooper (Gary) to Cooper (James Fenimore)*".

[57] Devlin, op. cit. p.8 passim; Geherin, op. cit. p.4-5 passim; Sedato, op. cit. p.20 passim, Rzepka, op. cit. p.8 passim. Also 'The Elmore Leonard Interviews', *CrimeCulture*.

[58] Sedato op, cit. p.30.

American voice, James M Cain,[59] his writing perhaps boiled harder than Leonard's but of whom Dutch was a fan, and John dos Passos, in particular *Manhattan Transfer*, for its transposition of cinematic language to literary technique, again maybe less a direct influence than a building block of narrative language.[60] Maybe trying too hard to establish academic credentials, Rzepka quotes Camus and Sartre as indirect influences on Leonard, who is on record confirming recollections of reading the two authors in his college days,[61] but even in his post-Western phase it would be hard to detect direct traces of Camus' or Sartre's style in Leonard, and as for their ethics, either due to a different sensitivity or to the exigencies of American commercial publishing, Leonard's novels always provide for a closure, good or bad, which is markedly absent in the fiction of the two classic existentialists.[62] Inevitably, Dashiell Hammet and Raymond Chandler are also frequently cited in connection with Leonard, but the author stated on several occasions he never felt that influence, pointing out he never wrote a whodunit.[63]

After *For Whom the Bell Tolls*, the second major canonical influence on Leonard's writing was Georgie V Higgins' *The Friends of Eddie Coyle*, a crisp 1970 crime thriller which is about 90% dialogue and is often ranked at the very top of the genre, which Elmore himself said helped him "find

---

[59] Geherin, op. cit. p.98 passim.
[60] Sedato op. cit. p.27.
[61] Rzepka op. cit. p.208, footnote 26.
[62] *A contrario*, Kris Mecholski makes a persuasive case for the impact of 20th Century existentialism in Leonard's work in *The Mozart of the Motor City*, Rzepka op. (ed) cit. p.81.
[63] Indeed, Sedato writes (op. cit. p.71): "*Anche in Leonard il crimine, di solto un assassínio, viene scoperto quasi súbito ma, a differenza della tradizione a enigma, anche il colpevole dell'omicidio viene rivelato nelle prime pagine del romanzo*"

his sound".[64] Again perceptively, Sedato considers that the reading of *The Friends of Eddie Coyle* didn't represent a significant change in Leonard's writing style so much as an encouragement for him to persist in his own.[65]

Much less mentioned, but mentioned by Leonard himself, with perhaps excessive elation, as his greatest influence, is Richard Bissell, in particular his novels about the Mississippi River, *A Stretch on the River* (1950) and *High Water* (1954).[66]

A final note on jazz, in particular 50's-60's bebop and hard bop. "I listen to jazz and it inspires me to write", Leonard told Rzepka, who goes on to associate improvisation and West Coast cool with Dutch's writing style.[67] Acknowledging jazz as one of several of Leonard's sources of inspiration doesn't necessarily imply, in my view, a correlation between jazzy improvisation and the meandering narrative structures Leonard developed from the late 60s on. Jazz was part of the mid-century cultural ecosystem Leonard portrays, as much as cars, bars, guns, hotels and motels. In this regard, one excerpt of *Glitz* seems to merit transcription: Jazz singer Linda muses "(...) *most of what I have to play, you take it out of a can and heat it over a low fire. Some of it's OK, some riffs you can have fun with, fool around. But you do the same kind of pop stuff every set, the computer music, key in a little bossa nova - I feel like an engineer, I ought to be wearing a white lab coat with a row of pencils in the pocket. Once in a while, I play with my own guys we throw the charts away and break loose, take some chances.*

---

[64] Geherin, op. cit. p.10. See also Challen op. cit. p.76; Devlin, op. cit. p.16-17; Rzepka, op. cit. p.20 passim.
[65] Segato, op. cit. p.34.
[66] Leonard to Geherin in Geherin op. cit.
[67] Rzepka, op. cit. p.43, and Rzepka, *Pitching Cinematic Identification in Get Shorty*, op. (ed) cit. p.129. Also 'The Elmore Leonard Interviews', *CrimeCulture*.

Who's doing that and getting paid? Nobody. McCoy Tyner, Gil Evans, maybe a few other guys. Let the audience keep up if they can - why not? They can tap their toes if they want, but it's a head trip too. Where were going - who knows? Let's find out, feel it and play it, look for an opening and break out... Do you know what I mean?".[68] Yes Linda/Elmore, we do (nothing wrong with feeling like an engineer musician with a row of pencils in your pocket, though, think Kraftwerk).

Themes

Elmore Leonard's published fiction, a few short stories and *Touch* (1987) excepted, be they Westerns, historical novels or capers, follow a standard dramatic pattern: a protagonist, mostly male, encounters difficulties of a dangerous nature and normally overcomes them, or, more rarely, falls victim of them, as in *Swag* (1976), by using cunning and/or violence, frequently with the help of a co-protagonist of the opposite sex.[69]

The foremost characteristic of Leonardian fiction is the Leonardian "cool", to some extent derived from the aforementioned Hemingway "code", the τέχνη Rzekpa comments on extensively:[70] a sort of oral and behavioural minimalism, to move, as Sade Adu sang back in her 1984 hit *'Smooth Operator'*, "with minimum waste and maximum joy", or as the Bahavad Gita preaches, to act the act you have to act without growing fond of the act or expecting

---

[68] Elmore Leonard, *Glitz*, 1985, p.223 (Harper Torch 2002 edition).
[69] See J Cawelty, *Mistery, Violence and Popular Culture*, Popular Press, 2004, p.160. Quoted in Sedato, p.165 footnote 2.
[70] Rzepka op. cit. p. 12 passim.

the consequences of the act,[71] or, like the Nike sportswear brand advertised in the 80s, to "just do it".[72] But Leonard's protagonists are very seldom efficient cool automata, they are normally average(ish) Joes or Janes victims of circumstance who develop or reveal heroic (in the etymological sense) qualities to overcome the problems they face.[73] This is Leonard's main empathetic device, to have people like you or me face a series of unfortunate events and, by confronting them, to triumph, unlike you or me probably would. "Leonard novels are about marginal people, small people incompetent even at petty crime, or (...) about quiet professionals who are underestimated".[74]

Indeed, Elmore Leonard's *Weltanschauung* diverges little from that of the average American, and therein may lie some of its gravitational power.[75] His characters are individualistic,[76] evince an unconscious belief in a sort of existential free will, and, - especially, but not exclusively, the bad girls/guys - are seldom above marked vanity and/or stupidity,[77] acting in the absence or unreliability of a normative or institutional framework,[78] left to, or opting for,

---

[71] *Bahavad Gita*, Chapter 2, verse 47. available at: https://www.holy-bhagavad-gita.org/chapter/2/verse/47 (accessed 28 September 2021). The responsibility for the free version in the main text is mine alone.

[72] Or, to add yet another attempt at definition, "their (Leonard's protagonists) existential tendency to perfect what they do best and leave others to do what they do best [Kris Mecholski, Rzepka op. (ed) cit. p.81].

[73] *Hombre*'s (1961) John Russel and *Valdez is Coming*'s (1970) Valdez come to mind as exceptions.

[74] George F Will, in the introduction to *Dutch Treat*, a compilation of Leonard's short fiction published in 1984. Quoted in Challen, op. cit. p.155.

[75] Devlin, op. cit. p.99.

[76] Segato, op. cit. p.172. In the same vein, in his essay on Leonard, Joseph Hymes perceptively characterizes Leonard's novels as *Bildungsromane*, adding that the reader never identifies with his characters, as they are too individual. "*High Noon in Detroit: Elmore Leonard's Career*", Joseph Hymes, *The Journal of Popular Culture*, Volume 25 (3) – Dec 1, 1991. Available at: https://www.deepdyve.com/lp/wiley/high-noon-in-detroit-elmore-leonard-s-career-B9otXRSBS0 (accessed 30th of August 2022)

[77] Devlin, op. cit. p.19 passim.

[78] "Leonard's trust in social organization is limited". Devlin, op. cit. p.115.

their own devices as they endeavour to obtain loads of money, either illicitly or with some kind of angle, whilst avoiding the sweat and tears part and parcel of the American Dream, which is the real American dream.

As a sort of "progressive" corollary of this all-American individualism, starting with his early western short stories and novels, Elmore showed interest in and sympathy for culturally diverse outsiders and underdogs, often making them protagonists. He characteristically develops his characters through dialogue, making their speech pattern and important layer of identification, be they cowboys, Indians, "frontier" women, African Americans (rendering jive with such unbiased and un-patronizing vividness African American readers often thought Leonard was black!) or Hispanics.[79]

Gender awareness was for Leonard more of a learning process. In his early Western phase his female characters were secondary and formulaic, usually the wholesome stoic bride and mother to be or the disruptive harlot.[80] *Last Stand at Saber River* (1959) introduces an important innovation in Leonard's fiction: Lorraine Kidston, the Yankee usurper's daughter, who teases Southern usurped confederate vet Paul Gable and plays both sides to stave off boredom, the stereotypical wanton psycho which will appear in some later works, often crucial for plot development, of which the most notable example is Nancy Hayes in *The Big Bounce*. This may not necessarily be a paragon of gender enlightenment, but it does bear noticing that Leonard was as much if not more creative with male psycho characters.

---

[79] Devlin, op. cit. p.33-35, Rzepka, op. cit. p.61 passim.
[80] But cf. Segato, op. cit. p.48-49, who points out that often in Elmore Leonard's early short fiction women take central roles in plot development and at least one main role (*The Colonel's Lady*, 1952). Segato further notes that the role ascribed to Apache and Mexican women is often unusually perceptive for the standards of 50s Western pulp.

As alluded to previously, the marriage with Joan Shepard signaled a number of important developments in Leonard's life and work. Specifically regarding gender, the writing of *The Switch* (1978), which is dedicated to Joan, inaugurates a new awareness, as Leonard's second wife reportedly shares with Chicago Free Press journalist Kate Warbelow the distinction of having inspired Leonard's development of female characters: Warbelow having pointed out to Leonard she thought his fiction portrayed women like Mickey Spillane's, Leonard, with characteristic coolness, mused he didn't think it was true but if the journalist felt so there must be something to it, so he proceeded to change his approach.[81] From love interest and moral supporters to Ibsen's Nora offspring (e.g. Karen from *Gold Coast*, 1980) or fully fledged main character (e.g Mickey from *The Switch*) the Leonard woman took almost 3 decades to come of age, but of age she came.

Other recurrent characteristics of Leonard's fiction are typical of coeval American fiction, especially of the noir vein: protagonists carrying the past (ex-cons, war vets, divorcees with estranged families, with a particular incidence of fathers missing little daughters, eg. *Swag*, *Switch* or *Stick*), or tutor-apprentice relationships not unlike those frequent in the work of that other great American anarcho-individualist, Robert A Heinlein. More particular of Leonard, and one of the defining traits of his fiction, is the last moment allegiance switch of the hero or the villain and the frequent latent symbiosis of both.

A word on the catholic question: as we saw, Leonard came from a Catholic background and was exceptionally devout until his detox in the late 70s, when his faith appears

---

[81] Challen, op. cit. p.85, Geherin op. cit. p.55, Rzepka p.63-65 passim.

to have moved to some sort of direct deist/non-denominational variety. The available literature, Leonard's interviews and Leonard's fiction give relatively little clues as to most aspects of his personal life, alcoholism excepted. Nonetheless, two scholars devote significant attention to religious reverberations in Leonard's work, Sedato to the point of having written an entire book on the subject and Rzepka identifying a tetralogy of "Catholic" books in Leonard's opus, namely *The Hunted* (1977), *Touch* (published 1987 but written 10 years before), *Bandits* (1987) and *Pagan Babies* (2000). Sedato's writing leaves the impression he is a Catholic himself so his sensitivity to catholic themes may be especially, maybe even excessively, enhanced. As for Rzepka, he admits the AA program "put some distance between Leonard and Catholicism", but this would have been only in the late 70s.[82] Perhaps more helpfully, Devlin contributes Leonard "has grafted onto his Catholicism – in its less restrictive and authoritarian forms - the largely Emersonian optimism and trust in self-reliance that has become the unofficial doctrine of the USA despite two World Wars and the Holocaust. (For Leonard) the church is mostly a distant memory".[83] I would tend to agree. I feel in Leonard mostly an American existential individualism taken matter-of-factly in stride, without anguish or exaltation.[84] There is an ethos but next to no metaphysics (here Sartre would disagree), even less religion, less even Christianity, least so of the Catholic variety.[85] There is no spiritual quest in Leonard. Existence very much precedes essence (here

---

[82] Rzepka addresses this matter extensively in p.185-200 op. cit.
[83] Devlin op. cit. p.100, 115.
[84] In his essay *Nostalgia and Authenticity in Elmore Leonard's Conflicted Heroes*, Michael Scrivener develops this idea further. Cf. Charles Rzepka's edited *Critical Essays on Elmore Leonard: If It Sounds Like Writing*, Wiley Blackwell, Hoboken, New Jersey 2020.
[85] Leonard did write an unsold and unpublished story titled *Jesus Saves*, Cf. Rzepka p.92.

Sartre would agree). God is either absent or so present as to not even warrant mention.

Style

The stylistic analysis of Elmore Leonard's writing benefits significantly from the testimony of the writer himself, who wrote a book on the matter, titled *Elmore Leonard's 10 Rules of Writing*, published in 2007. Although famous, these rules bear reproduction here:

- Never open a book with weather.
- Avoid prologues.
- Never use a verb other than "said" to carry dialogue.
- Never use an adverb to modify the verb "said": "...he admonished gravely".
- Keep your exclamation points under control. You are allowed no more than two or three per 100,000 words of prose.
- Never use the words "suddenly" or "all hell broke loose."
- Use regional dialect, patois, sparingly.
- Avoid detailed descriptions of characters.
- Don't go into great detail describing places and things.
- Try to leave out the part that readers tend to skip.

Leonard added: "My most important rule is one that sums up the 10: if I sounds like writing, I rewrite it."[86]

About 30 years previous, in *Swag*, my favourite Leonard novel, its main character Frank Ryan proclaimed his 10 rules for success and happiness (in crime) as follows:

---

[86] Or, as Chili Palmer, his character in *Get Shorty*, says: "I'm not gonna say any more than I have to, if that."

- Always be polite on the job. Say please and thank you.
- Never say more than is necessary.
- Never call your partner by name — unless you use a made-up name.
- Dress well. Never look suspicious or like a bum.
- Never use your own car.
- Never count the take in the car.
- Never flash money in a bar or with women.
- Never go back to an old bar or hang out once you have moved up.
- Never tell anyone your business. Never tell a junkie even your name.
- Never associate with people know to be in crime.

Taken together, these two sets of rule epitomize Leonardian cool, in form and content, if you will forgive the pleonasm.[87]

The rest of this section's text will be comparatively superfluous but I will try to contribute a few remarks. Leonards' fiction is dialogue driven and, at least since the late 50s, written with the screen in mind, systematically using basic narrative techniques developed in the 20th Century, such as "invisible" narration, interior monologue or multiple subjectivity, the latter being a Leonard specialty, who changes viewpoints seamlessly and frequently. [88]

---

[87] Rzekpa speculates rather fancifully that Leonard's cool, him being a Philosophy major and all, is ultimately rooted in Aristotle's *Nichomachean Ethics* (op. cit. p.40), which may be true but only insofar as all post-scholastic societies, be their background the Christian, Jewish, Muslim ethical traditions or a mixture thereof, can be said to be the grandchildren of the Stagirite's philosophy.

[88] Rzepka op. cit. p.13 passim. Revealingly, Leonard only wrote one novel narrated in the first person, *Hombre*.

Leonard's writing most celebrated feature is the so-called "Panasonic ear",[89] the realistic, deadpan "authentic dialogue built of sentences that no real person would utter (...)" with "an absolute economy of language".[90] As per his 10 rules, Leonard is economic with regionalisms, and, rather unlike Cormac McCarthy – a writer with whom Leonard shares striking similarities in dialogue style, although curiously none of his biographers point this out – he seldom "integrates" Spanish.[91] Dialogue, and dialogue driven plot, is Leonard's consensually acknowledged distinctive feature, but if he does tower over most of the competition in this particular, this seems to me to be a sign of excellence rather than of originality, as many coeval literature explores the same device.[92]

Essentially due to constraints derived from film rights, Elmore Leonard never developed series, like crime writers often due, and seldom used the same characters more than once, although he sometimes reused names he found catchy in different characters in different novels. Developing characters and then randomly letting the plot change course several times, a bit like soap opera scriptwriters do in function of audience ratings, is typical of Leonard's style,[93] as is another corollary of the commercial orientation of his fiction: to concoct implausible, even contrived

---

[89] J D Reed, *A Dickens from Detroit, Time Magazine*, 28 May 1984. The "Panasonic" and Dickens connotations became trademark descriptions of Leonard and his work, cf. Sedato p.57 passim, Rzepka op. cit. p.1 passim.
[90] C Lehman-Haupt, *Books of the Times; A Couple Shares Challenges in an Elmore Leonard Novel, New York Times*, 13 April 1989, p.18, quoted in Sedato, op. cit. p.114 footnote 1.
[91] Although Leonard does sometimes do so with jive. I borrowed the Cormac McCarthy allusion from Sedato, op. cit. p.33.
[92] Examples abound. Beside the aforementioned Cormac McCarthy and George V Higgins, I could randomly mention P H Newby, whose *Something to Answer For* (1968) I just happen to have finished reading.
[93] Rzepka complements with "the flawless manner in which (Leonard) intersects separate plotlines in scenes that, if they appeared in a book by

plot devices and render them believable through dialogue – or subsumed inner monologue – based character development.[94]

Elmore Leonard started from standard conventional Westerns and progressed during the 60s and 70s to increasingly rambling thrillers to achieve the hallmark of his writing, perfectly encapsulating my second favourite definition of Art: it is what you can get away with.[95] Elmore Leonard's own favourite novels were *Freaky Deaky* (1988) and *Tishomingo Blues* (2002).

Periodization

Mainly with a view to invite refutation, I would offer the following periodization of Leonard's literary work:

- The early Western phase (1951- 1961): five novels and 30 plus short stories published, all Westerns. The second novel, *The Law at Randado* (1954) witnessed an important evolution of Leonard's writing style, from plot oriented to character oriented.[96]
- The early caper phase (1969-1974): five novels published. After an 8 year publishing hiatus, *The Big Bounce* is Leonard's first long format masterpiece

---

any other writer, would seem like contrived coincidences": Rzepka, *"It's the way they're done": Style and Legerdemain* in *Out of Sight* [Rzepka, op. (ed) cit. p.138].

[94] In an interview with JM Lyczac for *Armchair Detective* in 1983 Leonard explained: "I begin with characters... Add a few more characters... and see what happens. I do not know myself what's going to happen until I'm well into the story and I see how the characters interact". [Quoted in Rzepka, op. (ed) cit. p.175].

[95] My favourite is Samuel Beckett's (quoted from memory): "the fact that there is nothing to express, nothing to express it with, no power to express, no desire to express, together with the duty to express".

[96] Cf. Sedato, op. cit. p.52.

and announces the single biggest thematic change in his career, so much so that Devlin calls it "the 'first' book"; subsequently, Leonard's style would develop and mature and subject matter diversify, occasionally returning to the Western and sporadically experimenting with "period" fiction;[97]
- The Detroit phase (1974-1980): seven novels published, including the aforementioned "Detroit Five". This was a period of further thematic and stylistic consolidation and of financial independence, although mostly derived from scriptwriting;
- The Florida phase (1980-1985): six novels published. Marriage with Joan, distancing for church and alcohol, joining AA. Moves Detroiters to Florida, gradually adds humour to his fiction, gains full financial independence as writer;
- The Christian interlude (1987-1988): comprising *Bandits*, *Touch* and the screenplay of *The Rosary Murders*;
- The peripatetic apogee (1988-2013): from *Freaky Deaky* to *Raylan*, Leonard is now a semi-permanent resident of the New York Times best seller list and his novels return to Florida and Detroit with frequent diversions to Missouri, Italy and beyond, his writing achieves its zenith.

Position in American literature

Geherin, writing in 1989, proclaimed Elmore Leonard "America's greatest living crime writer".[98] Martin Amis, not known for profligacy in praise, considered him "the closest

---

[97] Devlin, op. cit. p.51.
[98] Op. cit. p.134. Of course, this, being written in a biography of Leonard, should be taken *granum salis*.

thing America has to a national novelist" (although I can't think of any country that has, wants or needs a "national" novelist) and told him "your prose makes Raymond Chandler look clumsy".[99]

The back covers of Leonard's books abound with similar evaluations, for once not exclusively self-serving. Leonard was one of the foremost US writers of the second half of the 20th century and early 21st, if one of the foremost 5 or foremost 50 I don't know .[100] To me, he stands shoulder to shoulder with E L Doctorow, Philip José Famer, Ursula LeGuin, Cormac McCarthy, Joyce Carol Oates or Thomas Pynchon, to name alphabetically half a dozen of my personal favourites.

Elmore Leonard's writing's distinctive features, the "Panasonic" dialogue, the meandering plot and the final allegiance switch, were personal and uncommunicable. There were westerns, noirs and capers before him and there continued to be after him. Leonard has direct descendancy in his son, Peter Leonard, who carries his legacy and one of his characters, Raylan, with his own style and at his own level. But an important part of Leonard's legacy is up on the screen: the cool/light comedic caper/thriller popularized after the mid-90s and which continues to grace film theatres periodically to this day.[101] True, this legacy is not Leonard's alone, it can be traced to Dutch's fellow writer/friend/arch-competitor New Yorker, Donald Westlake, whose *Cops and Robbers*, adapted to the screen

---

[99] Interview with Charlie Rose in 1999, *Youtube*, available at: https://www.youtube.com/watch?v=U1QNdBRUedU (accessed 28 September 2021).
[100] Martin Amis, Saul Bellow and Joyce Carol Oates are among the many renowned "serious" writers who admired Leonard. Cf. Rzepka, op. (ed) cit. p.2.
[101] '*The Great Elmore Leonard Renaissance of the Late 90s*', Zach Vasquez, May 2020, *CrimeReads*, https://crimereads.com/the-great-elmore-leonard-renaissance-of-the-late-90s/ (accessed 28 September 2021).

in 1973 (Aram Avakiam) can be said to have inaugurated this sub-genre more than two decades *avant la lettre de* Leonard.

Elmore Leonard's body of work warrants no further legacy. For decades, the Dickens of Detroit, as he is often called, or the "poet laureate of assholes with revolvers" as that primer of my younger years, the *New Musical Express*, put it and Leonard preferred, blazed the grey zone between the haiku and the wisecrack. His novels and short stories and, mediated, the films, remain available for your pleasure.

Part II:
The Films

3:10 to Yuma (1957)

> 3:10 to Yuma: 92 minutes. Columbia Pictures. Release date: 7 August 1957.
>
> Directed by Delmer Daves; written by Halsted Welles; produced by David Heilweil.
>
> Cast: Glenn Ford as Ben Wade, Van Heflin as Dan Evans, Felicia Farr as Emmy, Leora Dana as Ms Alice Evans, Henry Jones as Alex Potter.
>
> Cinematography: Charles Lawton Jr. Editing: Al Clark. Art direction: Frank Otaling. Music: George Duning. Costume design: Jean Louis.
>
> Awards: Fårö Island Film Festival, Best Feature Film 1957; National Film Preservation Board, 2012.

The Story

"Jim, I don't have anything against you personally... this is what I get paid for, but I just want it understood that if you start across the seven feet between us, I'm going to pull both triggers at once – without first asking you to stop" (Scallen, *Three-Ten to Yuma*, edition consulted: *The Complete Western Stories*, Weidenfeld & Nicholson, London, 2017, p.182)

3:10 to Yuma was the 10th short story Elmore Leonard published, sold for 90$ to *Dime Western Magazine* and included in the magazine's March 1953 issue.[102]

Synopsis: Arizona, late 19th Century. Rancher Paul Scallen is deputized to bring outlaw Jim Kidd to justice. He

---

[102] James F Devlin, *Elmore Leonard*, op. cit., 1999), p.134.

takes him to a hotel room in the town of Contention, where they are to wait for the 3:10 train bound for the federal prison in Yuma. Jim Kidd's cronies are waiting outside the hotel to ambush them when the time comes to go the train station, stacking the odds heavily against outgunned Scallen. During the nerve-wracking wait Kidd permanently tries to "play" Scallen,[103] enjoining him to let him go, unsubtly pointing out that the sum of 200$ (the pay for the job, which he desperately needs to save his land from drought) is scarcely worth losing his life and leaving his wife a widower and his children orphans.

3:10 to Yuma's plot is clearly inspired by *High Noon* (Fred Zinnemann, 1952) a major coeval box success and a landmark in the history of the "psychological" western.[104] As in *High Noon*, it has been observed, the countdown suspense cliffhanger plot particularly resonated with audiences at the height of the Cold War nuke scare.[105]

Since his first published stories in 1951, Leonard evinced exceptional talent for setting and development in that most difficult of literary forms, the short story. *3:10 to Yuma* is arguably his first masterpiece, and Leonard's celebrated talent for dialogue is already apparent. It was his first major success[106], his first story to be sold to Hollywood (Columbia Studios, for 4.000$[107]), and also the first productive outcome of Leonard's business relationship with literary agent H N Swanson.

---

[103] In Devlin's expression, "a *Blut und Boden* homesteader", op. cit., p.42.
[104] Devlin, op. cit., p.32; David Geherin, *Elmore Leonard*, (Continuum, New York, 1989), p.21; Charles J Rzepka, *The Work of Elmore Leonard*, (Johns Hopkins University Press, Baltimore, 2017), p.68.
[105] Steven McVeigh, *The American Western*, (Edinburgh University Press, 2007); quoted in Rzepka, op. cit., pp.68-69.
[106] Geherin, op. cit., p.21.
[107] Devlin, op. cit., p.134; Geherin, op. cit., p.21; Rzekpa, op. cit., p.75.

The Director – Delmer Daves

Californian Delmer Lawrence Daves (1904-1977) was just too young to be one of the classics of the Hitchcock-Hawks generation, and not quite young enough to belong to the post WWII Ray-Brooks one. Also talent-wise he seems stuck in the middle: no one ever considered him a genius but his filmography includes many an effort which cannot be brushed aside as fodder.[108] Beside the film here under examination, consider *Dark Passage* (1947) and *Jubal* (1956, which preceded *3:10 to Yuma* in Daves' filmography, at the time somewhat hyperbolically hyped as the Western *Othello*), to name but two.

Born in San Francisco two years before the earthquake, Daves moved to Hollywood before the advent of sound. His early days were auspicious: he co-directed James

---

[108] Although he does has some distinguished advocates, namely Kent Jones (Criterion Collection's 2013 DVD edition booklet of *3:10 to Yuma*: https://www.criterion.com/current/posts/2766-3-10-to-yuma-curious-distances ; of course, this being a DVD booklet, the text could hardly be disparaging), Jonathan Rosenbaum (*'The Delmer Daves Problem*, Jonathan Rosenbaum, December 4 2019, https://www.jonathanrosenbaum.net/2019/12/the-delmer-daves-problem) and Betrand Tavernier ('The Ethical Romantic', *Film Comment*, January-February 2003, https://www.filmcomment.com/article/delmer-daves-bertrand-tavernier), the latter, no stranger to hyperbole, considered *3:10 to Yuma*" a magnificent parable of liberty" (Kent Jones, loc. cit.).

On the "opposite" side, with which I would tend to hold, the weight is perhaps heavier: in his seminal work *The American Cinema, Directors and Directions 1929-1969* (E P Dutton & Co, New York, 1968) Andrew Sarris referred to Daves, who he included in chapter VI of his book, "*Lightly Likeable*", as "the property of those who can enjoy stylistic conviction in an intellectual vacuum". More ambiguously, Manny Farber, in a November 1957 digression on underground films, refers to Dave *en passant* as a "backwoods primitive" (*Farber on Film*, Library of America, 2009, p 497). Finally, the University of California Press' encyclopedic *History of American Cinema* (10 volumes, 1994-2006) fails to mention Daves's name even once.

Cruze's *The Covered Wagon* (1923)[109] and co-wrote, albeit uncredited, Erich von Stroheim's *Queen Kelly* (1929). After spending the 30s scriptwriting romantic comedies and musicals, he graduated to directing in 1943, initially sticking to his comfort zone but later (1947) branching out to noir, horror, war, adventure and drama, but mostly Westerns, all of which he steered fluently - his style notably and perhaps excessively partial to the high angle shot - but somehow falling short of leaving a deep personal imprint, a sort of a poor man's Michael Curtiz, or, in Kent Jones's expression, "a casualty of the auteur theory".[110] On this matter, Jonathan Rosenbaum wrote: "The issue (...) isn't only that Daves has been seriously underrated for his best work, but also that his worst work has cast these achievements in an unjustly unfavorable light. Film artists should be judged by their best films, and Mann's *Serenade*, Ray's *Flying Leathernecks*, or Hawks's *Sergeant York* certainly don't undermine the strengths of *The Naked Spur*, *Johnny Guitar*, or *Rio Bravo*. The difference in Daves' case is that there might actually be more *Youngblood Hawkes* in his oeuvre than *3:10 to Yumas*."[111] Whilst not disagreeing with Rosenbaum's main argument, one might also add that if *3:10 to Yuma* is Delmer Daves' *Rio Bravo*, then he sure ain't no Howard Hawks.

The Film

3:10 to Yuma was adapted to the screen by Halsted Welles (1904-1990) who extended the short story's (which

---

[109] Jean Tulard, *Dicionaire Du Cinéma* (Éditions Robert Lafont, Paris, 1982), p.204. However, IMDbPro credits Delmer Daves as prop man in this film's crew.
[110] Kent Jones, loc. cit.
[111] Jonathan Rosenbaum, loc. cit.

had been optioned for 5,000$, an interesting sum at this stage of Leonard's career)[112] plot to retell in a different context the events leading to the capture of Ben Wade (Jim Kidd renamed), which take up about the first half of the film.

Somewhat anachronistically and incongruously in light of the film's subsequent tone, the proceedings start in old B-movie serial fashion: as a cattle drive passes by, not 2 minutes in there's a stage coach hold up and one of the assailants, as it happens Wade (Glenn Ford, appearing in the second of a string of three films with Delmer Daves) shoots one of the passengers dead without batting an eyelid. All this is witnessed by happenstance bystander rancher Dan Evans (Paul Scallen renamed, played by Van Heflin[113]), who is forced to "loan" horses to the assailants and returns home to tell the events to his disapproving wife (Leora Dana). This scene contrasts with a following one in which Wade, having arrived at Contention with his crew, flirts with saloon bartender Emmy (Felicia Farr) in the sole romantic interlude of the film (still practically mandatory by late 50s conventions) lending him a likeable side[114] and contrasting him with Evans before the female gaze.[115] Role fulfilled, Emmy disappears from the film. In the meantime, Evans has followed Wade to Contention and assisted

---

[112] J Sutherland, *Financial Times* epitaph, 23 August 2013, https://www.ft.com/content/701bc100-0a87-11e3-9cec-00144feabdc0 (accessed 28 September 2021).

[113] Hopelessly miscast. Reportedly (Kent Jones, loc.cit.) Glenn Ford was offered the part but opted for Wade instead, upon advice from John Barrymore never to turn down the part of the bad guy.

[114] In Rosenbaum's expression, an "unpredictable and multileveled killer-hipster and delicate gangleader-womanizer". Loc. cit.

[115] And "normalizing" non-marital romance in a Western, a relatively risqué innovation at the time. Cf. Graham Fuller, 'The Psychological Western', *BFI*, 6 May 2019, https://www2.bfi.org.uk/news-opinion/sight-sound-magazine/features/deep-focus/psychological-western (accessed 15 January 2021).

the town's sheriff in Wade's arrest, subsequently being entrusted to guard him in a hotel room, at which point the film basically follows the short story's plot.[116]

The dynamics between Wade and Evans in the film differs significantly from that between Kidd and Scallen in the story and the *huis clos* dramatic tension of the original text is considerably diluted by the "extended" plot of the screenplay - something that Elmore Leonard pointed out at the time, although he later changed his mind and came to judge the film one of the best adaptations of his writing.[117] Another heavyweight early detractor, none other than Howard Hawks,[118] considered it disingenuous that the plot's tension should be based in Wade threatening Evans when, in light on the situation, it should be the other way around; "correct" in theory, this doesn't come across, at least to me, in the film, and Glenn Ford's performance in this context is one of the film's strengths.

Slick framing and editing, gorgeous black and white cinematography (a sign of "arty" intent at a time when Westerns were massively going Technicolor and/or Cinemascope[119], by Charles "Buddy" Lawton Jr., who *inter alia*

---

[116] The plot background extension, introducing an element of ambivalence to Evans'" recruitment", reflects, perhaps subconsciously, it has been suggested, the moral dilemmas of the blacklist era, which was at its peak during *3:10 to Yuma*'s production. Cf. *BFI*, loc. cit.

[117] Kent Jones, loc.cit.

[118] Tavernier, loc. cit. IMDb reports this film was a deciding factor in Hawk's decision to direct *Rio Bravo* (1959) 'a return to more optimistric, less revisionist westerns'.

[119] Noted by *Sydney Morning Herald* critic Paul Byrnes in his review of the 2007 remake, cf. Paul Byrnes, '3:10 To Yuma', *The Sydney Morning Herald*, January 26 2008, https://www.smh.com.au/entertainment/3-10-to-yuma-20080126-gdryd4.html (accessed 15 January 2021). Reportedly, cinematographer Charles Lawton Jr used red filters on his lenses "to give the landscape an even more starkly parched look, befitting the story's setting amid a lengthy drought". Available at *IMDb* https://www.imdb.com/title/tt0050086/trivia/?ref =tt trv trv (accessed 18 January 2022).

photographed Orson Welles' 1947 *The Lady from Shanghai*)[120], several "signature" shots (cowboys lining up diagonally at saloon counter when Wade comes to Contention, funeral parade along empty street before Evans leads Wade to train station), dialogue often evocative of Leonard's writing[121] (mainly several lines given to Henry Jones, typecast as the town drunk) give the film a polish that distracts from, without, in my view, managing to fully compensate, the relative weakness of the general premise: a not very convincing B-plot wrapped in a late 50s "psychological" package. The lame lyrics of the title song ("there is a lonely train they call the 3:10 to Yuma...", sung by Frankie Lane) soaring along the closing credits, while Ms Evans waves the departing train goodbye (escape made possible in part to a last minute change of heart by Wade, possibly another blacklist Freudian slip, but stretching the limits of credibility, even back in the day) are ultimately an appropriate epilogue to the film's unevenness. The circumspect Leslie Hallywell said it perhaps best: "Tense, well-directed but talky (...) excellent performances and atmosphere flesh out an unconvincing physical situation".[122]

For posterity, however, *3:10 to Yuma* became a "sturdy film with a solid, but not iconic, reputation".[123] It was selected in 2012 by the US Library of Congress for the National Film Registry as being "culturally, historically or aesthetically" significant.[124]

---

[120] Delmer Daves reportedly said supplementary lighting was avoided whenever possible to retain "natural" shadows, a relative innovation at the time and an unorthodox practice to this day. Cf. Leslie Hallywell, *Hallywell's Film Guide 7th Edition*, Paladin, London, 1989, p. 1027.

[121] Leonard admitted from early on in his career he wrote dialogue with film in mind, see for all (...)

[122] Hallywell, loc. cit. p. cit.

[123] *Cineaste*, loc. cit.

[124] 'Complete National Film Registry Listing', *Library of Congress*, https://www.loc.gov/programs/national-film-preservation-board/film-

3:10 to Yuma (2007)

3.10 to Yuma. 122 minutes. Lionsgate, 2007. Release date: 31 August 2007.

Directed by James Mangold, Written by Michael Brand, Derek Haas, Halstead Welles and Elmore Leonard (story). Produced by Cathy Conrad.

Cast: Russel Crowe as Ben Wade, Christian Bale as Dan Evans, Peter Fonda as McEnroy, Ben Foster as Charlie Prince, Gretchen Mol as Ms Evans, Vinessa Shaw as Emmy.

Cinematography: Phedon Papamichael. Editing: Michael McCusker. Sound: David Betancour. Music: Marco Beltrami. Art Direction: Greg Barry.

Awards: Western Heritage Awards Bronze Wrangler for Theatrical Motion Picture.

The Director – James Mangold

NYC born (1963) James Mangold belongs to the small group of film directors (Richard Fleischer and Jean Renoir come to mind) who are offspring of renowned artists themselves: both his parents are famous painters.[125] Of artistically affluent Jewish origin, Mangold studied cinema with Alexander MacKendrick at the California Institute of the

---

registry/complete-national-film-registry-listing/ (accessed 15 January 2021).
[125] 'Robert Mangold', *Wikipedia*, https://en.wikipedia.org/wiki/Robert_Mangold (accessed 15 January 2021); 'Sylvia Plimack Mangold', *Wikipedia*, https://en.wikipedia.org/wiki/Sylvia_Plimack_Mangold (accessed 15 January 2021).

Arts[126] – he refers to the British director as his mentor – and at New York's Columbia University with Milos Forman.[127]

Mangold's filmography is eclectic. From neo-noir to comedy, superhero (his strongest connotation may be his Wolverine diptych) to westerns, he has been commercially successful in all: since *Identity* (2003), none of his films grossed less than 100 MUSD at the box office globally, and *Logan* (2017, occasionally, if to me incomprehensibly, referred to as the best superhero film ever) grossed an impressive 619 MUSD.[128] His first film, *Heavy* (1995), was selected for the Cannes Film Festival Director's Fortnight[129] and won the Special Jury Recognition for Directing at Sundance.[130] More recently (2019), *Ford versus Ferrari* received Oscar nominations for Best Film and Best Sound Mixing and won Best Film Editing and Best Sound Editing.[131] Mangold is currently tipped to sit behind the camera in the forthcoming Indiana Jones sequel.

Mangold's direction is comfortable with the mechanics of the FX-fuelled blockbuster whilst retaining an element of intimacy and psychodrama, revealed by his oft-noted and oft-criticized propensity for the lingering close-up. His

---

[126] John Esther, 'Avoiding Labels and Lullabies: An Interview with James Mangold', *Cineaste*, 2007, https://web.archive.org/web/20120206122326/http://www.cineaste.com/articles/an-interview-with-james-mangold.htm (accessed 15 January 2021).
[127] *Cineaste*, loc. cit.
[128] '3:10 to Yuma', *Box Office Mojo*, https://www.boxofficemojo.com/title/tt0381849/?ref_=bo_se_r_1 (accessed 15 January 2021). Interestingly, the only exception to this rule is precisely *3:10 to Yuma*, which grossed a comparatively modest 70 MUSD.
[129] 'Quinzaine 1995', *Quinzaine*, https://www.quinzaine-realisateurs.com/edition/1995/ (accessed 15 January 2021).
[130] '1995 Sundance Film Festival', *Sundance Institute*, http://history.sundance.org/events/30 (accessed 15 January 2021).
[131] 'The 92nd Academy Awards | 2020', *Oscars*, https://www.oscars.org/oscars/ceremonies/2020 (accessed 15 January 2021).

eclecticism makes it difficult to detect common themes or threads in his oeuvre, but diehard auteurists have pointed out to a slick if bland style, as well as to a recurring preference for the morally ambivalent protagonist, generally outsiders or fringe figures.[132] His wife Cathy Conrad produced all his films from *Cop Land* (1997) to *Knight and Day* (2010) – a sort of producing Alma to his directing Hitch.

The Film

3:10 to Yuma is not so much a new adaptation of Elmore Leonard's short story as a remake of Demer Daves' film.[133] Mangold himself described the project as a new take on "that wonderful Halstead Welles script"[134], and Welles is co-billed as scriptwriter.

The story line follows closely that of the previous film, expanding the background further to show Evans' (Christian Bale) plight with the local landowner who is trying to kick him out of his small ranch. As soon as Evans takes the job of escorting Wade (Russel Crowe, spot-on if occasionally irritating as psycho-coolster outlaw) the dynamics between the two becomes the emotional fuel of the film in a more dominating way than in Daves' version: both men are subject to similar social pressures, but respond in opposite ways. On the surface, the film holds for Evans, but Wade's

---

[132] In Jonah Jeng's suggestively cinephile expression, in a *3:10 to Yuma* review for online magazine *Paste*, a " Yojimbo-like fascination with the flawed hero", cf. Jonah Jeng, 'Walking within the Lines: The Films of James Mangold', *Paste Magazine*, March 6 2017 https://www.pastemagazine.com/movies/james-mangold/walking-within-the-lines-the-films-of-james-mangol/ (accessed 15 January 2021).

[133] The Criterion Collection DVD remaster of Delmer Daves' film referred to in the previous chapter was released to coincide with the première of Mangold's version. Cf. J. Hoberman in his review of the film in the *Village Voice*. J. Hoberman, 'Still Waiting for That Train', *The Village Voice*, August 28 2017, https://www.villagevoice.com/2007/08/28/still-waiting-for-that-train/ (accessed 15 January 2021).

[134] Cineaste, loc. cit.

likeability, and the fact that Evans is portrayed as a lame-legged Civil War vet, - one of this version's script's Freudian innovations - induce in the audience a degree of conflicting loyalty. Not to read too much of a neo-Marxist subtext in *3:10 to Yuma* (unless Breitbart are indeed right, in which case bless 'em), but in this film big money, in the person of rich ranchers and railway company executives, are the ruthless engines of progress: when detained and indicted by the latter, Wade notes: "notice he didn't mention the people I've killed".[135]

3:10 to Yuma is dramatically effective, sustaining tension throughout without ever lapsing into the wham-bam fatigue that often afflicts Hollywood action blockbusters. A baroquely gritty portrayal of the Old West, as much indebted to Sergio Leone as to Lawrence Kasdan, if longer on violence and shorter on irony, the script introduces dramatic detours involving an injun shootout and an altercation with railroad thugs which add to, or rather, superfluously prolong, the action, but provide for additional entertainment. Particularly enjoyable is an initial sequence straight out of spaghetti in which Wade's posse chases a stagecoach and Pinkerton agent passengers shoot back with a machine gun.

The "greek choir" to the dynamics of the relation between Wade and Evans is Evans' oldest son Bill (Logan Lerman) who follows along fascinated by Wade and frustrated by what he thinks is his father's cowardice. The roles of Evan's wife (Gretchen Mol) and Wade's flirt (Vinessa Shaw) are relatively symmetrical to those of the original version but here exist mostly for decorative effect (both actresses are former fashion models) complementing the CGI papier maché Monument Valley Wild West backgrounds. In this

---

[135] Pointed out by J. Hoberman, loc. cit.

version, the Hawksian doubt remains, and is thus verbalized by Wade: "what the hell are you doing out here Dan? You have a family to protect". In this film as in the previous, the answer is "plot necessity", and again, this is not, in my view, the film's biggest weakness, but rather the videogamey final action sequence, (although it provides for a surprisingly different ending from that of the first version, which will not be disclosed here).

At any rate, script, direction, the proverbial "production values" and overall performances – beside Bale and Crowe, Peter Fonda as grisly bounty hunter McEnroy and Ben Foster as Wade's latently homoerotically adoring chillingly über-sadistic second in command Charlie Prince, arguably both actors' finest – more than compensate. I belong to the minority that considers that Mangold's film is, on balance, a better film, or at any rate provides for more gripping viewing, than Daves'.[136] Resonances of Elmore Leonard's world, however, bar the occasional dialogue line, are all but absent.

---

[136] This minority includes Robert Ebert, cf. *'This train's got the disappearin' Western blues'*, RogerEgbert.com (2007), https://www.rogerebert.com/reviews/310-to-yuma-2007 (accessed 18 January 2021); and Richard Schickel, who wrote in *Time* "Who says remakes are always inferior to the original film? And who says the Western is dead?", quoted in *Variety*, November 15 2007, by Steve Chagollan, who also shares this view, cf https://variety.com/2007/film/awards/3-10-to-yuma-1117976062/ (accessed 18 January 2022).

Border Shootout (1990)

> *Border Shootout* (aka *The Law at Randado*). 88 minutes. Turner pictures 1990.
>
> Release date: 14 April 1992 (video release).
>
> Directed and written by Chris McIntyre; produced by Chris McIntyre and Grant Johnson.
>
> Cast: Glenn Ford as Sheriff John Danaher, Michael Ansara as Chuluha, Michael Forest as Earl Beaudry, Russell Todd as Clay Jordan, Michael Horse as Dandy Jim, Cody Glenn as Kirby Frye, Charlene Tilton as Edith Hanasain.
>
> Cinematography: Dennis Dalzell. Editing: Grant Johnson. Sound: Lisa Pinero. Music: Coley Music Group. Costume designer: Linda Cocuzzo.

The Story

"And that's where he found her and did what he had to do, what had been the customary act of a cheated Apache male longer than anyone could remember. A woman without a nose could not easily fall into adultery again" (*The Law at Randado*, edition consulted: Harper Torch 2002, p.6)

The Law at Randado was Elmore Leonard's second novel. It was published by Houghton Miffin in 1954, like the previous one (*Bounty Hunters*, 1953), also a western.[137]

---

[137] *Elmore Leonard*, http://www.elmoreleonard.com/ (accessed 19 January 2021).

Synopsis: Kirby Frye, a young Deputy Sheriff in Randado,[138] Arizona, witnesses powerlessly two Mexican cattle theft suspects be lynched by a cattle baron's men.[139] Armed with nothing but the law's reason, cunning and nerves of steel, except of course the standard issue Colt 45, Frye takes on the cattle baron, Phil Sundeen, and his men, concluding in a masterfully written final showdown in which Frye outwits Sundeen in a whisky drinking contest.

Typical of early Leonard fiction, this novel is a conventional, even clichéd, western story, upgraded by the author's dialogue - indeed the first instance of Leonard's typical dialogue virtuosity in long fiction and plot development. Like his later caper heroes, Leonard's western's main characters are courageous, uncompromising and clear about their objectives – but not invincible or fearless, often outmanoeuvering their foes by playing them against one another.

The Law at Randado heralds two innovations which would be frequent in Leonard's future novels, namely (i) the counterintuitive ending, in which a clever deceit, a last minute deal, a change of heart or a realignment of allegiances replaces the expected final showdown with something more clever (if sometimes, perhaps intentionally, somewhat anticlimactic) and (ii) the evolution from plot driven to character driven fiction, which would dominate virtually

---

[138] Frye is a protegé of Sheriff John Danaher, an instance of the "mentor-mentee" relationship which occurs frequently in Leonard's fiction, cf. Rzepka, op.cit. p 52. Rzepka further points out to analogies between Frye's past and Leonard's own and plausibly suggests protagonists such as this one or Evans in *3.10 to Yuma* are to some extent projections of the author (op cit. p.53).

[139] Lynching being "a topic that had been treated in American literature by William Faulkner, Thomas Wolfe, and Erskine Cladwell in the years between the two world wars and culminated in Walter van Tilbur Ckark's *The Ox Bow Incident* (1940), which Leonard had seen in its powerful film version during the war", Devlin, op. cit., p.41.

all subsequent Elmore Leonard writing.[140] Otherwise, conventionality and trite narrative premise notwithstanding, the book remains a rewarding read.[141]

The Director – Chris McIntyre

Information on director Chris McIntyre is thin on the ground, ciber or otherwise. Birthplace and date unknown, he reportedly directed one episode of the TV series *The Catlins* (1982-1985), his feature debut being the effort under review. Subsequently he directed seven more unremarkable lo-budget action programmers.[142]

The Film

Border Shootout is not really a film adaptation of *The Law at Randado*, but rather a Western very loosely inspired on the novel, retaining the characters of Kirby Frye and Phil Sundeen, the city of Randado as location [dialogue lines repeating at the vaguest pretext "(...) the law at Randado" punctuate the film about every 5 minutes] and the lynching as plot device, although in the film this is performed by a town mob and Sundeen conspires with the US Cavalry to steal cattle for beef to supply cavalrymen and connives to put the blame on the Mexicans, hence the lynching. The confusing script includes subplots involving Indians, an older sheriff who shows up occasionally to help put things

---

[140] Segato, p.52.
[141] Geherin considers that Leonard had not at this stage yet mastered the novel format and that *The Law at Randado* suffers from loose ends and disconnected plot development. Geherin, op. cit. p.35-26. "Disconnected" plot development is often apparent in Leonard's novels, and he freely admitted he often started writing books without knowing how or where they would end, just "allowing" the characters to egress as felt appropriate.
[142] 'Chris McIntyre', *IMDbPro*, https://pro.imdb.com/name/nm0570730/filmography (accessed 19 January 2021).

right whenever they seem to get out of hand (Glenn Ford, appearing again in a Leonard adaptation - of sorts - 33 years after *3:10 to Yuma* and once again the best thing in the film) and a mail order bride having an adulterous affair with Sundeen (Charlene Tilton, second best thing).

There's not much more literature available about this film than there is about its director. Devlin reports the film "attracted little attention and has just about slipped out of sight. Although (it has) a serviceable plot, (it is) a clumsy production with slow motion shootouts a la Sam Peckinpah and musical motifs reminiscent of the spaghetti Western (...) anachronistic dialogue and the least convincing Indians ever".[143] Else, there's a piece of amateur criticism linked in the relevant IMDb page that considers that "although *Border Shootout* is not a good movie, it is a surprisingly likeable one", but concludes the film "looks like a cheap TV movie, and, as poor as the quality of the direction is, it still far outshines the editing, which is truly atrocious".[144]

Both these reviews err vastly on the side of kindness. *Border Shootout* is a weird object, a 50s B script with an 80s 3d rate treatment. And it's a very bad film. Very bad. Take it from someone who's seen thousands. Bad as in no one would see it except if they have to write about it in a book bad, bad as in I thought they stopped doing films this bad somewhere in Southeast Asia or Latin America sometime back in the mid-70s bad, bad as in I can't believe nobody involved said anything bad. Acting, direction, editing and production are dismally incompetent, wardrobe out of 80s MTV videoclip leftovers, fake tan Caucasian Indians out of

---

[143] Devlin, op.cit. p.138, the only reference to this film I detected in the available literature.
[144] Richard Cross, 'Movie Review: Border Shootout (1990)', *20/20 Movie Reviews*, 27 January 2012 http://www.2020-movie-reviews.com/reviews-year/1990-movie-reviews/border-shootout-1990-movie-review/ (accessed 19 January 2021).

central casting deliver sitcom witticisms, fight scenes which wouldn't cut the mustard in 30s Poverty Row, I could go on, it's jaw-dropping, one only wonders how Glenn Ford ever got involved in this. I'll conclude by stating *Border Shootout* doesn't contribute much for the appreciation of Elmore Leonard's work on film. For full disclosure, I saw it in a YouTube version[145] that looked like a VHS transfer copy, or at least presented similar level quality, which may not have helped.

---

[145] Classic Rob, *Border Shootout (1990) - Glenn Ford*, September 26 2020. Available at https://www.youtube.com/watch?v=XZw5TBf1mz8 (accessed 19 January 2021).

The Tall T (1957)

The Tall T. 78 minutes. Columbia Pictures 1957. Release date: 2 April 1957. Directed by Budd Boetticher. Written by Burt Kennedy. Produced by Harry Joe Brown.

Cast: Randolph Scott as Pat Brennan, Richard Boone as Frank Usher, Maureen O'Sullivan as Doretta Mims, Arthur Hunnicut as Ed Rintoon, Skip Homeier as Billy Jack, Henry Silva as Chink, John Hubbard as Willard Mims.

Cinematography: Charles Lawton Jr. Editing: Al Clark; Sound: Lisa Pinero; Music: Heinz Roemheld. Art Direction: George Brooks

The Story

(Frank Usher) looked at Brennan and nodded towards Mims. "Where´d you find him?" "We just met". "Do you go along with what he´s saying?" "If I said yes" Brennan answered "you wouldn´t believe me. And you´d be right". A smile almost touched Frank Usher´s mouth. "Dumb even talking about it, isn´t it?" (*The Captives*, edition consulted: *The Complete Western Stories*, Weidenfeld & Nicholson, London, 2017, p 33)

The Captives, on which *The Tall T* is based, was the 19th short story published by Elmore Leonard, first appearing in the February 1955 issue of *Argosy* magazine. Its significantly longer than most Leonard's short fiction output, running 32 pages in 7 short chapters.[146]

Synopsis: Arizona, 1880s. A stagecoach is held up at a way station by a small gang of gunslingers. Passengers include Pat Brennan, who happened to get a lift by the stagecoach after having lost his horse in a bet to get credit to buy yearlings for his ranch, and newlyweds Willard and Loretta Mims, Loretta being the daughter of a local copper baron, fact which Willard reveals to Frank Usher, the head of the gang, in a ploy to tempt him to collect a ransom from his father in law, an abject attempt to escape the situation which turns predictably sour, it being up to Brennan to save the day in typically Leonardian fashion: by playing Usher and his men against each other.

The Captives is a standard cliffhanger featuring a number of Elmore Leonard's recurring early themes: an occasional bystander accidentally caught in someone else's business, the ambiguous sociopath who feels an affinity with the protagonist, and the unfavourable portrayal of big money. Leonard develops this conventional premise with clockwork precision. Dialogue, as usual, carries most of the action, and is among the best Leonard ever wrote. The suspense is tempered by the "mind my own business/do the right thing" moral dilemma, typical of Leonard and more broadly of XXth Century US culture. *The Captives* reveals

---

[146] Being therefore, strictly speaking, a novelette. The 30 short stories published by Elmore Leonard, all of them Westerns, run typically some 15 pages, the standard length of publication for monthly pulp magazines in the 1950s and 60s. *The Captives*, *Trial of the Apache* (1951) and *Law of the Hunted Ones* (1952), are the exceptions, running 30 pages or more each. The lengths mentioned refer to: Elmore Leonard, *The Complete Western Stories* (Weindenfeld & Nicholson, London, 2017). The original compilation of these stories was published by Harper Collins, New York, in 2003.

extraordinary maturity and is one of the author's masterpieces, in any format. It was the second short story Elmore Leonard sold to Hollywood, "apparently"[147] by H N Swanson, and like *3.10 to Yuma*, it was produced by Columbia Pictures.

The Director – Budd Boetticher

Oscar "Budd" Boetticher (1916-2001) was born in Chicago and raised in Indiana by wealthy adoptive parents. Educated at Culver Military Academy and Ohio State University, Boetticher went to Hollywood in 1939, after a stint in Mexico where he learned bullfighting, which would remain a lifelong passion and a subject matter of several of his films.[148] After a number of odd jobs and assistant director assignments, he graduated relatively quickly to direction with *One Mysterious Night* (1944) a low budget crime programmer, continuing to direct mostly noirs until switching to mostly westerns in 1949 with *The Wolf Hunters*.[149] To no detriment to the remainder of his output, Boetticher's reputation rests inly in the seven westerns he directed between 1956 and 1960, all written by Burt Kennedy,[150] produced by Harry Joe Brown, scored by Heinz Roemheld, shot

---

[147] Devlin, p.147, footnote 10.

[148] Boetticher later retracted: "It was different then. I never try to sell bullfighting today". Michael Wilmington, *'Tall in the Director's Chair : Budd Boetticher made some of the best-remembered Westerns of '50s and '60s; they don't make 'em like that (or him) anymore'*, LA Times, 29 November 1992, https://www.latimes.com/archives/la-xpm-1992-11-29-ca-2438-story.html (accessed 26 January 2021).

[149] Interestingly mirroring the career of another director Boetticher is often associated with, Anthony Mann, who also started with noir before moving to the "adult/psychological" Western. Manns first noir was *Strangers in the Night* (1944) and his first Western *The Furies* (1950).

[150] To whom Boetticher gracefully gave most credit for the quality of his westerns: "What was different about my Westerns was the beautiful job Burt Kennedy did in the original screenplays.". *LA Times*, loc. cit.

on Lone Pine locations, photographed by Charles Lawton Jr[151] (except one), and featuring Randolph Scott in the main role.[152] *The Tall T* was the second film of this series.

Budd Boetticher was long dismissed – to the extent that he was even noticed – as a mere workaday B-movie director, until his "discovery", or perhaps "reception", by none other than *Cahiers du Cinéma* co-founder André Bazin, who, in a lengthy text about *Seven Men from Now* in the August/September 1957 issue of the magazine[153] considered this film the best post WWII Western he had seen.[154] In classical *Cahiers* style, this fringe opinion triggered a scholastic debate following the customary trend "OK, the film is good, but is the director good?" to "OK the director is good, but is he an auteur?" until some 10 years later the "yeas" can be said to have had it: Andrew Sarris considered Boetticher "one of the most fascinating unrecognized talents in the American cinema".[155]

The contemporary consensus is that Boetticher is "one of the architects of the modern adult Western".[156] Less restrained, Jean Tulard proclaims *"Boetticher ou le cinema americain par excellence"*.[157] But the greatest praise must

---

[151] Who coincidentally also photographed Delmer Daves' *3.10 to Yuma*, also released in 1957 (cf. supra p xxx), which was therefore for Elmore Leonard a very good year, the first of many.

[152] Cf. Rick Thompson's text on *The Tall T* in *Senses of Cinema* (May 2006, https://www.sensesofcinema.com/2006/cteq/tall_t/, accessed 26 January 2021), a very perceptive analysis of the film and otherwise a useful reference source.

[153] *Cahiers du cinéma*, #74, August/September 1957. This text is available in English in *Cahiers du Cinéma – The 1950s* (Harvard University Press, Cambridge, Massachussets, 1985) pp.169-172, translated by Phillip Drummond.

[154] Although he conceded *The Searchers* (John Ford, 1957) and *The Naked Spur* (Anthony Mann, 1953) were strong contenders, cf. loc.cit.

[155] Sarris, loc cit, chapter *"Expressive Esoterica"*, pp.124-125.

[156] David A Cook, *A History of Narrative Film*, 2nd Edition (W H Norton & Company, New York 1990) p.502.

[157] Tulard, op. cit., p 88.

have come from Sergio Leone who, spotting Boetticher once in a film festival in Milan, reportedly snapped: "Budd, I stole *everything* from you!".[158]

Budd Boetticher was one of the greats. He is usually mentioned along the exponents of the "psychological" western, e.g. Mann, Ray, Daves or Zinnemman, but, with due credit to these, Boetticher is an artist of a different magnitude. I don't particularly see merit in ranking directors like tennis players, but for illustrative purposes I will state Boetticher is on a par with John Ford, Howard Hawks, Fritz Lang, King Vidor and Raoul Walsh as one the greatest Western directors ever.[159] He is the Euripides of the Wild West, taking John Ford's wide open landscapes and turning them into oppressive outer spaces, big sky peeking from the top third of the screen like a basement window, accentuating the characters' contingency, a "male antagonism with no audience required for the showdown",[160] a world where "the moral (...) is (...) simple (...): everyone loses".[161]

The Film

The Tall T follows closely its literary source, including whole dialogues reproduced verbatim, with the exception of the first 20 minutes or so, in which the background story leading to Pat Brennan (Randolph Scott,[162] uncharacteristi-

---

[158] *LA Times*, op. cit.
[159] I exclude here the "primitives" James Cruze, D W Griffith or Thomas H Ince.
[160] Sarris, loc. cit p 125.
[161] Jim Kitses, 'Horizons West', *Directing The Western from John Ford to Clint Eastwood*, London, 2004.
[162] Whom Devlin unkindly calls "the poor man's Gary Cooper". Devlin, op.cit., p 136. As we've seen, Elmore Leonard often said Gary Cooper was an early role model for his main characters, what Segato calls a "(...) *uomo taciturno e deditto a l´azione*". Segato, op. cit. p. 19.

cally smilingly congeniality providing contrast for resoluteness) hitchhiking by a dust road is enacted (as in *3.10 to Yuma*, it seems again here 50s scriptwriters felt short story plots were insufficient to fill a feature length film).

Released, as alluded to previously, in the same year as *3.10 to Yuma*,[163] *The Tall T* simply blows the other film away. Shot, like all other six films of the Boetticher/Kennedy etc polyptych, in Long Pine, some 300 Km north of Hollywood. Boetticher films the area's mountain and rocks, often in plongé, with little room for the sky, accentuating the oppressiveness of the captives' situation and suggesting a dry texture evocative of the sets of *Waiting for Godot*,[164] the film is both unmistakably Boetticher and a remarkably sensitive "rendering" of Leonard in several ways, namely:

- The delivery of Leonard's dialogue, in particular by Scott, Richard Boone as Frank Usher and Henry Silva as Chink, Usher's psycho henchman;[165]

- The dynamics between Brennan and Usher, portrayed less as two sides of the same coin as Usher as wannabe Brennan, an outlaw victim of circumstance who longs for a wife and a ranch;

- Brennan playing Usher's partners against one another;

---

[163] In a double bill with *Hellcats of the Navy* (Nathan Juran, 1957), which is revealing of the standing Boetticher had in the industry at the time.
[164] Finding everywhere affinities, perhaps far-fetched, with Samuel Beckett's work, is one of my weaknesses, for which I apologize to the readership. Leonard's gift for catchy if implausible character names (e. g. the Mims) is another characteristic he shares with the divine Irishman, and which Burt Kennedy was shrewd enough to keep, unlike the adapters of *3.10 to Yuma*, which is not to say, in fairness, that the latter's character names are not effective.
[165] "There's not a dead or even a plain line in the film: they all sing". Rick Thompson, loc. cit.

- A typically early Leonardian female character, Doretta Mims (Maureen O´Sullivan, made up to look "plain", uncharacteristically for a love interest in a mid-50s film) essentially a damsel in distress/prospective rancher wife, who Usher and his men use to cook, and Brennan uses as sexual bait to trick Usher's men. [166]

The Tall T is an iconic Western. Its only weakness, if it is a weakness, is the incomprehensible, if typically western and catchy, title, derived from the name of the Tenvoorde ranch which appears early in the film but is otherwise unrelated to the plot: the title was "reportedly slapped on the film after it was finished by a producer, and (...) Boetticher and Burt Kennedy were (...) bewildered (...)".[167]

---

[166] Jim Hitt, *The American West From Fiction (1823-1976) into Film (1909-1986)*, McFarland 1990, p.233, quoted in Devlin, p.136.
[167] Michael Grost, 'Budd Boetticher', *Mike Grost*, http://mikegrost.com/boettich.htm#TallT (accessed 26 January 2021).

Last Stand at Saber River (1997)

> *Last Stand at Saber River*. 96 minutes. TNT TV 1997. Release date: 19 January 1997. Directed by Dick Lowry. Written by Ronald M Cohen. Produced by Michael Brandman and Tom Selleck.
>
> Cast: Tom Selleck as Paul Gable, Suzy Amis as Martha Cable, Keith Carradine as Vern Kidston, John Carradine as Duane Kidston, Tracey Needham as Lorraine Kidston.
>
> Cinematography: Rick Waite; Editing: William B. Stitch; Sound: David Brownlow; Music: David Shire; Art Direction: Vaughan Edwards.

The Story

> *"You´re telling me to go after them. To shoot them down like some animal." "Exactly". "That´s called murder." "It´s also called war". Cable shook his head. "As far as I´m concerned the war´s over". Janroe watched him closely. "You don´t stop believing in a cause just because you´ve stopped fighting".* (*Last Stand at Saber River*, edition consulted: Phoenix, London, 2005, pp 45, 46)

Last Stand at Saber River was the 4th novel written by Elmore Leonard, like the previous three, a Western, and the 2nd, by writing chronology, to be adapted to the screen. It was published in 1959 by Dell Publishing.

Synopsis: Arizona, 1865. Paul Gable is a Confederate vet returning home from war to his wife and children, to find his land occupied by the Yankee Kidston brothers Duane and Vern. He uses "patience and weigh alternatives and (...)

be sure of a situation before he acted"[168] to overcome his difficulties.

Last Stand at Saber River is "the most predictable and conventionally heroic of Leonard's Westerns"[169], but it does feature an important innovation in Leonard's fiction: Lorraine Kidston. Also typical for Leonard, in a final plot twist the Kidstons become Vernon's allies in a conflict against a murderous die-hard rebel. Unlike most Elmore Leonard Western fiction, however, the period is not the "classical" 1870-1880s frontier era, but rather the final days of the Civil War, historical background which is brought to bear significantly in the dramatic developments.[170] *Last Stand at Saber River* reveals Leonard's growing maturity in handling the novel format and, like everything the author published, is never less than a rewarding read, but occupies a secondary position in Elmore Leonard's body of fiction.

The Director – Dick Lowry

Oklahoman Dick Lowry is a prolific director (about 50 films directed between 1975 and 2011, mostly for TV) who has deserved no scholarly attention. The literature available, beside laconic IMDb and Wikipedia entries which mention also filmographies as actor and/or producer, mostly in

---

[168] *Last Stand at Saber River*, p.2 (ed. cit.). Quoted in Rzepka p. 59. In pp.59-61 Rzepka develops *a propos* Paul Gable the "central features" of the Leonardian protagonist's τέχνη.

[169] Geherin, p.27; similarly Devlin p 41: "conventional but conventionally satisfying", and Segato, p 52: "*una narrazione chi se potrebbe definire canonica*".

[170] A relatively rare device for Leonard. Other instances include the Israeli-Palestinian conflict in *The Hunted* (1977) and the Rwandan civil war in *Pagan Babies* (2000).

his own films, is limited to an article in *The Oklahoman* celebrating local boy making it in Tinseltown.[171]

The Film

Last Stand at Saber River departs from and develops several aspects of the novel, in a globally coherent and consistent manner, while remaining close to its original structure and premise. In the film, the dynamics between Gable (Tom Selleck, who also produced and delivers a surprisingly nuanced performance for a usually wooden actor) and his wife, who recurrently guilt-trips him for abandoning the family to go to war, is developed beyond its scope in the book. Also, post-war Yankee-Dixie resentment plays a more prominent role in the Gable/Kidston (played by David Carradine, Keith Karradine and Tracey Needham) relationship, adding climax to the final Gable/Kidston alliance, although its final resolution is different from that of the novel, in one of the rare instances in which departure from the original plot disservices the film.

Last Stand at Saber River received next to no critic attention. Devlin, the only Leonard biographer to say anything about the film, considers it "thoughtful but undistinguished"[172], an evaluation which may be both too much and too little. Sensitively scripted and competently, if conventionally, directed and produced (art direction, namely, is above par for a TV production) the film is a worthy variation on Leonardian themes, developing its own "personality" while remaining within the general narrative structure

---

[171] Jim Miller, "'Oklahoma kid' Dick Lowry graduates to screen movies Film director finds Sooner background makes up for later start', *The Oklahoman*, 28 April 1983. Available at: https://oklahoman.com/article/2022753/oklahoma-kid-dick-lowry-graduates-to-screen-movies-film-director-finds-sooner-background-makes-up-for-later-start (accessed 2 February 2021).
[172] Devlin, op. cit, p.138.

of its literary base – and, as often happens with film adaptations from Leonard's work, reproducing whole chunks of dialogue. An unnecessarily slow start and a few final cartoony stampedes and shootouts, which don't exist in the book and sit ill with the overall tone of the film, make the film worse than it needed to be.

Hombre (1967)

> *Hombre*. 111 minutes. Twentieth Century Fox 1967. Release date: 21 March 1967. Directed by Martin Ritt. Written by Irving Ravetch and Harriet Frank Jr. Produced by Martin Ritt and Irving Ravetch.
>
> Cast: Paul Newman as John Russel, Richard Boone as Grimes, Fredric March as Favor, Diane Cilento as Jessie, Cameron Mitchell as Bradie, Barbara Bush as Audra Favor, Margaret Blye as Doris, Martin Balsam as Henry Mendez.
>
> Cinematography: James Wong Howe; Editing: Frank Bracht; Music: David Rose; Art Direction: Jack Martin Smith and Robert Emett Smith. Budget: 5.8 MUSD. Box Office: 14.1 MUSD

The Story

> *"I´m thinking"* Russell said, *"wether to kill you right now or wait till you turn around,"* (*Hombre*. Edition consulted: Orion, London, 2017, p 104)

Hombre was the 5th and last novel of Elmore Leonard's early Western phase. From then on he would write mainly crime fiction and capers (although he returned to the West three times in the 70s for novels and twice for short stories in the 80s and 90s). The publishing of *Hombre* (sold by Marguerite Harper to Ballantine Books in 1961 for 1.250$)[173] also marks the moment Leonard quit his day job

---

[173] Devlin, op.cit, p.12, Geherin, op cit, p.8. There is some confusion in the available sources regarding the value and significance of this sale, as some biographers, including the two cited, refer to a supposedly small difference between this amount and the 1000$ Leonard would have gotten for *3.10 to Yuma*, the first short story he sold. As mentioned previously, Devlin

at an advertising agency to devote himself to writing full time.[174] He wouldn't publish another novel until 1969, the completely different but landmark *The Big Bounce*, to which I will revert in the following chapters.

Synopsis: Arizona 1880s. Jack Russell, a white man raised by the Apache who works as policeman in an Indian reservation, takes a stagecoach on a business trip related to a recent inheritance, fellow passengers including Indian reservation agent Alexander Favor, his posh wife Audra, and boorish roughneck Cicero Grimes. Alexander is eloping with reservation money and Grimes, aware of this, plots to hijack the stagecoach, resulting in a confrontation between him and his cronies and the other passengers. These, in spite, or rather due to, racial bias, rally behind Jack Russell, who reluctantly resorts to the standard Leonardian hero skill set to overcome the situation, finally making the ultimate sacrifice to rescue Audra – who at various points during the narrative shows her contempt and dislike of Indians and specifically of Russell – who the Grimes gang held hostage to exchange for the money, as her husband watches passively.

Hombre is the "tightest and most gripping"[175] of Leonard's Western novels. Essentially an extended variation on *The Captives* with several of Leonard's recurrent themes present, e.g. the cool, detached hero who abides by his own code – at one point even "betraying" the white flag convention, in one of the novels surprising twists – the

---

refers this sum was actually 90$, and not 1000$, which seems more plausible considering the time elapsed, inflation, the general market price difference between short stories and novels and not least the difference in Leonard's standing in the publishing market in 1961 as compared to 1953. I have therefore retained the smaller sum.

[174] Devlin, op.cit, p10.
[175] Ibid.

negative portrayal of wealth and greed, the absence, or inobservance, of institutional normativity etc.[176] However, a few typical elements the reader would have been led to expect are absent - a sign of the evolution of Leonard's writing at this time: it is written in the first person, the only Leonard novel in which this narrative device is used,[177] and the cliffhanger suspense isn't resolved by cunning but rather by physical courage and ultimately, and counterintuitively, by self-sacrifice.[178]

Hombre was elected one of the 25 best Western novels of all time by the Western Writers of America in 1977.[179] It was sold to 20th Century Fox for 10.000 USD in 1965, a further important step toward Leonard´s financial independence as a full-time writer.[180]

The Director – Martin Ritt

Martin Ritt (1914-1990) born in Manhattan to a Jewish family, started working in theatre after college (St. Johns), getting involved in the New Deal's Federal Theater Project, where he became acquainted with Marxism and the radical left, leading to a life-long association with progressive politics, including being blacklisted in 1951, at a time when he

---

[176] Karine Powers, in her piece on *Hombre* [*The Man with Five Names*, Rzepka, op. (ed) cit. p.95-111] notes that "the many named" John Russell is a precursor of "the complicated protagonists" of spaghetti Westerns, such as The Man With No Name in Sergio Leone's *Dollars* Trylogy (1964-1966), or Sergio Corbucci's *Django* (1966). Ms Powers' illuminating analysis is otherwise mainly centered on *Hombre's* racial and identity subtexts in the context of the US's coeval civil rights movement.

[177] Devlin, op. cit, p 44, Geherin, op. cit. p.29. Karine Powers (loc. cit. p.102) notes the first person narrator, although supposedly writing in 1884, betrays "the same cultural and imaginative knowledge as Western movie fan (...) He introduces John Russell in panning close-up".

[178] Devlin, op. cit, p 44, Rzepka, op. cit, p.190.

[179] Geherin, op. cit. p 30, Rzepka, op. cit, p.72.

[180] Challen, op. cit. p 57, Rzepka, op. cit, p.75.

was active as actor and director in television, subsequently supporting himself by teaching at the Actors Studio (where his students included James Dean)[181].

Once the Red Scare decreased intensity, Ritt returned to the industry, having his first shot at film direction with *Edge of the City* (1957),[182] going on to direct a number of renowned, mostly "socially engaged", films – often working with Paul Newman, with whom he co-founded a production company – including *The Long Hot Summer* (1958), *Hud* (1963, with Newman) an adaptation of John Le Carré's *A Spy Who Came in from the Cold* (1965), *The Molly Maguires* (1970), *The Front* (1976, broadly fictionalizing his own experience during the Red Scare)[183] and *Norma Rae* (1979).

Martin Ritt is considered the embodiment of Liberal Hollywood, a reputation that may have done him more scholarly harm than good: "Uneven (....) sometimes too didactic, (...) attitudinizing (...) ponderous"[184], "*Cinéaste généreux, il represente l'aile libérale du cinema americain (...) Pas un grand metteur en scéne mais un bon temoin des defauts de la societé americaine*"[185]. This kind of evaluation is typical of an academic establishment which, however progressive, tends to retain an "Art for Art's sake" bias, and while not inaccurate, feels somewhat unfair. Ritt's best films – which should be the measure of his worth – are slickly, if conventionally, directed, unobtrusively effective, bereft of rhetorical flourish and relay their "message" without piety

---

[181] Tulard, op. cit. p.656.
[182] Paul Buhler and Dave Wagner, *Radical Hollywood,* The New Press, New York, 2002, p.444.
[183] Aliis and Ronald Radosh, *Red Star Over Hollywood*, Encounter Books, San Francisco, 2005, p.245.
[184] Eric Rhode, *A History of the Cinema from its Origins to 1980*, Pelican Books, New York 1979 p.619.
[185] Tulard, loc. cit.

or indoctrination stated or implied. *Hombre* is one such case.

The Film

Hombre follows very closely the book's narrative structure and, as often in adaptations of Elmore Leonard to the screen, there's some plot background development before the start of the novel's narrative, as John Russell (Paul Newman, adequately poker-faced, in his last role for Ritt)[186] goes to town to collect his inheritance. Also, and as usual, vast amounts of dialogue are reproduced verbatim from the book.

An early "transition" western, as a gritty "realist" look was taking over the tailored cowboy image (the film's opening credits display period photos completely unrelated to the plot and Paul Newman spends the first 20 minutes wearing a black wig, underscoring his Apache heritage).[187] Strikingly photographed by James Wong Howe,[188] the film carries the narrative effectively, focusing

---

[186] *Hombre* was marketed as a Paul Newman vehicle, the title resonating with the audience, being the 4th film of the decade featuring Newman in the main role with a single word title starting with an H. The other 3 were *The Hustler* (Robert Rossen, 1961), *Hud* (also directed by Martin Ritt, 1963) and *Harper* (Jack Smight, 1966). See Roger Egbert, 'Hombre', *Roger Egbert*, https://www.rogerebert.com/reviews/hombre-1967 (accessed 9 February 2021).

[187] Which reportedly cost 450$, cf. Devlin, op. cit. p 136. In 1967, at the dawn of hippiedom, it was cool to affect or invoke an Indian (they still didn't say "native American" back then) connection/background, real or imagined, so blue-eyed Newman with an apache wig was a winning proposition.

[188] One of the greatest cinematographers of classical Hollywood, Guangdong born 10 times Oscar nominated 2 times winner James Wong Howe (real name Wong Tung Jim) had a career that spanned from the silent period to the 70s. He pioneered deep focus cinematography, the use of wide angle lenses and crab-dollies. With Hal Mohr and others he popularized, mainly at Warner Bros, the chiaroscuro cinematography often associated with German expressionism that European emigrés brought to

on drama rather than social comment, the odd allusion to the plight of the natives or the insensitivity of the moneyed classes incidental and contextualized enough not to be distracting or moralizing. Alexander Favor (Fredric March, characteristically nuanced) is weak rather than cruel, his wife Audra (Barbara Rush, typecast) more a victim of sociocultural tunnel vision than bigotry, Cicero Grimes (Richard Boone, in his second baddie role in a Leonard adaptation, playing it Anthony Quinn style) a standard telluric outlaw. The only superfluous concession to coeval convention is the flirt between John Russell and Jessie (Diane Cilento, deservedly getting many of the best lines as a Hawksian salt of the earth gal), the "governess" of Russel's inheritance, which is more developed in the film than in the novel.

Hombre had fair box office and retains a solid, maybe slightly underrated, reputation. Bosley Crowther, who pontificated as *New York Times* film critic during virtually the entire classical period (actually starting and ending a bit late: 1940-1967) perceptively if slightly dismissively described it thus: "Take a large portion of *Stagecoach*, a small chunk of *The Treasure the Sierra Madre*, a dash of *Broken Arrow* (...) put them all together (...) give it to Martin Ritt to pan-roast in his Western culinary style. What will you get? You'll get '*Hombre*' (...)", and gave the film 4 stars out of 5, which seems about right.[189] Less forgivingly, *Sight and*

Tinseltown in the 30s (which was also convenient for shadowing/disguising dodgy or rehashed sets in low budget films). Almost all of Howe's best work was in black and white, *Hombre* being a relative exception. See John Russell Taylor, *Strangers in Paradise – Hollywood Emigres 1933-1950*, Faber & Faber, London 1983, Clive Hirshhorn, *The Warner Bros Story*, Crown Publishers, New York, 1981 and 'James Wong Howe', *Wikipedia*, https://en.wikipedia.org/wiki/James_Wong_Howe (accessed 9 February 2021).

[189] Crowther, *New York Times*, 22 March 1967; available at: *The New York Times*, https://www.nytimes.com/1967/03/22/archives/screen-an-able-

Sound founder Penelope Houston, writing at the time for *The Spectator*, considered: "Strikes a not very satisfactory balance between traditionalist themes (...) and interludes for reflection on race prejudice (...)".[190]

But this was a minority report. *Hombre* is an authoritatively scripted and directed Western. As Crowther, and others, pointed out[191], the action is allowed to develop in long silent sequences, and the setting selection, foremost the final abandoned mine showdown, superlative.

---

hombrewestern-recipe-served-skillfully-at-astor.html (accessed 9 February 2021). Interestingly. 1967 was also the year of Bosley Crowther's famous polemical disparaging review of *Bonnie and Clyde* (Arthur Penn, 1967), which sealed his future reputation as a conservative and outdated critic.
[190] *The Spectator*, 21 April 1967. Available at *The Spectator Archive* http://archive.spectator.co.uk/article/21st-april-1967/26/cinema (accessed 9 February 2021).
[191] Devlin, op. cit. p.136.

The Big Bounce (1969)

> *The Big Bounce*, 102 minutes. Warner Bros/Seven Arts 1969. Release date: 5 March 1969. Directed by Alex March. Written by Robert Dozier. Produced by William Dozier.
>
> Cast: Ryan O'Neal as Jack Ryan, Leigh Taylor-Young as Nancy Barker, Van Heflin as Sam Mirakian, Lee Grant as Joanne, James Daly as Ray Ritchie, Robert Webber as Bob Rodgers.
>
> Cinematography: Howard Schwartz; Editing: William Ziegler, Music: Mike Curb; Art Direction: Audrey Blasdel.

The Story

"And to each of the three who didn´t escape, close to them, her head on their shoulders, she said, `do you know what I´m going to do?´ Each of the three whispered, `No, what are you going to do?´ And she answered, `I´m going to tell your wife you were seen taking advantage of a sixteen-year-old girl, that´s what.´ And she did, too." (*The Big Bounce*, edition consulted, Harper Torch, New York, 2003, p.52)

The Big Bounce was the 6th novel published by Elmore Leonard. It was his first crime novel and it signalled a radical change in subject matter, dramatic structure and literary style, after an 8 year publishing hiatus. The reason for this change was prosaically commercial: in the 60s the literary Western was considered to be moribund as a popular genre. Subsequently, Leonard's reputation outside the scholarly circuit was to be almost exclusively associated with crime and caper fiction.[192] *The Big Bounce* was rejected no less than 84 times by publishers, which reportedly didn't discourage agent H N Swanson as, after some rewriting and a title change from *Mother, This is Jack Ryan* to the definitely catchier *The Big Bounce*, it was finally sold for 50.000$, consolidating Leonard's financial independence.[193]

Synopsis: Michigan Thumb, 1960s. Ex-con Jack Ryan is given a chance at a new beginning working at Mr Majestyk's (no relation with the character in Leonard's later eponymous novel, Leonard just liked the name) beach resort, where he gets involved with Nancy Hayes, a young psychotic seductress whose idea of fun,[194] or "bounce" (hence the title) is "sexually entrapping the fathers of the kids she babysits and throwing rocks though, or shooting out, strangers windows to prove something to her unloving mother and absent father – none of whom could care less".[195] Nancy plans to have Jack steal a $50,000 payroll from Ray Ritchie, her older married millionaire sugar daddy, unleashing a game of violence and double cross between Jack and Nancy, with several unexpected plot twists – namely, the payroll steal plan is dropped half unexplained half way through the book – and an intriguingly open ended ending.

A definite milestone in Leonard's work, *The Big Bounce* merits extensive analysis from most Leonard's biographers,

---

[192] Although Leonard's crime novels were often "infused with Western tropes", cf. R. Sanders, Common Criminals and Ordinary Heroes, in Armchair Detective, 1989, quoted by Kris Mechalski, Rzepka, op. (ed) cit. p.81.
[193] Devlin, op. cit., p.135, Challen, op. cit., p 61. A further sign that Leonard wrote increasingly with film in mind, the novel's film rights were sold before the novel itself was published.
[194] "a nastier version of Lorraine Kidston", Devlin, op. cit. p 13.
[195] Rzepka, op.cit., p.83.

Devlin revealingly titling the chapter devoted to it in his work "*The First Book*".[196] Indeed, *The Big Bounce* marks the single most significant evolution in Elmore Leonard's writing and is one of his greatest novels. Set in the Detroit area, where Leonard lived and worked for most of his life, the novel has several autobiographical references (Mr Majestyk's reminiscences of WWII, Jack Ryan's alcoholism) and Leonard said Jack Ryan (the first in long line of ex-con main characters[197] and a "surly jerk who keeps making mistakes he regrets")[198] became the model for all is future protagonists.[199] Typically for Leonard, the novel's plot drifts randomly to a conclusion that seems to hint at a sequel that never was to be.[200] *The Big Bounce* has aptly been compared to *The Great Gatsby* and Jack Ryan and Nancy Hayes to a latter day Gatsby and Daisy Buchanan.[201]

The Director – Alex March

Alex March (New York, 1921 – Los Angeles 1989) was a proliferous but obscure TV producer and director active between 1953 and 1984, who directed three unremarkable feature films, one of which was *The Big Bounce*.[202]

---

[196] Devlin, op. cit., p.51.
[197] Geherin, op. cit., p.34.
[198] Ibid.
[199] Rzepka, op. cit., p.5.
[200] Although Jack Ryan reappeared in *Unknown Man #89* (1977).
[201] Devlin, op. cit., p.53.
[202] The most complete (which is not saying much...) source of information on Alex March can be found here: 'Alex March', *Fandom*, https://dallas.fandom.com/wiki/Alex_March#External_links (accessed 16 February 2021).

The Film

Released the same year of the novel's publication, *The Big Bounce* tells the same story the book does and, as always in Leonard adaptations, the original dialogue saved the scriptwriter a lot of work, and most of the best. There are some differences: the place is California instead of Michigan, the relationship between Jack Ryan (Ryan O'Neal, playing it sulky pin up), who is now a Viet vet as well as an ex-con, and Nancy (then O'Neil spouse Leigh Taylor-Young, playing wanton mischief and volatile histrionic modes on demand), no longer contrasted by age and social class and its several triangle ramifications, take centre stage, making the film more a melodrama with incidental criminality than a crime thriller. Also, the final outcome is somewhat sanitized to allow Ryan to retain a good guy aura and to dilute the novel's amorality.

Elmore Leonard hated the film, considering it the worst he ever saw, and described it in a letter to H N Swanson as "a 1957 situation TV script with dirty words".[203] The coeval critical consensus concurred. A H Wyler wrote in *The New York Times*: "'Have you ever thought of doing something else?' Mr. Heflin asks our hero at one point.[204] It's a question that could have been put to almost everyone concerned with *The Big Bounce*."[205]

Fortunately, Andrew Sarris was there to save the day: "*The Big Bounce* has been reviled more than it has been reviewed, some critics going so far as to condemn it as the

---

[203] Challen, op. cit., p.63.
[204] Van Heflin, in his second appearance in a Elmore Leonard adaptation after *3.10 to Yuma* (1957) playing Sam Mirakian, a renamed Mr Majestyk.
[205] A. H. Weiler, '*Big Bounce' Arrives*', *The New York Times*, 6 March 1969. Available at: https://www.nytimes.com/1969/03/06/archives/big-bounce-arrives.html (accessed 16 February 2021).

worst film of the still new year. Don't believe it. The worst movies of any year are usually those exercises in cultural clout that wind out in most people's ten best list. *The Big Bounce* is far from being a good movie but it isn't dull and it isn't burned down with high-brow ballast. Alex March's direction (...) is fairly slick, bland, and painless (and) the plotting spares us the cheap sentimentality of last-minute conversions, repentances and revelations. (...) what I like best about it is the casual acceptance of the total corruption of our society from the top (...) to the bottom (...)."[206]

I hesitate to add to this seamless evaluation, except perhaps to venture *The Big Bounce* is actually not very far from a good film, even if that would be just with a small "g". Indifferent actor's direction does practically ruin most of Elmore Leonard's dialogue and March's bland style lends the proceedings a soap opera tang that erodes the novel's ethos, but still this is the film – so far – that most retains the flavour of Elmore Leonard's "main period" novels of mid-20th Century US suburban existentialism, the characters enacting their personal take on the American Dream, namely to make as much money as possible, preferably through ingenious illegal means, and then spend it emulating the imagined consumption pattern of people one or two socio-economical notches above them. Admittedly, period art direction and wardrobe, appreciated at 50 year-plus distance, may contribute significantly to that flavour.

---

[206] Andrew Sarris, 'The Nihilism of Nudity', *The Village Voice*, 20 March 1969. Available at: https://news.google.com/newspapers?id=yccpAAAAIBAJ&sjid=9IsDAAAAIBAJ&pg=4526,2133523 (accessed 16 February 2021). I would presume to suggest reading the remainder of this delightful text, not least because in the end Andrew Sarris, that most progressive of film critics writing at the height of the 60s sexual revolution, protests at what he considers sexploitation, gratuitous nudity etc. in the film, which for contemporary viewers errs, if anything, amusingly on the side of bashfulness.

The Big Bounce (2004)

> *The Big Bounce*, 88 minutes. Warner Bros. Release date: 30 January 2004. Directed by George Armitage. Written by Sebastian Gutierrez. Produced by George Armitage, Steve Bing and Jorge Saralegui.
>
> Cast: Owen Wilson as Jack Ryan, Sarah Foster as Nancy Hayes, Morgan Freeman as Walter Crewes, Willie Nelson as Joe Lurie, Gary Sinise as Ray Ritche, Charlie Sheen as Bob Rogers Jr, Vinnie Jonas as Lou Harris.
>
> Cinematography: Jeffrey L Kimball; Editing: Brian Berdan and Barry Malkin; Music: George S Clinton; Sound: Christopher S Aud; Art Direction: John Bucklin.
>
> Budget: 50 MUSD. Box Office: 6.8 MUSD

The Director – George Armitage

George Armitage was born in Connecticut in 1943 and moved to Beverly Hills in 1956 with his mother, who wanted to pursue a screenwriting career in Hollywood. After majoring in economics and political science in UCLA, Armitage entered the film industry in 1965 via the mailroom at 20th Century Fox (for 53$ a week).[207] Being a young hipster at a time when counterculture awareness was becoming a plus in the industry, he quickly climbed through the ranks, becoming junior associate producer in the studio's TV department the following year.

---

[207] Nick Pinkerton, 'Interview: George Armitage', *Film Comment*, April 2015. Available at: https://www.filmcomment.com/blog/interview-george-armitage/ (accessed 16 February 2021).

Armitage met indie mogul Roger Corman in 1967 when Corman was directing *The St. Valentine's Day Massacre* at Fox, and left the studio the same year to concentrate on scriptwriting, getting his first shot at writing and directing for Corman's New World Pictures in 1972 with *Private Duty Nurses*, the start of a long and fruitful relationship with Corman, if mainly as screenwriter and script editor: in the subsequent 50 years, Armitage sat behind the director's chair only seven times and to this day is known mainly by his two 90s cult hits *Miami Blues* (1990) and *Grosse Pointe Blank* (1997).

A fellow traveler of Corman's second generation recruits (along Jonathan Demme, Curtis Hanson, Monte Hellman or Paul Bartel) Armitage has been championed as one of the most underrated directors ever.[208] Scholarly attention has been otherwise all but absent. A fondness for location filming and for optimistic, upbeat characters and strong women characterize his films.[209] Stanley Kubrick is his favourite director and *Dr Strangelove* (Kubrick, 1964) his favourite film.[210] *The Big Bounce* is his last directorial effort to date.

The Film

The remake relocates to Hawaii and retains the original plot about 2/3 of the way, concluding with a series of surprising plot twists which are both entertaining and

---

[208] Mainly in *Film Comment*, first by Dave Kerr in the magazine's 1977 September/October issue, and later by Nick Pinkerton, loc. cit. supra.

[209] "(...) as a trouble making left winger I thought 'Let's do all we can to support (women)'" Armitage interviewed in Paul Rowlands' 'An Interview with George Armitage (Part 1 of 3)', *Money Into Light*. Available at: http://www.money-into-light.com/2016/12/an-interview-with-george-armitage-part.html (accessed 16 February 2021).

[210] Ibid.

Leonardian, but were absent from both the novel and the previous film version.[211] From the opening credits on, Henry Mancini-like jazzy background music ensures the audience of the lightness and coolness of the proceedings. Cameos by Harry Dean Stanton and Willy Nelson, especially in a delightfully Hawksian[212] domino-playing scene with Walter Crewes (Mr Majestyk/Sam Mirakian renamed again, efficiently played by Morgan Freeman) also contribute, and the dialogue, once more the best thing in the film – and, for once, occasionally improved from the original by Owen Wilson's (playing Jack Ryan with his usual Woody Allen-sounding delivery) frequent improvisations[213] – adding the final touch. On the minus side, Nancy Hayes (Sara Foster, insipid) is now a mischievous gold digger rather than a psycho, validating once again Hitchcock's dictum to the effect that a film is only as good as the bad guy (or in this case, girl) is bad.

The film was marketed as a comedy, so the final cut left out some explicit scenes and language[214] to ensure a PG-13 rating, to the dismay of Armitage, who complained that in the released version "nothing works" and the Leonardian flavour was absent, so he "left the picture after the second cut".[215]

The Big Bounce belongs to the post-*Pulp Fiction* (Quentin Tarantino, 1994) cool caper fad series of Elmore Leonard adaptations which started with *Get Shorty* (Barry Sonnenfeld, 1995) continued with *Jackie Brown* (Tarantino,

---

[211] Armitage told Nick Pinkerton Elmore Leonard assisted in the scriptwriting, but it seems unlikely the final plot changes were suggested by him. Cf. Nick Pinkerton, loc. cit.
[212] A tendency to proliferous allusions to Howard Hawks plagues me perhaps more than the similar tendency regarding Samuel Beckett, but in this particular case I can claim to be borne by Nick Pinkerton, loc cit.
[213] Ibid.
[214] Including the overdubbing of several f words, which is noticeable if one looks closely to the actors' lip movements.
[215] Ibid.

1997), *Out of Sight* (Steven Soderbergh, 1997) and the subsequent *Be Cool* (F Gary Gray, 2005). Whether due to the final cut emasculation Armitage – who never directed again – lambasted or not, the film was a critic and box office flop, returning 6 MUSD on a 50 MUSD investment. Elmore Leonard himself liked it even less than the version released 35 years previous and commented a propos, in an interview with *The Guardian* in 2004: "It's a mystery to me why people buy one of my books and then take out everything that made them buy it in the first place."[216]

This evaluation is unfair. *The Big Bounce* is and adaptation, not an illustration, of the novel and it functions well enough as light caper/one liner entertainment, surprising final plot twists managing to be both preposterous and plausible. Elmore Leonard might be not expected to accept that Armitage's vision would be different than his, but that's another matter. It's the matter of this book.

---

[216] Jeff Hudson, '*Detroit Spinner*', *The Guardian*, July 2004. Available at: https://www.theguardian.com/film/2004/jul/31/booksforchildren-andteenagers.elmoreleonard (accessed 16 February 2021).

The Moonshine War (1970)

> *The Moonshine War*. 100 minutes. MGM; 1970. Release date: 31 July 1970. Directed by Richard Quine. Written by Elmore Leonard. Produced by Martin Ransohoff.
>
> Cast: Patrick McGoohan as Frank Long, Richard Widmark as Dr Emmett Taulbee, Alan Alda as John W Martin, Melodie Johnson as Lizann Simpson, Will Geer as Mr Baylor, Joe Williams as Aaron, Suzanne Zenor as Miley Mitchell; Harry Carey Jr as Arley Stamper.
>
> Cinematography: Richard H Kline; Editing: Allan Jacobs; Music: Fred Karger; Sound: Franklin Milton; Art Direction: Edward C

The Story

> *"You pointing that at me, boy?" "No, suh, it pointing out of my arm" "I'm telling you you're pointing at me. (...) No n***** points a gun at me." "Mister, I ain't pointing the gun, it pointing itself." "Put it down." "I like to, but my finger caught in the trigger. I'm afraid to move it"* (*The Moonshine War*, edition consulted, William Morrow, New York, 2012, p.94)

The Moonshine War was the 7th novel written by Elmore Leonard. It was published by Doubleday in 1969, the same year as *The Big Bounce*. The action takes place during Prohibition, making this Leonard's first period novel, Westerns excepted.[217] It first saw the light of day as a 10 page script

---

[217] And one of only two, the other being *Cuba Libre* (1998) set before the Spanish-American War.

outline sold to MGM for 50.000$,[218] which was subsequently developed into a full novel, marking the first time Leonard adapted his own work for the screen. Impressed by this, H N Swanson, in a letter to Leonard dated 25 September 1968, wrote: "Any time you decide you want a career as screenwriter I am ready to run with you".[219] In the next few years Leonard would try his hand at scriptwriting a number of times, but most of the resulting output remains either unsold or unfilmed to date.[220] Exceptions will be addressed in due course.

Synopsis: Kentucky, 1931. Frank Long, a corrupt Prohibition agent, got word that Son Martin has 125.000$ worth of moonshine hidden somewhere and tries to use his authority to extract the location from him. Failing that, Frank calls in "Dr". Emmett Taulbee, the Leonard psycho of the hour, who deploys more violent methods in getting what he wants whilst affecting a faux Southern courtesy, causing Frank to change his mind and assist Martin in using the standard Leonard hero skill set, this time leveraged by a significant stock of dynamite, to keep the booze and the money.

The Moonshine War retains some of the flavour of Leonard's earlier Western novels and a loose-jointed rambling plot with unexpected twists and turns with some shifting loyalties before the final showdown. The novel features one of Leonard's signature scenes, in which the heavies on duty force a young couple to strip in the middle of a diner, just for the fun of it.[221] A gripping read, mostly, as always, due

---

[218] Devlin, op. cit. p.14. Rzepka, somewhat misleadingly, seems to imply the screenplay was written before the novel (op. cit. p.99).
[219] Devlin, loc. cit, note 14.
[220] Geherin, op cit. pp.40-43, Rzepka, op. cit. p.92.
[221] Pp.70-76 of the edition consulted, William Morrow 2012. Stage-setting scenes of cowardly bullying, designed to dispose the reader against the villains whilst contrasting their victim's behaviour with the bravery and

to dialogue, *The Moonshine War* lacks the irony that characterize Leonard's best fiction.[222]

The Director – Richard Quine

Detroit born Richard Quine (1920 -1989) moved to LA with his family at the age of 6 and pursued a calling as child actor that continued to adulthood. He nourished ambitions of becoming a leading man in film, but as his career plateaued around fourth or fifth billing in the early 40s, Quine switched to directing and producing in TV and film.

In July 1951 he signed a seven-year contract with Columbia, where he became the studio's main director for musicals and sophisticated comedies, going on to direct *The Sunny Side of the Street* (1951) *My Sister Eileen* (1955),[223] *Bell, Book and Candle* (1958) and *Paris When it Sizzles* (1964), among several others, generally with considerable commercial success and some critical acknowledgment, if mostly of the lowbrow variety. From the late 60s on, Quine's style and genres fell out of public favour and his films became sparser and less successful, his final film being *The Prisoner of Zenda* (1979). Afflicted by depression and poor health, Richard Quine took his own life with a gunshot to the head in 1989.

---

cunning of the heroes, are typical of early Leonard. See, for instance, the scene in *Hombre* in which Frank Braden cowers an ex-soldier into relinquishing his stagecoach ticket, pp.27-31 of Weidenfeld & Nicolson 2017 edition.

[222] Devlin reads in *The Moonshine War* echoes of Erskine Caldwell, op. cit. p.105. I only know Caldwell, through John Ford´s adaptation of *Tobacco Road*, and on that basis I would tend to agree. But by that rationale you could also see in *The Moonshine War* (the film) echoes of Lil´Abner...

[223] Which Quine co-wrote with Blake Edwards. Quine and Edwards shared a marked stylistic affinity and established a close working relationship throughout the 50s and early 60s, co-writing, co-directing and reciprocally directing each others' screenplays.

Richard Quine was a respected professional in the industry at the height of his career, but his name was virtually unknown to the general public and generally ignored by the critical establishment. The dean of French film historians, Georges Sadoul, considered him "second rate, with some success in musicals"[224] and even the usually reliable Andrew Sarris dismissed Richard Quine as "an inoffensive imitator of his betters".[225] More sensitively, if counterintuitively, Lindsay Anderson considered Quine's films "not merely well-directed films; there is a wry, disenchanted quality about them which betrays the presence behind the camera of an individual, a human being and a rather sensitive one".[226]

But as with Budd Boetticher and so many others, it was the *Cahiers du Cinema* that eventually righted the wrong, with a piece by chief MacMahonian Bertrand Tavernier in the magazine's July 1962 issue appropriately entitled 'Introducing Richard Quine'. The rest is film history: Jean Tulard considers him the *"grand maître de la comédie a la Columbia"*[227] and his virtuosity with wide screen formats, which Fritz Lang famously quipped were good only for filming snakes and funerals, has often been noted.

Again like Boetticher and others, this evaluation falls short and, again, perhaps shorter on the western shores of the Atlantic. Appropriately, another former *Cahiers* critic, none other than Jean-Luc Godard, mentioned Richard

---

[224] Georges Sadoul, *Dictionnaire des Cinéastes*, Editions du Seuil 1965. Sadoul's evaluation brings to mind Fred Astaire's legendary first screen test verdict: "Can't sing, can't act, can dance a little".

[225] Sarris, op. cit. p.264

[226] Joe Baltake, 'Richard Quine, at Columbia and Beyond', April 9 2018, *Moviegoer*. Available at http://thepassionatemoviegoer.blogspot.com/2018/04/richard-quine-at-columbia-and-beyond.html (accessed 21 March 2021).

[227] Tulard, op cit., pp.631-632. Tulard notes Quine owed to Blake Edwards the sense of burlesque.

Quine's *Pushover* (1954, which catapulted Kim Novak to the limelight) as having influenced *À Bout de Souffle* (1960).[228] Godard also once said that future historians would consider him the last of the primitives, not the first of the moderns. I would conversely contribute Richard Quine was both one of the last classics and one of the first postmoderns, his films accompanying the decline and fall of classic US cinema and revealing a self-referential sense of genre and convention absent in the generation he succeeded to and, consciously or not, sought to emulate.[229] His sophistication lacked the cruelty of Ernst Lubitsch or the vivacity of Stanley Donen, but there was plenty left over, nonchalance thickly disguising wounded sadness.

The Film

Since Elmore Leonard adapted his own novel to the screen the issue of fidelity to the original is mute, sufficing to state that the film retains almost the entirety of the plot and dialogue of its source.

The influence of, or rather reference to, *Bonnie and Clyde* (Arthur Penn, 1967)[230] is clearly visible in *The Moonshine War*, and, very appropriately considering its director, the film is one of the first indications retro was becoming a thing at the turn of the 70s.[231] If the book was said to have

---

[228] See *Cahiers do Cinema, The 1960s*, Harvard University Press, 1986, edited by Jim Hillier, p.48 note 5. Coincidentally, Fritz Lang's aforementioned remark is also from a Godard Film: *Le Mépris* (1963).

[229] John Sturges, to whom I will revert in a subsequent chapter, strikes me similarly.

[230] Devlin, op.cit, p.14.

[231] Preceded by, other than *Bonnie and Clyde* itself, *Thoroughly Modern Milly* (George Roy Hill, 1967) and *Hello Dolly* (Gene Kelly, 1969), and succeeded by *The Sting* (George Roy Hill, 1973) and even, to some extent, *The Godfather* (Francis Ford Coppola, 1971), to name but the most notorious examples.

resonances of William Faulkner or Erskine Caldwell, the film can be said to resonate of John Ford[232] (so much so that the characters even sing *Oh My Darling Clementine* and *Shall Gather at the River*).

Not particularly well received at the time,[233] and hated by Leonard himself,[234] *The Moonshine War* is consistently entertaining and one of the rare cases in which Leonard's dialogue is brought to full effect, be it dramatic, comedic, or pathetic, and, as in Boetticher in *The Tall T*, a film in which the director manages to comment creatively on his literary source while remaining true to his own vision, in Richard Quine's case a misanthropic lyricism.

To no detriment to Quine, and exceptionally in Leonard adaptations, much of the pleasure of the film derives from the acting, or rather, overacting, namely of Richard Widmark as "Dr" Emmet Taubee, of country singer Lee Hazlewood as "Dr" Taubee's typically Leonardian psycho henchman, the brilliantly named Dual Metters, playing it hillbilly languid rather than the usual highly strung sadist, and last, and in this case somewhat least, of Melodie Johnson as Taubee's halfwit moll Lizann Simpson. The flip-side of this coin is that so much attention is dispensed to the baddies that the notional protagonists take definite second seat, Alan Alda uncharismatically strained – the exact opposite of Leonardian cool- as supposed leading man Son Martin, the remaining cast sitting worthy to allow for the aforementioned trio to shine.

The plot develops flawlessly from beginning to Leonardian anticlimactic end, the unorthodox focus on the

---

[232] Brings to my mind in particular, for some reason, *The Sun Shines Bright* (1953).
[233] Hellywell calls it a "downright peculiar hillbilly melodrama, interesting only in fits and starts" (op. cit. p. 694). Downright peculiar, certainly, but that's a compliment, and the interest is sustained.
[234] Challen, loc. cit.

unsympathetic villains being perhaps the reason for the lukewarm critical reception and Elmore Leonard's dislike. But to me he disliked erroneously: same as, say, *Batman Returns* (Tim Burton, 1993) is the best film of that franchise in spite of, or perhaps because, the virtual absence of Batman to the benefit of Danny de Vito's Penguin, in *Moonshine War* Richard Quine characteristically followed Hitchcock's aforementioned bad guy dictum, to effective effect.

Valdez is Coming (1971)

> *Valdez is Coming*, 90 minutes United Artists 1971. Release date: 9 April 1971. Directed by Edwin Sherin. Written by Roland Kibbee and David Rayfiel. Produced by Ira Steiner.
>
> Cast: Burt Lancaster as Valdez, Susan Clark as Gay Erin, Frank Silvera as Diego, John Cypher as Frank Tanner, Richard Jordan as R L Davis, Barton Heyman as El Segundo, Hector Elizondo as Mexican rider.
>
> Cinematography: Gábor Pogány; Editing: James T Heckert and George Rohrs; Music: Charles Gross; Sound: Bud Alper; Art Direction: José María Tapiador.
> Box Office: 4.7 MUSD (USA 3 MUSD)

The Story

"He says get me a bottle, you run." "I get it, I don't run". (*Valdez is Coming*, p.14. Edition consulted, Orion, London, 2005)

Valdez is Coming was Elmore Leonard's 8th novel. It was published by Fawcett Gold Medal in 1970. It immediately succeeded *The Moonshine War* and it is the first of his three returns to the Western after *The Big Bounce*.

Synopsis: Town constable Bob Valdez mistakenly kills an innocent man at the behest of rich rancher Frank Tanner, so he feels the least that can be done, once the mistake is established, is to compensate the innocent man's Indian widow with 200$, half of which to be contributed by Tanner himself. Tanner doesn't see things this way, and after an animated exchange with Valdez he has his men tie the latter to a heavy wooden cross and send him to the desert to face what seems like certain death. But Valdez luckily survives and duly seeks redress, having word reach Tanner that "Valdez is coming", ensuing a series of confrontations with Tanner's men culminating in a typical Leonardian showdown.

Valdez is Coming is familiar Elmore Leonard territory. It is essentially an expansion of the short story *Only the Good Ones*,[235] in which Bob Valdez and Frank Tanner had previously appeared, Valdez being resurrected for the purposes of the novel, which also borrows from previous short stories *The Hard Way*[236] and *Saint with a Sixgun*.[237] Conventionally, even stereotypically heroic,[238] *Valdez is Coming* suggests Leonard might be tiring of Westerns.[239] But the novel was seen by the author as a major turning point, both commercially and in terms of writing maturity: "it started with *Valdez is Coming*" he told Challen," I was staring to loosen up with that one".[240]

Indeed, if *Valdez is Coming* can be considered to be the climax of Leonard's conventional Western virtuosity (*Hombre* being, for this purpose, "unconventional") it is not without development and innovation relative to hitherto acquired Leonardian narrative structure. Valdez himself, for

---

[235] First published in *Western Roundup*, New York, MacMillan, 1961.
[236] *Zane Grey's Western*, August 1953.
[237] *Argosy*, October, 1954. All the aforementioned stories have since been republished in several compilations, the definitive being *Elmore Leonard: The Complete Western Stories*, HarperCollins, New York, 2004.
[238] Geherin, op. cit., p.36. Devlin sees passages of what he considers outright Hemingway pastiche (op. cit. p 45) which I must confess don't strike me as such. Perhaps less farfetched, Segato sees echoes of Herman Melville's *Billy Budd* (op. cit. p.48 note 8) in *Valdez is Coming*. Surprisingly for an author who reads so much into Leonard's catholic background, Segato fails to mention the crucifixion scene, the novel's "signature" scene, in his book.
[239] Geherin, op. cit., p.37.
[240] Challen, op. cit., p.71.

instance, switches from victim to avenger in extreme fashion: all he wants is to collect money to provide some measure of compensation to the widow of a mistakenly executed man, but in the process he kidnaps a woman and does all the killing in the book:[241] 12 men shot dead, including the mistaken execution...[242] The final allegiance switch and "peaceful" conflict resolution, *par contre*, are vintage Leonard.

With *Valdez is Coming*, beside further consolidating his financial independence (the novel's film rights were sold for 45.000$) [243] Leonard learned (...) "how to become invisible behind the ventriloquy of free indirect discourse".[244]

The Director – Edwin Sherin

Pennsylvanian Brown graduate Korean war vet Edwin Sherin (1930 – 2017) was an American theatre and television director and producer, who distinguished himself foremost on the stage on Broadway, in London and Washington DC, winning Pulitzer and Tony awards for *The Great White Hope* in 1974 in a decades-long career in which he staged many classical repertoire plays, from Shakespeare to Eugene O'Neill.

On TV he directed dozens of episodes of the popular series *Law and Order*, *Hill Street Blues*, *Moonlighting* and *LA*

---

[241] Female characters in *The Captives* and *Hombre* suffer similar fates, cf. supra.
[242] Michael Scrivener, in his aforementioned article [Rzepka, op. (ed) cit, p.21] also points this out, in the context of what he qualifies as the "Sartrean hypocrisy" of several Leonard protagonists.
[243] Devlin, op. cit., p.14
[244] Rzepka, op. cit., p.66.

Law. For the big screen he only directed twice, both in 1971, *Valdez is Coming* being one of them.[245]

The Film

This being the first film for which Elmore Leonard wrote the script himself, the point of putative fidelity to the novel becomes again mute,[246] it sufficing to state that the film follows very closely the novel's plot and, perhaps revealingly considering the screenplay's authorship, it relies comparatively less on Leonard's dialogue and frequently allows the action to unfold through visual means. Still, much of the dialogue is taken verbatim from the book, although, as often in film adaptations of Leonard, the delivery mostly fails to convey the deadpan effect it has in the written page.

The film was received generally negatively upon release. Vincent Canby, who succeeded Bosley Crowther as resident *New York Times* film critic and de facto East Coast arbiter of cinematic taste, detected "(...) A lot of fancy flourishes, which I associate with Mr. Sherin's stage work".[247] Elmore Leonard reportedly didn't like the film either. More forgiving, Devlin, the only Leonard scholar to comment on the

---

[245] Patrick Shanley, 'Edwin Sherin, Director of 'The Great White Hope' on Broadway and 'Law & Order,' Dies at 87', May 5 2017, *The Hollywood Reporter*, https://www.hollywoodreporter.com/news/edwin-sherin-dead-pulitzer-prize-winning-theater-director-was-87-1000761 (accessed 21 March 2021). IMDb claims Sherin was Burt Lancaster's personal, and surprise, choice for director.

[246] I might here interject that the same applies to Samuel Beckett's translations of his own work to and from English and French but, considering what I wrote previously about my excessive tendency to find analogies with Beckett, I will not make such an interjection.

[247] Vincent Canby, *The New York Times*, film review, "'Valdez Is Coming': Burt Lancaster Stars in Vengeful Western," April 10, 1971. Not quite spot on, I would argue, although it does seem to suggest that the sensitivity of Andrew Sarris and his coreligionists was beginning to permeate the mainstream.

film, considers that "Not quite in the league of *Hombre*, *Valdez is Coming* is still furlongs ahead of the average horse opera".[248]

My personal judgement would fall somewhere in between. Edwin Sherin's direction is certainly more understated, maybe even sedated, than his lively TV police and detective dramas and comedies would lead to expect, but Burt Lancaster is effective at playing Valdez as a meekly righteous rather than stoically defiant Mexican and the main cast (Susan Clark, John Cypher, Richard Jordan and Frank Silvera) more than hold their own (as kidnapee on the verge of Stockholm syndrome, cowardly cruel boss, usual psycho-sadist henchman and hardboiled but ultimately standup desperado, respectively). Action sequences are adequately enacted and Sherin modestly but effectively appropriates John Ford and Sergio Leone's scenography of deserted landscapes and white adobes.[249] By no means least, the final confrontation scene does perfect justice to, no to say surpasses, that of the novel, ending the film with a bang that allows the viewer to forget some of its shortcomings.

---

[248] Devlin, op. cit., p.138.
[249] Shot in Spain, cf Devlin, op. cit., p.137.

Joe Kidd (1972)

> *Joe Kidd,* 88 minutes, Universal Studios 1972. Release date: 19 July 1972. Directed by John Sturges. Written by Elmore Leonard. Produced by Sidney Beckerman.
>
> Cast: Clint Eastwood as Joe Kidd, Robert Duvall as Frank Harlan, John Saxon as Luis Chama, Don Stroud as Lamarr, Stella Garcia as Helen Sanchez, James Wainwright as Mingo, Gregory Walcott as Mitchell.
>
> Cinematography: Bruce Surtees; Editing: Ferris Webster; Music: Lalo Schifrin; Sound: John R Alexander and Walden O Watson; Art Direction: Henry Bumstead and Alexander Golitzen.
>
> Box Office: 7.3 MUSD (USA 6.3 MUSD)

The Story

Joe Kidd: *What's the matter, you run out of nerve?*

Joe Kidd was the first screenplay written by Elmore Leonard and adapted to the screen that didn't originate from previous fictional material. The first of four screenplays he wrote which never found their way to novel format, it was written at a time when Leonard's was working primarily for the screen, selling a number of screenplays that, although not all filmed, supported him financially while he matured his skills as a crime/caper writer.[250] *Joe Kidd* was bought by Clint Eastwood in 1971 and made it to the screen the following year.

---

[250] Devlin, op. cit., p.138; Geherin, op. cit., p.43; Rzepka, op. cit., p.92.

Synopsis: New Mexico, early 1900s. Mexican American Luis Chama (John Saxon) leads a peasant fight against vicious land baron Frank Harlan (Robert Duvall), who hires ex-bounty hunter Joe Kidd (Clint Eastwood) to assist him, the latter becoming gradually estranged by Harlan's brutal methods, switching sides toward the end of the film, which concludes, as usual, with a showdown.

The plot borrows heavily from Leonard's first novel (*Bounty Hunters*, 1953) and revisits much of the thematic of his Western canon, e.g. the unfavourable portrayal of economic power, the unsentimental sympathy for the underdog, the shifting allegiance of the non-committed protagonist or the lopsided dramatic resolution, with vengeance served with a twist.

The Director – John Sturges

John Sturges (1910-1992) entered RKO in 1932, where we worked as an assistant to David O Selznick[251] and in the editing department, in such films as *Of Human Bondage* (John Cromwell, 1934) and *Gunga Din* (George Stevens, 1939). After Air Force service in World War II he returned to Hollywood, getting his first shot at directing in 1946 with *The Men Who Dared*, a B noir, the first of several. In 1949 he directed *The Walking Hills*, his first Western, the genre for which he was subsequently to be mostly renowned. Sturges' breakthrough to the major league was *Bad Day at Back Rock* (1955) a film about the then controversial sub-

---

[251] Michael Barson, 'John Sturges', *Encyclopaedia Britannica*, 1 January 2021, https://www.britannica.com/biography/John-Sturges (accessed 21 March 2021).

ject matter of racial discrimination against Japanese-Americans after the war, which won critical acclaim and his only Oscar nomination.[252]

Today, Sturges is perhaps best remembered for *The Magnificent Seven* (1960), a remake of Akira Kurosawa's *Sichinin no Samurai* (1954), which was selected for preservation in the United States National Film Registry by the Library of Congress as being "culturally, historically, or aesthetically significant".[253] Certainly more significant for the history of popular culture, not to mention public health, an excerpt of the film's score (by Henry Mancini) was for decades associated with commercials for Marlboro cigarettes. Kurosawa once personally told Sturges he loved the remake, and Sturges considered this the proudest moment in his career.[254]

Sturges has an uneven reputation. Georges Sadoul dryly asserts the great Sturges was *"l'autre"*, John being only good at Westerns and even then only as good as the scripts he was given.[255] The *Cahiers du Cinema* didn't like him

---

[252] 'The 28th Academy Awards | 1956', *Oscars*, https://www.oscars.org/oscars/ceremonies/1956 (accessed 21 March 2021). I hasten to interject that IMHO the history of US cinema and that of Oscar nominations and awards are things quite, quite apart.

[253] Stephen Price, *The Magnificent Seven*. Available at: https://www.loc.gov/static/programs/national-film-preservation-board/documents/magnificent_seven.pdf (accessed 21 March 2021).

[254] 'Died Today (August 18th) – Director John Sturges (The Great Escape, The Magnificent Seven)', August 18 2016, *Festival Reviews*, https://festivalreviews.org/2016/08/18/died-today-august-18th-director-john-sturges-the-great-escape-the-magnificent-seven/ (accessed 21 March 2021). I'll leave considerations about Sturges' awareness of Japanese obligatory politeness and his taste in Japanese directors for another occasion.

[255] *"L'autre"* being, of course, Preston. Sadoul, op. cit., p.238. No contest, but being a lesser director than Preston Sturges should hardly be taken as diminishing.

much either: André Bazin blasted his adaptation of Hemingway's *The Old Man and the Sea*.[256] On cue, Sarris called him ""The American Kurosawa, tortured, humourless and self-consciously social". [257]

More generous, Tulard, whilst insisting that *"il vaut surtout pour les Westerns"* added *"libre aux puristes de lui préférer Daves ou Mann"*.[258] Cook and others point out to his innovative use of widescreen.[259] The highest praise was perhaps lavished by John Carpenter: "John Sturges was one of cinema's greatest action directors (...) For my money, he's also a candidate for one of last century's most underrated directors, period".[260]

John Sturges was to noir and Western what Richard Quine was to the musical and the sophisticated comedy: a "transition" director, catching the tail-end of the classical studio system soon enough to be in it but late enough for self-reference and nostalgia to sneak in. Like many of his contemporaries, he could be over-serious, and John Carpenter's assertion is certainly more than a little hyperbolic, but John Sturges was a relevant director and the history of the Western wouldn't be the same without his best films.

---

[256] *Cahiers du cinéma*, July 1958, p.85. Of course, blasting film adaptations of prestigious literary works was one of the *Cahiers*' favourite sports.
[257] Sarris, op. cit., p.202.
[258] Tulard, op. cit., p.746. Agree on Daves, not so sure on Mann.
[259] Cook, op. cit., p.498. Cook lists Sturges with the coeval cofounders of the "psychological" Western, mentioning Boetticher et. al., and goes on to contrast this "realist" tradition with that of John Ford (p.511), an assertion which can be qualified, with kindness, as dated.
[260] For full disclosure, this quote comes from the cover notes of a book on Sturges: *Escape Artist: The␣FIlms and FIlms of John Sturges*, Glenn Lovell, Wisconsin University Press, 2008.

The Film

Intended as a Western comeback for Sturges and marketed as a Clint Eastwood vehicle (the introductory close-up shot of Eastwood is standard classical Hollywood style), *Joe Kidd* mostly failed at both.

Box office was fair to middling (7,4 MUSD) and critical reception lukewarm. *The Village Voice*'s Michael McKegney considered the film a "mild comeback, dull and heavy in the manner of *OK Korral* and *Last Train to Gun Hill*" and rightly considered Budd Boetticher "did much better with similar material and less means".[261] In the same vein, Jean Tulard considers Joe Kidd *"traduit un incontestable essouflement" (...) trop marqué(...) pour l'influence du Western spaghetti*".[262] Ambiguously, the *Encyclopedia Britannica* considers the film "arguably (John Sturges') best film since *The Great Escape*".[263] Not without reason, Hallywell calls it a "rough and tumble star Western with untenable moral attitudes".[264]

As mentioned above, the film recovers many of Leonard's recurrent themes, with no value added. Eastwood's iconic cool, Duvall histrionic evil, Bruce Surtee's cinematography and some very well scouted location landscape insufficiently compensate for formulaic to clumsy plot development, subpar (for Leonard's standards) dialogue and

---

[261] Michael McKegney 'Film: Maverick with a Cause', 31 August 1972, *The Village Voice*. Available at: https://news.google.com/newspapers?id=FONLAAAAIBAJ&sjid=NIwDAAAAIBAJ&pg=6308,1699459 (accessed 21 March 2021)
[262] Tulard, loc. cit.
[263] Michael Barson, 'John Sturges', *Encyclopaedia Britannica*, 1 January 2021, https://www.britannica.com/biography/John-Sturges (accessed 21 March 2021).
[264] Hallywell, op. cit., p.539.

John Saxon's caricature Mexican. A final sequence of a locomotive ramming into a saloon – part of Joe Kidd's plan to win the day - although preposterous, does allow for the film to end on a merry note. Nevertheless, *Kidd* is an unquestionably inferior coda to John Sturges' Western oeuvre.[265]

---

[265] Sturges was an alcoholic and his drinking interfered chronically with shooting, causing a tense relationship with Eastwood, who disapproved of what he understandably considered unprofessional behaviour (*IMDb*, https://www.imdb.com/title/tt0068768/trivia/?ref_=tt_trv_trv; accessed 18 January 2022).

Mr. Majestyk (1974)

> *Mr. Majestyk*, 103 minutes, United Artists 1974. Release date: 17 July 1974. Directed by Richard Fleischer. Written by Elmore Leonard. Produced by Walter Mirisch.
>
> Cast: Charles Bronson as Vince Majestyk, Al Lettieri as Frank Renda, Linda Cristal as Nancy Chavez, Lee Purcell as Wiley, Paul Koslo as Bobby Kopas, Frank Maxwell as Det. Lt. McAllan, Alejandro Rey as Larry Mendoza.
>
> Cinematography: Richard H Kline; Editing: Ralph E Winters: Music: Charles Bernstein; Sound: Harold M Etherington; Art Direction: Sam Gordon.
>
> Box Office: 129.000 USD (USA)

The Story

> *"It seemd easier to get out of jail than it was to get back in"* (*Mr Makestyk*, edition consulted: William Morrow, New York, 2012, p.73)

With *Mr. Majestyk*, Elmore Leonard "reversed the book to movie process"[266]: Written at the height of his screenwriting phase, *Mr Majestyk* reuses an idea Leonard first considered in a previous unsold script, based on migrant farm workers (*Picket Line*, 1971). Initially an outline for a Clint Eastwood vehicle, *Mr Majestyk* was eventually bought by Walter Mirisch for a film with Charles Bronson in the leading role.[267] It was published by Dell in 1974, the same

---

[266] Challen, op. cit., p.78; see also Geherin, op. cit., pp.10, 42.
[267] Devlin, op. cit., pp.15, 138.

year as the film's release, being Leonard's 10th novel, and the 7th adapted to/from the screen.

Synopsis: Arizona, 1970s. Vincent Majestyk (as mentioned previously, no relation to *The Big Bounce*'s Walter) is a smalltime farmer who is trying to get his melons picked before the end of the season. After confronting a hustler who tries to impose on him a crew he doesn't want to hire, Majestyk is arrested for assault and ends up sharing a jail bus with mob operative Frank Renda (again a name taken from an unrelated character in a previous Leonard work, *Escape from Five Shadows*, a 1956 Western novel which hasn't been adapted to the screen so far), subsequently partnering with Renda to escape but finally pulling a Leonardian switch to square things with the law.

Mr Majestyk is basically a western transposed to the mid 20th century, with mid 20th century USA traits, such as increasing multiculturalism and social awareness thrown in (the crew Majestyk hired is Mexican and the one peddled on him is "Anglo").[268] Vincent Majestyk is like Frank Ryan, an ex-con and a war vet, who uses Leonardian cool, namely, unlike Frank Renda, not getting emotional about his predicaments, to succeed.[269]

The Director – Richard Fleischer

Richard Fleischer's (1916 – 2006) directorial career spanned from the height of the classical period through New Hollywood all the way to the movie brat generation. Born in Brooklyn to a Polish-Jewish family (his father being none other than animation pioneer Max Fleischer, creator of Betty Boop and arch-rival of Walt Disney), after studies at Yale Drama School, Fleischer joined RKO in 1942, where

---

[268] Rszepka, op. cit., p.62.
[269] "Being cool means not taking it personally". Rszepka, op. cit., p.111.

he directed shorts, documentaries and "flicker flashbacks" (silent comedy samplers), graduating to feature direction with *Child of Divorce* in 1947, the same year the documentary *Design for Death*, co-written with Theodor Geisel (aka Dr Seuss) won him his only Oscar. Subsequently he directed mostly B noirs till poetic justice visited in the form of an invitation by... Walt Disney, to direct *20.000 Leagues Under the Sea*, in 1954. Having gotten to the A-list, Fleischer stayed there for over 30 years, there ensuing a dazzlingly eclectic career which included numerous big-budget, tentpole films and major box-office hits. He retired from directing in 1987 but remained active in the industry in various forms, including as head of merchandizing for Betty Boop.

Fleischer was commercially successful and had a solid reputation as journeyman and "replacement director", filling in when directors were removed or removed themselves from projects due to artistic or other differences. Otherwise, hardly anyone took him really serious except (who else?) the *Cahiers du Cinema*, through the pen of Jacques Rivette, who, in a seminal piece in the magazine's December 1955 issue, considered Richard Fleischer one of four "indisputable front-rankers" US directors in need of serious attention.[270] But this long remained a minority report. In the very same venerable publication, Luc Moullet, reviewing *The Vikings* (1958), astonishingly proclaims Fleischer is *"mal a l'aise dans la superproduction"*.[271] And Andrew Sarris, for once totally off the mark, incomprehensibly files Richard Fleischer under "Strained Seriousness"

---

[270] Jacques Rivette, *"Notes sur une révolution"*, *Cahiers du Cinéma* No.54, December 1955. The four were Richard Fleischer, Samuel Fuller, Joseph Losey and Edward G Ulmer. Three out of four right, that's not bad.

[271] *Cahiers du cinéma* No.92, March 1959. The review is otherwise an exceptionally perceptive appreciation of Fleischer's style.

and considers his career "sputtered to 50%" after *Narrow Margin* (1952)[272], a film that is also singled out by Jean Tulard, who *par contre* qualifies Fleischer's career as a *"carriére en dents de scie oú, malgré tout, les bons films l'emportent sous les mediocres"*.[273]

I never saw a mediocre Richard Fleischer film so I woudn't know. Make no mistake: Fleischer easily is the greatest director to have graced the pages of this book so far, Budd Boetticher excepted. From gritty kitchen sink to SciF FX, from the Middle Ages to the bottoms of the sea, there's no genre he didn't illuminate, pulling several times his own weight in the secular labour of casting the tinsel in Tinseltown. A sort of Ed Wood without the talentlessness, Richard Fleischer was hallowed with the reckless *je ne sais quoi* essential to put the twinkle in the eye of the spectator. In this, Fleischer stands shoulder to shoulder with the likes of Stanley Donen.[274]

<u>The Film</u>

Since the film preceded the book on this one, the question of fidelity to the original should be put in reverse, except it needn't, as both coincide almost perfectly, with the exception of a location change from Arizona to Colorado.

---

[272] Sarris, op. cit., p.192. At the time still on probation for auteurist fundamentalism, Sarris justifies his evaluation by claiming directors should be judged by the weighted average of the entirety of their work and not their best work only (wrong).
[273] Tulard, op. cit., p.281; Sadoul, op. cit., p.120. says basically the same.
[274] There is a website dedicated to Richard Fleischer's memory where abundant material can be sourced: www.richardfleischer.com . Fleischer also wrote an autobiography: *Just Tell Me When To Cry*, Carrol & Graf, New York, 1993.

The first thing that stands out about *Mr. Majestyk* is it represents the strongest argument for an auteurist perspective of the film adaptations of Elmore Leonard's work so far, if one was looking for one. The film is much more Fleischer than Leonard. Let's do this the nice way and start with the bad and end with the good. On the bad side, practically the entire cast is miscast. Charles Bronson, whose vehicle this film is, a hairstyle second only to Boris Johnson's notwithstanding, is no better than he would be expected to be as *Mr. Majestyk*.[275] Al Littieri, who played Solozzi to perfection in *The Godfather* (Francis Ford Coppola, 1972) goes for a histrionic rendering of Frank Renda that robs the character of the sinister quality it has in the book, and Lee Purcell plays Renda's moll Wiley as if she mistook the role for that of a *Vogue* consultant. Also, and as so often in Leonard film adaptations, actor's direction or lack thereof ruins the dialogue's effect almost completely.

On the good side there's the Fleischer touch, which in this film could be labelled as "Sam Peckinpah meets the Keystone Cops". The tone is action adventure rather than crime thriller as Fleischer, the most cartoony director this side of Frank Tashlin, has Charles Bronson escape shooting attempts by flying through back windshields, make phone calls in public phone booths where newspaper clips report of people complaining of the price of gas, or Renda's henchmen indulge in a watermelon shootout extravaganza. The films consists about 50% of car chases and explosions[276] and Leonard's ethos is present only as back-

---

[275] Devlin kindly calls him "wooden", op. cit., p.138.
[276] As Devlin pus it, Mr. Majestyks' truck "seems to spend as much time in the air as on the ground", op. cit., loc. cit. *Variety* (31 December 1973) wrote "the narrative makes little sense unless used as a study in pathology". Available at: https://variety.com/1973/film/reviews/mr-majestyk-1200423204/ (accessed 18 January 2022).

ground: the Draconianly transactional nature of the US penal system is illustrated by one of the few exchanges where Leonard's deadpan is retained: police detective to Majestyk: "you're on your own"; Majestyk's reply: "I've been on my own since the beginning".

Mr. Majestyk is a very watchable film, and Richard Fleischer's visual inventiveness is apparent throughout, but is neither vintage Leonard nor vintage Fleischer.

The Ambassador (1984)

> *The Ambassador*, 97 minutes, Northbrook Films 1984. Release date: 11 January 1984. Directed by J Lee Thompson. Written by Max Jack. Produced by Yoram Goblus and Menahem Golan.
>
> Cast: Robert Mitchum as Peter Hacker, Ellen Burstyn as Alex Hacker, Rock Hudson as Frank Stevenson, Fabio Testi as Mustapha Hashimi, Donald Pleasance as Minister Eretz, Chelli Goldenberg as Rachel, Michal Bat-Adam as Tova.
>
> Cinematography: Adam Greenberg; Editing: Mark Goldblatt: Music: Dov Svelter; Sound: Michael John Bateman; Art Direction: Yoram Barzilai.

The Story

> *"Whether you're faking one or the other it isn't worth the state you get yourself in."* (*52 Pickup*, edition consulted: William Morrow, New York, 2013, p.31)

Fifty-Two Pickup was Elmore Leonard's 11th published novel, and the 8th adapted to the screen. It is the first instalment of the five novels set in Detroit Charles Rzepka calls the "Motor City Five"[277] and Leonard's first big commercial success in the crime novel format,[278] establishing his reputation as a thriller writer and setting the direction of his work for the next two decades.[279]

Synopsis: Harry Mitchell, a small Detroit businessman having an affair with a younger woman, nude model Cini Fisher, is being blackmailed by gangsters who ask for

---

[277] Rzepka, op. cit. p.100.
[278] Gehrein, op. cit. p.32.
[279] Devlin, op. cit. p.15.

52.000$ else they will divulge a film of Harry and Cini's goings on to Harry's wife. Leonardian plot twists ensue, as Harry goes "divulge and be damned" and confesses to his wife, which causes gangsters to murder Cini in a way that seems to frame Harry and blackmail him again for this, at which point Harry ingeniously plays gangsters against each other and ultimately tricks them into falling prey to their own greed.

Fifty-two Pickup is one of Elmore Leonard's most important works, a major turning point which first brought together "all the strands typical of the Leonard thriller",[280] and an early example of the influence in his work of George V Higgins' *The Friends of Eddie Coyle*", as previously mentioned, an acknowledged watershed read for Leonard - Harry Mitchell is the umpteenth Jack Ryan type, a regular guy "energized when cornered"[281], and another instance of an older man with a younger mistress and of a typical caper series of unexpected developments. It has a harder edge than most previous Leonard fiction, however, and in particular Cini's assassination is unusually graphic and violent for Leonard's hitherto standards, as he seldom did away with likeable, or at least not unlikeable, characters.

Fifty-two Pickup was posthumously (2014) selected for inclusion in the Library of America's compilation *Elmore Leonard: Four Novels of the 70s*.

The Director – J Lee Thompson

J Lee Thompson (1914-2002) was a British playwright and wunderkind scriptwriter who inter alia worked as dia-

---

[280] Devlin, op. cit. p.55. Devlin considers *Fifty-two Pickup* a better novel than *The Big Bounce*. I disagree. See also Geherin, op. cit. pp.44 and 45.
[281] Rzepka, op. cit. p.103.

logue coach in Alfred Hitchcock's *Jamaica Inn* (1939), graduating to directing with *Murder Without Crime* (1950), subsequently directing mostly gritty social dramas, having is biggest hit in the UK with the thriller *Ice Cold in Alex* (1958), which won four BAFTA nominations, including Best Film, and established Thompson's reputation as rising star of British cinema.[282]

It was not to be. Lured by Hollywood, Thompson rose to international fame with *The Guns of Navarone* (1961), which was the start of a long and eclectic career that includes many kitschy if sprightly wide screen big budget action films, from mock-historic to SciFi, often featuring Yul Brynner, Gregory Peck or Charles Bronson, the most famous of which are *Tarass Bulba* (1962), *Kings of the Sun* (1963), *McKenna's Gold* (1969), two *Planet of the Apes* franchise instalments, namely *Conquest of (...)* and *Battle for (...)* (1972 and 1973, respectively) and the Indiana Jones rip-off *King Solomon's Mines* (1985).

His British artistic and American commercial success notwithstanding, Thompson remained ignored or underrated by critics and academia throughout his life. In an article revealingly titled *"L'Impossible Cinema Anglais"*,[283] Alain Tanner, *a propos Woman in a Dressing Gown* (1957) calls him *"prétentieux"*, and decrees his *Ice Cold in Alex*, Thompson's most renowned film at the time, to be a lame plagiarizing of *Le Salaire de La Peur* (Henri-Georges Clouzot, 1953, admittedly probably the best thriller ever). Upon

---

[282] *BAFTA*, http://awards.bafta.org/keyword-search?keywords=Ice+Cold+in+Alex (accessed 20 April 2021).

[283] *"Impossible"* due to alleged massive US cultural colonization, resulting in Hollywood films having a 70% share of coeval British screens. *Cahiers du cinéma*, #89, November 1958, p.30.

his passing in 2002 his obituaries were suitably kinder, generally labelling him a competent action/adventure craftsman with a brilliant past in British 50s film industry.[284]

The Film

Having sold the film rights to the novel in 1973 for the eponymous film which will be reviewed subsequently, Elmore Leonard re-sold them the following year to Israeli film company *Noah Film* for 35.000$.[285] Intellectual property rights in Israel at the time must have been exceptionally strict, as the changes in plot, characters and location introduced for this film were so vast I suspect if they had gone ahead and filmed the adapted screenplay without having paid Leonard no-one would have shouted plagiarism. Still, this was an auspicious deal for Leonard, who visited Israel during production and liked the country greatly, not least as the trip gave him a pretext to take a break from his then ongoing AA detox,[286] and so much so that he later used Israel as setting of a subsequent, and to date unfilmed, novel: *The Hunted* (1977).

As for *The Ambassador*, Detroit becomes Israel, Harry Mitchel becomes the US Ambassador to Tel Aviv (Robert Mitchum, ageing relatively gracefully), the blackmail angle involves footage of Ms Ambassador (Ellen Burstyn, doing her best in the apparent absence of acting direction) having sex with a local lover who turns out to be an important PLO operative, and an ambassador's head of security (Rock Hudson, doing his version of the Burstyn act) is added, upon whom befalls the task of sorting out the intricacies of

---

[284] See inter alia *The Guardian*, London. 4 September 2002. p.20; *The Washington Post*, 8 September 2002. p..C09; or *Variety*, #388 (9 – 15 September 2002) p.63.
[285] Devlin, op. cit. p.139.
[286] Devlin, op. cit. p.17, Geherin, op.cit. p.51.

a plot involving the PLO, Mossad, KGB, the ambassador bewilderingly lame attempts to impress upon Israeli and Palestinian young fanatics the virtues of peace, patience and understanding, while the Israeli Defence Minister (Jack Palance, remarkably managing to look convincing) pops up occasionally to pontificate cynically/philosophically, till eventually good will appears to be vindicated and even the estranged couple take a very deep breath and give it another chance.

Not before, however, a snappy helicopter/car chase bloodily interrupts one of the ambassador's mediation attempts, Ms Ambassador narrowly escapes a bombing, and a few jazzy editing episodes remind us of J Lee Thompson´s English heyday, although he does make a complete mess of a final bloody massacre in which unidentified extremists mow down Israeli and Palestinian youths who were energetically disagreeing with each other.

To be fair, the film tries to strike a conciliatory, however unsubtle, note in its portrayal of a conflict that endures to this day, including commendable references to the Shoah. That doesn't begin to compensate for the clumsy mix of spy thriller, political parable and conjugal morality play its creators, intentionally or not, ended up concocting. As for Elmore Leonard, there's no trace of him either in letter or in spirit, although I retained a one-liner that would do him no shame: Burstyn to Mitchum: "This isn't the Holy Land, this is holier-than-thou land!".

Hallywell summed it up best: "aged stars go gloomily through some tasteless paces in this politically unwise pseudo-thriller".[287]

---

[287] Hallywell, op. cit. p.31.

Fifty-Two Pickup (1986)

> *Fifty-Two Pickup*, 110 minutes, Canon Group, 1986. Release date: 7 November 1986. Directed by John Frankenheimer. Written by John Steppling. Produced by Yoram Goblus and Menahem Golan.
>
> Cast: Roy Scheider as Harry Mitchell, Ann-Margaret as Barbara Mitchell, Vanity as Doreen, John Glover as Alan Raimy, Robert Trebor as Leon Franks, Lonny Chapman as Jim O´Boyle, Kelly Preston as Cini, Doug McClure as Mark Averson.
>
> Cinematography: Jost Vacano; Editing: Robert F Shugrue: Music: Gary Chang; Art Direction: Russell Christian.

The Director – John Frankenheimer

New Yorker John Frankenheimer (1930 – 2002) belongs to the generation of directors who made the reverse path of their predecessors of the 30s and 40s, namely by starting in TV and then moving on to the big screen. Frankenheimer directed over 150 feature films for TV during the 50s, ranging from adaptations of stage works (Shakespeare, Eugene O'Neill, Arthur Miller) to original teleplays by Rod Serling, Paddy Chayevsky, or Gore Vidal, making his big screen debut with *The Young Stranger* (1957), his most famous title remaining *The Manchurian Candidate* (1962) an elaborate political thriller about a presidential assassination attempt that happened to be released less than one month before the murder of President John F Kennedy, thus ensuring the perennial notoriety and typecasting of its director.

Frankenheimer was thereafter strongly associated with the progressive left, and chose or was chosen to direct purportedly "intense" social/political films, with a propensity for a rhetorically "expressionistic"[288] style that made him a critic's darling in the US during the height of the Cold War. In the 70s and 80s his star sunk, both due to changing public tastes and health problems related to severe alcoholism, but he enjoyed something of a comeback from the 90s onwards, winning four Emmy Awards for best director, three of which consecutive,[289] the last of which, *George Wallace*, also received a Golden Globe Award.[290]

John Frankenheimer's critical reputation is stronger on the western shores of the Atlantic than on the eastern. Cooke considers him an "important" director[291] and in his heartfelt eulogy Robert Ebert wrote that "he had his ups and downs, but the ups were glorious".[292] Even Steven Spielberg once said John Frankenheimer was his major influence![293] The French were less enthusiastic: unimpressed, the venerable George Sadoul dismissively considered he

---

[288] Frankenheimer said in an interview to the *Cahiers du cinéma* he wanted to bring to the big screen the experimentalism that was allowed at the time in TV. Cf. *Cahiers du cinéma* #94, April 1959, p.24. Naturally, it was not so much that the coeval TV industry was particularly fond of experimentalism than that the tight production deadlines and live broadcast methods of TV imposed a much freer style of direction than that of the film industry's screenplay-to-set process.

[289] Search criteria: "John Frankenheimer", *Emmy's*, https://www.emmys.com/awards/nominations/award-search (accessed 20 April 2021).

[290] Search criteria: "John Frankenheimer", *Golden Globes*, https://www.goldenglobes.com/awards-database (accessed 20 April 2021).

[291] Cooke, op. cit. p.891.

[292] Roger Ebert, 'John Frankenheimer: A master craftsman', *Roger Ebert*, July 8 2002, https://www.rogerebert.com/interviews/john-frankenheimer-a-master-craftsman (accessed 20 April 20210.

[293] Steven Spielberg interviewed by Richard Combs, *Sight and Sound*, Spring 1977 issue.

"more or less" held the promise of his his 1st film with "Hollywood fabrications" such as *The Birdman of Alcatraz* (1962) or the *"rocambolesque" Manchurian Candidate*.²⁹⁴ Kinder, Jean Tulard admitted *"il apparaît long temps comme l´un des grands espoirs du cinema américain"*, that didn´t quite hold his promise, musing (in 1982) *"Frankenheimer est jeune (...) atttendons maintenant les réussites"*.²⁹⁵

True to form, Andrew Sarris begged to differ: "a director of parts at the expense of the whole" who betrayed his TV roots for an "all embracing academicism (...) sweating over his technique".²⁹⁶ Without disagreeing with Sarris, I would not disagree with Eric Rhode either, who, on the other side of the Atlantic but still in the Anglosphere, considered Frankenheimer "(...) the most brilliant of the directors to emerge from TV", adding with characteristic perceptiveness that "for all his progressive stance he has something in common with such doom-laden myth makers as Fritz Lang and Stanley Kubrick".²⁹⁷

He wished, I would add. Seen from 2022, John Frankeinheimer's work looks clearly dated and at any rate overrated even in its time. Riding the wave of increasing permissiveness in cinema from the 60s onward, he indulged in a directing style that used and abused wide angle lens, elaborate dolly and travelling shots accentuated by loud and abrasive music, making films that, to quote Paul Attanasio's review of *Fifty-Two Pickup*, "practically watch themselves".²⁹⁸ Allergic to understatement, Frankenheimer

---

[294] Sadoul, op. cit. p.124.
[295] Tulard, op. cit. p.297.
[296] Sarris, op. cit. p.193, (Chapter 'Strained Seriousness', I'd say rather more appropriately than Richard Fleischer).
[297] Rhode, op. cit. p.620-621.
[298] Paul Attanasio, '52 Pick-Up', *Washington Post*, 12 November 1986. Available at: https://www.washingtonpost.com/wp-srv/style/longterm/movies/videos/52pickuprattanasio_a0ad6f.htm (accessed 20 April 2021).

often comes across, once shock value fades, as vacuously pretentious, a sort of Ken Russell without the redeeming loonyness. Oh, and Hurray for doom-laden myth makers.

The Film

Elmore Leonard is co-credited as screenwriter but reportedly his input was limited to retouching some dialogue,[299] which is immaterial as, quite unlike *The Ambassador*, the script of *Fifty-Two Pickup* follows the novel's plot and dialogue practically verbatim, minor changes being Detroit becoming LA, Harry's wife becoming an aspiring politician, hence Harry's reluctance to let his blackmailers divulge the compromising footage, and Gini being on the blackmail plan from the start. Also, a subplot involving a friend of the Mitchell's attempts to "console" Barbara after she learns of her husband's infidelities, significant in the novel as it establishes Harry's wife's character as a typically Leonardian heroin, is absent in the film.

Fifty-Two Pickup had a mixed and polarized reception. Devlin considers that, although "tough, coarse and not for the faint hearted" it is "vintage Leonard",[300] and Geherin calls him "one of the most successful cinematic treatments of any of Leonard's work".[301] Christopher Orr, in its aforementioned article, also considers *Fifty-Two Pickup* a "relatively capable adaptation" although it "emphasized the violence (...) at the expense of character and dialogue." Roger Ebert perceptively wrote the film "retains Leonard's

---

[299] See Devlin, op. cit. p.139 and Geherin, op. cit. p.47.
[300] Devlin, op. and loc. cit.
[301] Geherin, op. and loc. cit.

gift for terse, colorful dialogue" and affirms "it's Frankenheimer's best work in years".[302] In *The New York Times*, Janet Maslin aptly described it as "fast-paced, lurid, exploitative and loaded with malevolent energy (and) darkly entertaining (...)".[303]

A contrario, the *Encyclpedia Britannica* deems it "grisly and pointless",[304] and Paul Attanasio, in the aforementioned review, writes "John Frankenheimer has directed *Fifty-Two Pick-Up* in a style so devoid of nuance (...) so aggressively explicit that it might have been made for an audience of trained apes."

I am inclined to moderately side with the latter. *Fifty-two Pickup* is certainly a measure of the limits of John Frankenheimer's style. On the good side, the actors' delivery of Leonard's dialogue is mostly bereft of the declamatory clumsiness that usually plagues Leonard adaptations, and the acting is overall excellent, in particularly the three blackmailers (John Glover, Robert Trebor and Clarence Williams III) delightful as a sort of evil Three Stooges, a harbinger for countless future Tarantino characters and spinoffs thereof.

Otherwise, the Frankenheimer treatment is often seedy and its ponderousness sits ill with the borderline cartoony rollercoaster action of the script.[305] Roy Scheider's worthy performance notwithstanding, the film's tone robs his transformation from middle-aged middle-class successful

---

[302] Roger Ebert, '52 Pick-Up', *Roger Ebert*, https://www.rogerebert.com/reviews/52-pick-up-1986 (accessed 20 April 2021).
[303] Janet Maslin, 'Screen: '52 Pick-Up', A No-Frills Thriller', *New York Times*, November 7 1986. Available at: https://www.nytimes.com/1986/11/07/movies/screen-52-pick-up-a-no-frills-thriller.html (accessed 20 April 2021).
[304] Michael Barson, 'John Frankenheimer', *Britannica*, 15 February 2021, https://www.britannica.com/topic/52-Pick-Up (accessed 20 April 2021).
[305] Including a "porn party" scene, for which Frankenheimer recruited several of the time's prominent porn "stars" (IMDb, loc. Cit.)

business man to daredevil man of action of veracity, in particular in the final explosive denouement. Ultimately, *Fifty-Two Pickup* feels like an extended and pumped-up TV programmer rated R for language and nudity, partially redeemed by the evil Stooges.

Life of Crime (2013)

Life of Crime, 98 minutes, Lionsgate, 2013. Release date: 1 August 2013. Directed by Daniel Schechter. Written by Daniel Schechter. Produced by Ashok Amritraj.

Cast: Jennifer Aniston as Mickey Dawsonl, Yasiin Bey as Ordel Robbie, Isla Fisher as Melanie, Will Forte as Marshall Taylor, Mark Boone Jr as Richard Monk, Tim Robbins as Frank Dawson, John Hawkes as Louis Gara, Clea Lewis as Tyra Taylor, Charlie Tahan as Bo Dawson.

Cinematography: Eric Alan Edwards; Editing: Daniel Schechter: Music: The Newton Bros; Art Direction: Lisa Myers.

The Story

"Diana Vreeland." "Never heard of her." "Betty Bacall." "You mean Lauren Bacall?" Frank said. "Same one". Melanie said. "Yves St Laurent". "He´s the guy that makes clothes, women´s clothes". "Georgia O´Keefe". "Sounds like a stripper". "Wrong. Giancarlo Giannini". "Opera singer". "Wrong. Jeanne Moreau". "He´s a... writer". "She´s an actress. Jerome Robbins". "Who knows?" "I´m just giving you the easy ones. OK, Pat Buckley". "He´s the one, he´s gonna punch that fag, what´s his name, on TV." "Pat´s his wife... I think. Loulou de la Falaise". "For Christ sake." Frank said. (*The Switch*, edition consulted: Bantam, New York, 1978, pp.110-111)

The Switch was the 15th novel written by Elmore Leonard, being, chronologically, the 9th Leonard novel to be adapted to the screen. It was published by Bantam in paperback in 1978.

Synopsis: two Detroit ex-cons team up with a neo-Nazi to kidnap Mickey Dawson, the wife of successful businessman Frank Dawson, unaware of the fact that Frank is planning to dump Mickey and marry his lover, Melanie, and therefore has little interest in paying ransom. As the truth emerges, kidnapped Mickey evolves from country club spouse to Leonardian hero, reverse engineering a Stockholm Syndrome situation by playing the kidnappers against each other and them against Frank and Melanie, concluding in a Leonardian switch – hence the title – which will not be disclosed here, in consideration of those who haven't read the book.

The Switch is the fourth novel of Rzepka´s Motor City Five series and the first Leonard long work of fiction to have a female protagonist, Mickey, who essentially assumes the role male protagonists had in Leonard's books hitherto. Otherwise, it is essentially a variation of *Fifty-Two Pick-Up* and very much a recognizable Leonardian story, complete with the trio of criminals, the dysfunctional couple, Frank Dawson's alcohol problems and the final allegiance switch.[306]

But there's much that's new. The writing of *The Switch* coincided with Leonard overcoming his AA phase and with his second marriage, to Joan Shepard,[307] to whom the novel is dedicated, signaling also a shift to centre stage and 'emancipation' of female characters that would often occur in future fiction, exhibit A being Mickey Dawson, who Devlin, somewhat fancifully, considers Leonard's version of Ibsen's Nora from *A Doll's House*,[308] and exhibit B the reference to Susan Brownmiller's 1975 book *Against Our Will*, a 2nd generation feminist indictment of rape, during a

---

[306] Some of Leonard's early short stories had female protagonists, notably *The Colonel's Lady* (1952)
[307] Rzepka op. cit. p.120.
[308] Devlin op. cit. p.62.

scene in which Richard Monk, the dimwit neo-Nazi, tries to rape Mickey.

The Switch also shows the first signs of satire in Leonard's writing, and his "uncanny ability to take the pulse of mid-20th Century America", foremost in the condescending way ex-con Ordell Robbie, an African-American, interacts with neo-Nazi Monk.[309] The novel also offers evidence of Leonard's increasing maturity and ability to go beyond convention and formula in plot development.[310]

The Switch was also posthumously (2014) selected for inclusion in the Library of America's compilation *Elmore Leonard: Four Novels of the 70s*.

The Director – Daniel Schechter

Daniel Schechter is an American film director, editor and screenwriter, who gained some notoriety with his second feature film, the lo-budget *Supporting Characters*, which premiered at the Tribeca Film Festival in 2012.

Otherwise, most information publicly available on this director is related to the promotional activity surrounding the aforementioned film and *Life of Crime*, of which I deem apt to retain the following statement, in response to a question in an interview about what he thought was the most important thing he learned while making his adaptation of *The Switch*: "Easy: Elmore Leonard is a genius whose talent can't be overstated."[311]

---

[309] Devlin op. and loc. cit.
[310] Geherin op. cit. p.56.
[311] Nick Dawson, 'Five Questions with *Life of Crime* Director Daniel Schechter', *FilmMaker*, September 12 2013, https://filmmakermagazine.com/76026-five-questions-with-life-of-crime-director-daniel-schechter/#.X9OecXBKjIV (accessed 20 April 2021).

The Film

Life of Crime follows closely the plot of *The Switch* and, as usually in Leonard adaptations, borrows heavily from the novel's dialogue. The original title wasn't retained simply because it had already been used, for an eponymous romantic comedy co-directed by Josh Gordon and Will Speck in 2010, coincidentally also featuring Jennifer Anniston, who plays Mickey in *Life of Crime*.

The film was a long time coming, as director Daniel Schechter took the unusual initiative of "unilaterally" writing a script from the novel and then scouting who owned the film rights to try to sell it. Turned out Leonard just had gotten the rights back from a 30-year option in 2009 and it took Schechter a further year to persuade Leonard to give him the green light, so *Life of Crime* hit the screens some 35 years after the novel on which it is based was published, ending up as a late prequel to Quentin Tarantino's *Jackie Brown* (1997), itself an adaptation of Leonard's novel *Rum Punch* (1992), in which most of the main characters of *The Switch* reappear.

Life of Crime was chosen open the 7th Abu Dhabi Film Festival and to close the Toronto International Film Festival in 2013 and, having had its commercial release three weeks before Elmore Leonard's death on August 20th, 2013, at the age of 87, it merited a generally benevolent critical reception, often sprinkled with elegiac references to the original novel's author, who reportedly never got to see the final cut, but is listed as executive producer in the film, which is dedicated to him.[312] Matthew Taylor summed up the critical consensus in his review in *Sight and Sound:*" (...) while

---

[312] Kenneth Turan, 'Review:' Life of Crime 'is True to Mayhem and Humor of Elmore Leonard', *Los Angeles Times,* August 28th 2014,

the movie often seems feather weight, its tart flavour and brusque approach make it one of the more authentic stabs at Leonard in recent years". [313]

I can't say I agree. *Life of Crime* is mildly likeable, mostly due to what it retains from the original novel, but also to outstanding casting, as Anniston, but foremost John Hawkes and Yasijin Bey as kidnappers Louis Gara and Ordell Robbie, more than hold their own when compared with Robert de Niro and Samuel L Jackson, who played the same roles in the aforementioned previous sequel. Other than that, a couple of discrete Hitchcockian allusions (a tennis match, a shower drain shot, but maybe that's just me) and the priceless Beckettian nomenclature (ditto), the film comes pretty close to my own personal perception of Elmore Leonard's universe – which, besides subjective, is a characteristic rather than a quality – and the Detroit 1978 look is accurate without verging on the borderline mimicry that often afflicts contemporary period production design.

Nevertheless, the film sits uncomfortably between black comedy and soft crime drama, drifting along unable to distill the Leonardian juice said plot so seductively lends itself to, a few sequences excepted, namely the final switch, details of which won't be disclosed etc. *The Hollywood Reporter* said it best: "*Life of Crime* starts promisingly and ends with a smile but underwhelms in between."[314]

---

https://www.latimes.com/entertainment/movies/la-et-mn-life-of-crime-review-20140829-column.html (accessed 20 April 2021).
[313] Matthew Taylor, *Sight and Sound,* October 2015.
[314] 'Life of Crime: Toronto Review', *The Hollywood* Reporter, 8 September 2013, https://www.hollywoodreporter.com/review/life-crime-toronto-review-624065 (accessed 20 April 2021).

High Noon Part II - The Return of Will Kane (1980)

> *High Noon Part II – The Return of Will Kane*, 96 minutes, CBS 1980. Release date: 15 November 1980. Directed by Jerry Jameson. Written by Elmore Leonard. Produced by Edward J Montagne.
>
> Cast: Lee Majors as Will Kane, David Carradine as Ben Irons, Pernell Roberts as J D Ward, J A Preston as Alonzo, Michael Pataki as Darold, Kathleen Kennedy as Amy Kane, M Emmet Walsh as Harold Patton, Frank Campanella as Dr Losey.
>
> Cinematography: Harry J May; Editing: Lee Burch: Music: Richard McCurdy; Sound: Marvin Kerner; Art Direction: Adrian Gorton.

The Story

> Marshal J.D. Ward: *"the only law you got is this piece of tin worth about two bits..."* (drops his marshal badge on the justice of the peace's desk). *"Now you got nothin'."*

High Noon Part II was the second Elmore Leonard screenplay put to film that didn't come from or end up in novel format. The title is pretty much tantamount to a plot synopsis but for the sake of good order: Will Kane (Lee Majors), the brave sheriff played by Gary Cooper in the 1952 prequel, is now a cattle grower returning on a business trip to Hadleyville, the town where the first film took place, to learn the town is under the yoke of sadistic marshal J D Ward (Pernell Roberts), who rounds up a posse to capture and collect the ransom for outlaw Ben Irons (David Carradine). After a false start between Kane and Irons, a Leonardian allegiance switch takes place and the two men team up to confront Ward, action climaxing in a hotel room cliffhanger similar to that of the prequel or of the first *3.10 to Yuma*.

High Noon (the original one) was reportedly one of Elmore Leonard favourite films, and a clear influence on some of his early Western fiction, not least the short story adapted to the screen for the Delmer Daves film.[315] Also, in the same year *High Noon Part II* was broadcast, Elmore published *City Primeval,* the fifth and last the Motor City Five novels, which he subtitled *High Noon in Detroit*, so the connection is abundantly established.[316] More prosaically, Geherin, the only Leonard scholar to mention this film in passing, reports Leonard accepted this "dubious project", for which CBS paid 50.000$, simply because he needed the money.

The Director – Jerry Jameson

Jerry Jameson (1934) is a prolific TV director and producer who directed around 150 films and TV series episodes between 1971 and 2015, after cutting his teeth as editorial consultant during the 60s in some of the most iconic series of the era, e.g. *The Andy Griffith Show*, *I Spy* or *Mod Squad*.

The quintessential hack, specializing in low-budget disaster movies, the most famous possibly *Airport 1977*, with a penchant for gore and/or melodrama and wide-angle

---

[315] Devlin, op. cit., p.18.
[316] Rzepka, op. cit., p.92. Of the five, only the fist, *Fifty-two Pickup* (1974) was adapted to the screen, twice, as we´ve seen.

lens, Jerry Jameson's work has merited virtually no scholarly attention.[317]

The Film

High Noon Part II can be seen as a digest of recurrent Leonard Western themes, slickly if lazily regurgitated, into a competent if bland TV feature programmer that feels like an extended TV series episode and has production values to match.[318] The direction, for better and worse, is practically invisible behind industry routine and the occasional sparks of Leonard dialogue mostly afflicted by the usual curse of histrionic delivery. Lee Majors is the wooden personification of Leonardian uncool and it is left to David Carradine as villain turned co-hero and Pernell Roberts as unrepentant bad guy to give the film whatever edge it has. A few scenes, like the shootout in the midst of horses in the first Kane/Ward encounter, or the profanation of the white flag convention, echoing a similar scene in *Hombre*, stand out (and the first one was perhaps the inspiration of the similar one in James Mangold's *3.10 to Yuma* final scenes) but most crucial ones, like the final hotel room showdown, are bereft of tension.

Still, *High Noon Part II: The Return of Will Kane* is passable TV entertainment, and it's not everyday you get to see

---

[317] The above few lines are heavily indebted to the only source of information I found on Jerry Jameson, other than brief IMDb and Wikipedia entries, namely Howard S. Berger's 'Jerry Jameson: The Accidental Auteurist', 9 March 2017, *Beverly Cinema*, https://thenew-bev.com/blog/2017/03/jerry-jameson-the-accidental-auteurist/ (accessed 21 March 2021). The blog author's appraisal of Jameson's body of work is comprehensive and at times enthusiastic, and in this sense it does fill a void, although I must add that on evidence of *High Noon Part II* alone I don't see much of a case for the auteurish reappraisal the blog attempts.
[318] To illustrate: there was a composer's strike in Hollywood at the time so the film used music rehashed from the TV series *Return of the Saint* (1978-1979). *IMDb*, https://www.imdb.com/title/tt0080870/trivia/?ref_=tt_trv_trv (accessed 18 January 2022).

an 80s western that ends with a man shot dead on the ground and the one who shot him hugging his wife a few feet away from the corpse.

Gold Coast (1997)

> *Gold Coast*, 109 minutes, Chanticleer films 1997. Release date 28 September 1997. Directed by Peter Weller. Written by Harley Peyton. Produced by Richard Maynard, Jana Sue Memel and Peter Weller.
>
> Cast: David Caruso as Maguire, Barry Primus as Ed Grossy, Mark Helgenberger as Karen DiCilia, Jeff Kober as Roland Crowe, Wanda de Jesus as Vivian Onzola, Melissa Hickey as Martha Diaz, Rafael Baéz as Jesús Diaz, Richard Bradford as Frank DiCilia, Jim Coleman as Andre Patterson.
>
> Cinematography: Jacek Laskus; Editing: Dean Goodhill: Music: Peter Harris; Art Direction: Allen Terry.

The Story

"He said: I´m retired". "She said: From what". "He said: Industrial laundry business". "She said: are you in the Mafia?" "He said: That´s in the movies" (*Gold Coast*, edition consulted: Penguin, London, 1988, p. 11)

Gold Coast was the 18th novel written by Elmore Leonard, and the last to be published in paperback, by Bantam Books in 1980, as part of a two novel contract that included *Touch*.[319] *Gold Coast* was written before *City Primeval*, although it was published later in the same year, and is the first of several Leonard novels to take place in Florida.[320]

Synopsis: Mobster Frank DiCillia dies and leaves his wife Karen a gilded cage, a generous monthly stipendium and

---
[319] *Touch*, however, was eventually published by Arbor House in 1987.
[320] Challen, op. cit. p.96; Devlin, op. cit. p.20; Geherin, op. cit. p.63.

a mobster associate entrusted to supervise the execution of his will, which entails making sure Karen shall want for nothing but must never love again, as for some unexplained reason Frank doesn't want to be cuckolded from beyond the grave. So the mob hires local heavy Roland Crowe to act as DiCillia widow body guard, task involving, whenever necessary, persuasively discouraging potential suitors. Crowe subsequently falls for Karen and unimaginatively conceives of a scheme whereby it is he who will be the suitor of that which he is entrusted to protect, at which point in comes ex-con and typical Leonard hero Frank Maguire, who also falls for Karen, thereby setting the usual carrousel of twists and switches in motion.

As often in Leonard's "golden age" fiction, an implausibly Romanesque situation is sustained by hardboiled style, virtuoso dialogue and perceptive character study.[321] "Finger gently pressed on the pulse of Florida",[322] although Leonard imported a crew of Detroit characters, so as not to suddenly stray too far too quickly from his comfort zone, *Gold Coast* confirms the evolution and growing importance of female characters in Leonard's fiction, and Karen seems to me to be closer to Ibsen's Nora than *The Switch's* Mickey.

Gold Coast also marks the beginning of the golden era of Elmore Leonard on film. Until 1980, only 5 of his novels had been adapted to the screen, although another 4, as previously reviewed, would be in the future. From 1980 on, 15 of the 18 novels he was to write in the next 20 years were adapted to film or TV or in some cases (*Get Shorty*,

---

[321] Devlin (op. cit. p.79) sees here, especially in Karen's forced chastity, resonances of fairy tales, which strikes me as a bit meta. Leonard never thought of himself as anything other than a commercial writer and used implausible narrative conventions typical of "action" literature almost systematically throughout his career. Indeed, Devlin himself accurately refers to the portrayal of Karen as "Lauren Bacall stuff" (loc. cit).
[322] Devlin, op. cit. p.80, goes on to claim that Leonard's writing about Florida matches anything on the subject by Carl Hiaasen or even John Updike.

Pronto), to both, although often with a significant time lapse between book publication and film adaptation.

The Director – Peter Weller

Peter Weller (Wisconsin, 1947) is *Robocop*. He played the main role in the eponymous original film (Paul Verhoeven, 1987) and its sequel (Irvin Kershner, 1990) and that is the image he's most strongly associated with. Which is unfair, as Weller also featured prominently in David Cronenberg's *Naked Lunch* (1991), Woody Allen's *Mighty Aphrodite* (1995) and Michelangelo Antonioni's *Al di là delle nuvole* (1995), not to mention acting studies with Uta Hagen, stage performances in David Mamet and Tennessee Williams plays, among others, proficient jazz trumpet playing (Miles Davis is his hero) and a doctorate in Italian Renaissance Art History. An all-round all-American Renaissance man, if ever there was one.

Otherwise, and starting in 1993 and continuing to this day, Peter Weller was also a prolific, if comparatively obscure in that capacity, director of assorted TV series' episodes, having tried his hand twice at feature length efforts for the small screen, the second being the film adaptation of *Gold Coast*, possibly inspired by having previously played the main role in *Cat Chaser* (Abel Ferrara, 1989) an earlier adaptation of a subsequent Leonard novel, to be reviewed in due course.

The Film

Made 17 years after the novel's publication and banking on the success of *Get Shorty* (Barry Sonnenfeld, 1995), itself based on a subsequent Leonard novel, *Gold Coast* cannibalizes, as usual, most of the books dialogue and follows the plot mostly verbatim with two small but benign variations, namely a first sequence illustrating Frank's (James Caruso, adequate as on-duty Jack Ryan) release from prison, and the novel's initial scenes between Frank (Richard Bradford) and Karen (Mark Helgenberger, slightly strained as wannabe Kim Basinger) before Frank's death, which are moved to a flashback about a third into the film.

Peter Weller reveals itself a competent director, if a bit heavy on the close-ups, and manages to lend a neo-noir whiff to the proceedings, making *Gold Coast* a sort of poor man's *Body Heat* (Lawrence Kasdan, 1981). The main trio's delivery of Leonard's dialogue, the perennial litmus test of the Leonard adaptation, in particular Roland Crowe (Jeff Kober, easily carrying the weight), is above par, and the final climax is simultaneously appropriately Leonardian anticlimactic and evocative of both *Double Indemnity* (Billy Wilder, 1946) and *Notorious* (Alfred Hitchcock, 1946). In sum, a watchable, if unremarkable, illustration of the book.

Split Images (1992)

> *Split Images*, 90 minutes, Braun Entertainment Group 1992. Release date November 1997. Directed by Sheldon Larry. Written by Pete Hammill and Vera Appleyard. Produced by Richard Borchiver and Ken Gord.
>
> Cast: Gregory Harrison as Robbie Daniels, Robert Collins as Gossage, Rebecca Jenkins, as Angela Nolan, Steve Whistance-Smith as George Johnson, Nahanni Johnstone as Dorrie Vaughn, Maury Chaykin as Walter Kouza, David Hewlett as Gary Hammond, Melody Rayne as Patty Daniels, Dennis O´Connor as Jasinski.
>
> Cinematography: Perci Young; Music: Marty Simon; Sound: Steve Foster; Art Direction: Ian Brock and David Oren Charles.

The Story

He felt like everything was going to work out. He felt like talking. He felt he knew the guy coming in now. And when he found out he was right he didn´t know what to feel. (*Split Images*, edition consulted: Avon, New York, 1983, p.55)

Split Images was the 19th novel written by Elmore Leonard, sold to Arbor House, which succeeded Bantam Books as Leonard's publishing company, for the relatively paltry sum, at this stage of Leonard's career, of 7.000 USD. The book's sales were fair to middling but Arbor House turned out to be a more aggressive marketer than Bantam, publishing a full page advertisement to the novel in the *New York Review of Books* in which H N Swanson (admittedly not entirely disinterested) compared Leonard with Raymond Chandler and Scott Fitzgerald, resulting, not immediately in better sales, but equally if not more importantly in significantly augmented critical attention, including Leonard's first mention ever in *Newsweek* and encomia in *The Chicago Tribune* and *The Village Voice* ("the finest thriller writer alive").[323] *Split Images* also marks the beginning of Leonard's lifelong association with Greg Sutter, whom he met for an interview for the *Monthly Detroit* and thenceforth became his associate as researcher and location scout.[324]

Synopsis: Robbie Daniels, a Detroit gun-collecting multimillionaire, shoots a Haitian refugee who broke into his Palm Beach mansion. Enjoying shooting people and fancying himself a sort of freelance crime fighter, Daniels enlists Walter Kouza, a veteran of the Detroit Police Department, to assist him in planning the assassination of a local Latin-American drug dealer who, enjoying diplomatic immunity, is beyond the reach of the law. In steps Detroit PD Lieutenant Bryan Hurd, in Florida on leave from an initially supposedly unrelated investigation, who soon suspects Daniels' intentions and teams/shacks up with journalist Angela Nolan, who is working on a piece on Daniels, to foil the plot, succeeding only at the cost of (spoiler alert) Angela making the ultimate sacrifice.

Split Images, like *Gold Coast*, is set in Florida, but, again like *Gold Coast*, its characters are still Detroiters. It was initially thought as a sequel to *City Primeval*, but as the latter's film rights had already been sold (although the book as so far not been filmed), Leonard had to introduce a few minor changes in context and nomenclature to avoid legal issues.[325] The result of the new collaboration with Sutter is patent in the local detail, which is vivid without being cum-

---

[323] Geherin, op. cit. p.81.
[324] Challen, op. cit. p. 98; Geherin, op. cit. p.79; Rzekpa, op. cit. p.122.
[325] Devlin, op. cit. p.22; Geherin, op. cit. p.73; Rzekpa, op. cit. p.130.

bersome, and again, an implausible plot is pulled off by virtuoso treatment and the gritty realism of the police procedural minutiae resulting from Sutter's research. The dynamics between the four main characters is positively Mozartian, Daniels building upon the usual Leonard psycho killer, with an added layer of depth and social graces or, as Devlin puts it, like Shakespeare's Iago his malice"is motiveless but (he is) a victim of pride": atypically for a Leonard villain, Daniels teases Hurd with clues to his plans.[326] Also, Walter Kouza isn't the usual dimwit or psycho henchman but rather a hardened dirty Harry type bent on some "real action". In a further departure from personal convention, but also in a reflection of the development of Leonard's propensity for anticlimactic conflict resolution, he has Angela murdered after allowing her affair with Bryan to mature throughout the book to the point of evolving beyond a love interest subplot into the main emotional engine of the novel. *Split Images* is perhaps my third favourite Leonard novel so far, after *Swag*, which has to this day not been adapted to the screen, and *The Big Bounce*.

The Director – Sheldon Larry

Toronto born Sheldon Larry (1949) belongs to the group of "Leonard auteurs" who one could categorize as

---

[326] Devlin, op. cit. pp 81 and 82. Also, besides being a gun buff Daniels is also a video buff, a relative novelty in the early 80s, and his house is fully covered with surveillance cameras. Rzepka sees here an example of "mediated alienation" (op. cit. p.131), first to be detected in Leonard's work in the first pages of *The Big Bounce*, when the police examines in slow motion video footage of Jack Ryan's fight scene that triggers the novel. Alternatively, I would risk that Leonard, although a commercial writer, was cognizant of the trends of post-modern fiction that were breaking into the mainstream at the time *Split Images* was published, and understated suggestions of intertextuality, video art etc. might have been designed to earn academic respectability to complement his commercial success. If my theory is right, Leonard succeeded.

"illustrious unknowns" or thereabouts. Publicly available information on him is scarce, his main claim to fame being perhaps his 2011 indie musical *Leave It on the Floor*, which had a successful career in the festival circuit, including selections for the Toronto International Film Festival (maybe here the local boy factor was a factor), but also for the Berlinale, the Los Angeles Film Festival and the Chicago International Film Festival, among others.

Which is not to say his CV doesn't look interesting. Reportedly earning his spurs in the BBC, where he inter alia directed documentaries about Pasolini, Visconti and Zeffirelli (a penchant for Italian flamboyancy?) and had a chance to work with Monty Python, Sheldon Larry had a distinguished four-plus decade career as film, television and theatre director and/or producer, having worked with F Murray Abraham, Kevin Bacon, Christopher Plummer and Gena Rowland, among others, subsequently retiring to teach at the University of Southern California.[327] Finally, it might be worth mentioning that one of his favourite films, among those he directed, is *Split Images*.

The Film

Split Images the film takes *Split Images* the novel video/gun voyeur/murderer subtext and runs away with it. Minor but significant plot changes vis a vis the book include an opening sequence where Robbie Daniels (Gregory Harrison, not needing much in the way of acting classes to make crazy faces all the time) shoots dead, in the back, a hunting partner just for the thrill of it, establishing the character as an all-out psycho rather than the novel's power tripping trigger happy Dirty Harry type, and the murder of

---

[327] 'Sheldon Larry', *American Film Showcase*, https://americanfilmshowcase.com/experts/larry-sheldon/ (accessed 6 May 2021).

a female cop instead of Gary Hammond (Bryan Hurd renamed, played by David Hewlett with an 80s pompadour, giving Alan Alda a run for his money as the least convincing Leonard protagonist to date) love interest Angela Nolan, to allow for a happy end.

There's next to no literature available on this film, on or offline. The only Leonard scholar to make a passing reference to it is Devlin, who mentions that failure to release *Split Images* was a "minor setback" for the writer,[328] seeming to imply the film was initially produced with a view to theatre release and was eventually "downgraded" to television (but I could find no other source to confirm this). Else, the relevant IMDb entry reveals the film was nominated for the best sound for the now defunct Canadian Gemini awards.

As several other Leonard film adaptations, *Split Images* is a slightly weird creature. The director makes the simultaneous presence of firearms and video cameras pervasive, including TV installations *a la* Nam June Paik in Robbie's luxury home, and goes for broke in piling up references: slo-mo carnage with opera soundtrack *a la* Arthur Penn, analogies between cinephilia, modern technology and crime *a la Rear Window* (Alfred Hitchcock, 1954), *Blow Up* (Michelangelo Antonioni, 1967), or even *The Conversation* (Francis Ford Coppola, 1974), some effective (Robbie to Kouza, inciting him to keep filming as they chase and try to shoot a witness to a previous murder: "double feature, Walter, double feature!", a precursor of Joel Courtney's proclamation "production values!" during the train crash in JJ Abrahams 2011 Steven Spielberg pastiche *Super 8*), some lame (Gary's final words to Robbie, after - spoiler alert – doing him in: "is this live or is this Betamax?").

---

[328] Devlin, op. cit. p.142.

Still, *Split Images* is strangely effective, highly strung pathos *a la* William Friedkin partially compensating for occasional cheesiness. As in *The Moonshine War*, the novel's protagonist is practically obliterated and the real main character is the antagonist. The script uses quite a bit of the book's dialogue, although not as much as usually, but re-contextualizes it. This is very much film Sheldon Larry's film, for good (the court scene) and bad (the cringing sex scenes). Some of Leonard's fiction elements are there but they are ingredients for the stew, not the stew itself.

Cat Chaser (1989)

> *Cat Chaser*, 90 minutes, Vestron Pictures 1989. Release date 2 October 1989. Directed by Abel Ferrara. Written by Elmore Leonard and James Borrelli. Produced by Peter S Davis and William Panzer.
>
> Cast: Peter Weller as George Moran, Kelly McGillis as Mary DeBoya, Charles Durning as Jiggs Scully, Fredric Forrest as Nolen Tyner, Tomas Milian as Andres DeBoya, Juan Fernandéz as Rafi, Kelly Jo Minter as Loret, Phil Leeds as Jerry Shea, Roberto Escobar as Mario Prado.
>
> Cinematography: Anthony B Richmond; Editing: Anthony Redman: Music: Chick Corea; Art Direction: CJ Simpson.

The Story

"All over the world...the past was being wiped out by condominiums." (Cat Chaser, edition consulted: Avon Books, New York, 1983, p.59)

Cat Chaser was the 20th novel written by Elmore Leonard, published by Arbor House in 1982. It was sold by 10.000$, the last of the "budget phase" of Leonard's career, before things really shot off with the subsequent *Stick*,[329] to be addressed subsequently.

Synopsis: It's complicated: 1965 Dominican campaign vet Pompano Beach Florida motel owner George Moran, involved in a dangerous affair with Mary de Boya, spouse of Dominican drug dealer Andres de Boya, returns to Santo

---

[329] Geherin, op. cit. p.16.

Domingo on a whim to try and locate Lucy Palma, a member of the local resistance with whom he had had a fugacious fling back in the day, in the course of which quest he meets local hustler Rafi Amado, who ensures he can assist in finding Lucy. Failing that and returning to Florida, Moran has to deal with de Boya associates Nolen Tyler and ex-cop Jiggs Scully, who are in on Moran's affair with Mary and try to shake him down when in steps Rafi, having travelled from Santo Domingo with a hired hooker putting on a lame act as Lucy's supposed little sister, mourning Lucy's alleged death; when finally everyone is more or less on to everyone else's angle they come to the conclusion that the best solution for all concerned would be to kill de Boya and retain the 2 MUSD he – turns out – keeps around as emergency escape money, plot which very Leonardianly ends up with the demise of almost all concerned, except for and to the profit of the leading man and lady, who at the right moment exercised the prerequisite Leonardian cunning and cool.

By now Leonard was getting major league attention, e.g. *The New Yorker* considering him *a propos* its review of *Cat Chaser* a "gripping writer – a real first rate writer",[330] or the *New York Times*, finally noticing that Leonard was "better at dialogue than anyone else on the block".[331] More to the point, the *New York Review of Books* proclaimed "it has taken a little time, but Elmore Leonard is beginning to be taken seriously as a writer".[332] Famously, and revealing of Leonard's accruing street cred, *Heavy Metal* called him "an

---

[330] *The New Yorker*, 12 July 1982, p.197 quoted in Geherin, op. cit, p.138 footnote 31.
[331] *New York Times*, 11 June 1982, p.29 quoted in Devlin, op. cit. p.151 footnote 6.
[332] *New York Review of Books*, 5 May 1982, p.20, quoted in Geherin, op.cit, p.141 footnote 37. Geherin appropriately comments "a little time" was over 30 years...

especial pisser".[333] His biographers, though, were still warming up to his style: Geherin considers the novel is "unsure of plot, requires patience from the reader", although he concedes the book evinces "great improvisational flair",[334] whereas Devlin writes "In what is often Leonard's mode, the story wanders about in an erratic fashion until settling down and then growing unbearably suspenseful".[335]

Cat Chaser was another stepping stone in Elmore Leonard's financial and artistic emancipation, and one of his best novels so far (Top 5 or thereabouts for me). Recurrent themes abound: the Florida setting, the mafia mistress, the emancipated/ing woman, the psycho henchmen. Research on Trujillo's dictatorship by recently acquired assistant Greg Sutter lends flesh to a narrative that, typically for Leonard at this stage, changes course every 50 pages or so without ever seeming incongruous, dialogue developing character and character establishing plot motivation with jazzy harmony. To quote an anonymous review in Goodreads, "nobody writes a mess quite like Dutch".

The Director – Abel Ferrara

Bronx born of Italian/Irish parents (1951), Abel Ferrara was raised in the Bronx until his move to Peekskill aged 8, his directing style belying his self-described suburban idyll milieu[336]: a gritty urban hard-boiled post-punk neo-noir

---

[333] *Heavy Metal*, January 1984, p.4, quoted in Geherin, op. cit, p.141 footnote 39.
[334] Geherin, op. cit. p.82.
[335] Devlin, op. cit. p.23.
[336] Interview on the occasion of his May 2019 MoMA retrospective. Available at: *Lohud*, https://www.lohud.com/story/entertainment/2019/05/20/director-abel-ferrara-unrated-raramoma/3677852002/ (accessed 12 June 2021).

Weltanschauung, starting in 1976 with what has to be categorized as an "independent" porn film featuring himself and his girlfriend, directed under an alias. Forever independent, Ferrara proceeded to direct the grindhouse *The Driller Killer* (1979) and crime thrillers *Fear City* (1984, with Melanie Grifitth), *King of New York* (1990, with Christopher Walken) and his arguably most renowned *succés de scandale*, *Bad Lieutenant* (1992), with a celebrated high octane performance by Harvey Keitel in the title role; must confess I prefer Werner Herzog's 2009 remake with Nicolas Cage, though; none other than Martin Scorsese begs to differ and named the first version one of his top 10 films of the 1990s.[337] His latest media splash was *Welcome to New York* (2014), a mordant, if Manichean, fictionalization of the troubles of former IMF chef and French presidential hopeful Dominique Strauss-Kahn, with Gérard Depardieu in the title role.

Abel Ferrara is an interesting pairing for Elmore Leonard. More than Leonard and the aforementioned Scorsese, but certainly less than, say, Paul Schrader (who also directed a Leonard adaptation), Ferrara's Christian childhood trauma is patent in most of his films, as an unforgiving world of guilt and redemption, or lack thereof, darkens the fate of virtually all his protagonists. Very much the New Yorker and often filming on location on a string budget, Ferrara tends to repeatedly use the same actors (Willem Dafoe, Keitel, Walken) and, a stranger to understatement, to wear his Big Apple punk heart blood red on his sleeve. Confusingly, he cites Stanley Kubrick, Woody Allen, Per Paolo Pasolini (of whom he directed a biopic of sorts in 2014) and Rainer-Werner Fassbinder as influences. Maybe

---

[337] *Roger Ebert*, https://www.rogerebert.com/apps/pbcs.dll/article?AID=/20000226/COMMENTARY/41219001/1023 (accessed 12 June 2021).

the last two? At any rate, our man doesn't take himself seriously: "(...) don't worry about the films you're making; worry about the life you're living. You can talk about honesty in filmmaking. What honesty? It's not the films, man. (...)".[338]

The Film

Cat Chaser is another Leonard adaptation co-scripted by the author so presumably the (minor) plot changes and character variations were OK'd by him, the matter of fidelity to the original, always secondary anyway, being thus settled.

The film had a modest career and a lukewarm to indifferent critical reception, *Variety* considering it "another example of how difficult it is to transform a sharp and racy novel into a classy movie. Despite a fine cast and atmospheric direction by Abel Ferrara, the pic [from the novel by Elmore Leonard] doesn't quite make the grade, though it certainly is worth a look".[339]

I would wholeheartedly agree with the final sentence. Indeed, *Cat Chaser* can be said to be the reason I decided to write this book: to find out if it was out there, the "perfect" Leonard adaptation, true to the writer and to the director. There is, and this is it. "Historically" speaking, the film is an "early" Ferrara film, that is, made immediately before *King of New York* and *Bad Lieutenant* made him a household name, and it is also an "early" Leonard adaptation, preceding the main wave inaugurated in 1995 by *Get*

---

[338] Aã da Ruilova, "Abel Ferrara", *Interview Magazine*, 13 February 2013, https://www.interviewmagazine.com/film/abel-ferrara# (accessed 12 June 2021).
[339] 'Cat Chaser', *Variety*, 31 December 1988, https://variety.com/1988/film/reviews/cat-chaser-1200428039/ (accessed 12 June 2021).

Shorty. As a neo-noir it doesn't have nearly the reputation it deserves. The opening credits roll over black and white footage of the 1965 Dominican "campaign" as a very noir off-voice that will accompany the remainder of the film, doing its best to sound like Orson Welles in *The Lady from Shanghai* (1947), delivers Leonardian epigrams, only to be outdone by the perfect cast: Peter Weller as Moran, more effective as Leonard actor than as Leonard director, Kelly McGillis as Mary, an iconic a noir femme fatale, Frederic Forest as stumbling drunkard Nolan Tyler and, trumping them all, Charles Durning as Jiggs Scully, holding the world record so far for Leonard dialogue delivery, to no detriment to the rest of the cast, who all fare way above average in this department. Mild for Ferrara standards, the love story between Moran and Mary is as implausible as in the novel but nevertheless equally effective as dramatic leitmotiv. Occasionally grungy sound and image editing lends the film a B movie flavour that amplifies its power, contrasting with the scenes of Mary and/or the deBoya residence, lit *a la* Douglas Sirk and with McGillis' frequently changing wardrobe - designed *a la* Edith Head. All this and a Chick Corea soundtrack. It is interesting that Ferrara could manage to recruit such a cast at a time when he still was relatively unknown, and even more that he got away with so much frontal nudity and an M16 rating.[340]

---

[340] Including a rape scene which Kelly McGillis insisted in playing herself without a double and which, according to Ferrara, the actress ended up practically directing herself (c.f. *IMDb*, https://www.imdb.com/title/tt0105458/trivia/?ref_=tt_trv_trv, accessed 18 January 2022). Other sources claim McGillis found the experience so traumatic she considered giving up acting.

Stick (1985)

> *Stick*, 109 minutes, Universal Pictures 1985. Release date 26 April 1985. Directed by Burt Reynolds. Written by Elmore Leonard and Joseph Stinson. Produced by Jennings Lang.
>
> Cast: Burt Reynolds as Stick, Candice Bergen as Kyle, George Segal as Barry, Charles Durning as Chucky, José Pérez as Rainy, Richard Lawson as Cornell, Castulo Guerra as Nestor, Dar Robinson as Moke, Alex Rocco as Firestone.
>
> Cinematography: Nick McLean; Editing: William Gordean: Music: Joseph Conlan and Barry de Vorzon; Art Direction: Edward Richardson.
>
> Budget: 22 MUSD. Box Office: 8.5 MUSD (US and Canada)

The Story

"You been to Vegas?" "Couple of times". "You like it?" "How about cheap perfume covering up b.o.?" "There you are. Been to Vail?" (*Stick,* edition consulted: HarperTorch, New York, 2002, p. 271)

Stick was the 21st novel written by Elmore Leonard, published by Arbor House in 1983, which bought the paperback rights for 50.000$. It is dedicated "for Joan, always".

Synopsis: Ernest "Stick" Stickley is fresh out of prison (where he did time for a crime he committed in *Swag* seven years previous, a rare Leonardian comeback) and goes to Florida where he accepts a job as driver for big shot financial investor Barry, not before perambulating with former associate Rainy as sort of hanger-on in a drug deal gone wrong, in which Rainy dies at the hands of drug dealing operatives dope head Chucky and psycho Moke, incident from which Stick unilaterally derives the persuasion that the 5,000 USD owed for the deal should be paid to him (not unlike Valdez, in *Valdez is Coming*, decides it would be only fair that Frank Tanner should pay the Indian widow 100$ for the mistaken assassination of her husband). While working with Barry, Stick gets involved with Barry's part time mistress Kyle, who moonlights as financial adviser and who assists Stick in concocting a scam involving an implausible film production financing operation, which should more than compensate for the loss Stick feels he suffered in the initial drug deal. It all goes eventfully and entertainingly well until Stick ultimately comes undone in a relatively unimaginative final twist.

We're back in Florida, and our hero still comes from Detroit. Another ex-con, another man with a past involving an estranged wife and daughter (Mary Lou and Katy, whom we meet half way through the book, the latter's encounter with her father proving Leonard is as good at poignancy as at rejoinder) and whose ability, at least as per self-evaluation, surpasses his social standing, but who bears his condition stoically, although not insensitively to a possible angle. As he muses to himself (in a text that is a dazzling polyphony of free indirect discourse, inner monologue and shifting perspectives): "making money without working. It seemed the way to do it"; and, might one ask, what for? to "use it wisely (...) buy things. Buy a car, buy things for Katy, clothes, buy a truck, buy a business. Buy Wild Turkey instead of Early Times".[341]

---

[341] *Stick*, HarperTorch, 2002, p.366-367. Rzepka considers Leonard on a par with Jane Austen or Gustave Flauber in this department. Charles Rzepka (ed.), *Critical Essays on Elmore Leonard: If It Sounds Like Writing...* John Wiley & Sons, Hoboken, New Jersey, 2020.

Leonard's fiction has a reputation for meandering but *Stick* is downright Proustean.[342] Running almost 400 pages, after the introductory drug deal nothing much happens as the characters take their time getting acquainted to each other, not before page 270 does Stick's affair with Kyle start to develop and not before page 320 does the scam start to take shape, not that the reader notices or cares, as the meandering is a constant delight. Leonard betrays the effort of a man on the verge of 60 trying to keep up (barely), as references to computers, stock exchange dealings and even biotech colour the deals and scams Stick and Kyle witness, assist in or fantasize about. The introduction of a film production subplot in the last third of the book, in particular the scene where film producer, Joe Firestone (those names again) tries to pitch the financing of a film to a group of a drug dealers, may be self-referential irony, as may a paragraph which Leonard presents as an example of narrative drafting work in progress, complete with rewrites and deletions, a mischievous glimpse at his own creative process, concluding "boy, it's hard" (tell me about it).

Stick is yet another step in Leonard's ascent to the critical, commercial and popular Olympus. The novel received good reviews from reviewers who didn't normally review crime literature, such as the *New York Times'* Christopher Lehmann-Haupt or the *Washington Post*'s Pulitzer Prize winner Jonathan Yardley, the latter stating Leonard had "raised the hard-boiled suspense novel beyond the limits

---

[342] Leonard's biographers were still trying to come to terms with the style of their biographee: Devlin writes (op. cit. p.86) "*Stick* never really settles into one pattern", whereas Geherin (op. cit. p.94) offers: "Leonard is confident enough to include scenes that are extraneous to the main plot, yet which add to the richness of the book". As for Leonard himself, he explained, illuminatingly if unpersuasively: "Plots write themselves if the characters are right" (Devlin op. cit. p.92)

of the genre and into social commentary".[343] It was also selected as alternate book of the month by the Book of the Month Club, potentially opening a vast new audience to Leonard.[344]

The Director – Burt Reynolds

Michigan born (1936) Burt Reynolds was an all-American, all-70s/80s Hollywood star, with the string of divorces, bankruptcies and nightclub ownerships to prove it. After a University American football scholarship, a series of accidents caused him to shift to acting, - in theatre, TV and finally film [with *Angel Baby* (1961, his first feature)], entering the Motion Picture Almanac's top box office stars in 1973 (4th place) reaching the 1st place in 1978, which he retained till 1982, bowing out in 6th place in 1984.[345] He lost prominence in subsequent years but remained a face about Tinseltown until his death in 2018, aged 82.

His success was based mostly on sex appeal – in the 50s he was often cast as a Marlon Brando lookalike – and a dated masculine charm.[346] Never taken seriously as an actor, Reynolds had an exceptionally commercially successful career and was capable of both nuance and histrionics within the range he was typecast. Like many in his league, he tried his hand at directing, sitting behind the camera a dozen times between 1976 and 2000, both for the small

---

[343] Geherin op. cit. p.95. I must confess it never crossed my mind hardboiled could be anything other than social commentary.
[344] Geherin op. et loc. cit.
[345] Quoted in *David A Cook, A History of American Cinema* cit, volume 9 p.339.
[346] Circumstance often noted by contemporaries. Upon Reynolds' signing a seven year contract with Universal in the late 50s, agent Lou Wasserman snapped: "I don't care if he can act or not. Anyone who has this effect on women deserves a break" *Chicago Daily Tribune* 20 August 1959.

and the big screen, always featuring himself in one of the main roles. He is on record stating directing was what he liked to do most and what he thought he was best at.[347] This opinion was not largely shared. Reynolds' directorial work received next to no scholarly attention. Possibly because his dictionary was published around the time of Reynolds' career peaked, Tulard alone lists him and considers he *"révèle un temperament original"*.[348]

The Film

Stick's film rights were sold to Universal for 350.000$, making Leonard, who co-wrote the script, a full-fledged Hollywood big timer.[349] Also significantly, and unlike most Leonard film adaptations, the film was produced immediately after the novel's publication. It was finished in 1984, but due to reshooting was only released in 1985.[350] This delay was caused by Leonard, who, already disappointed that Roy Scheider, who was initially chosen for director, had been replaced by Burt Reynolds, after reading the first draft of the script wrote a long letter to Reynolds with objections, which Reynolds mostly accepted but the final product of which Leonard liked even less.[351]

Stick follows the novel's plot half way through, but removes Mary Ann from the family reunion to leave Stick (Reynolds, in a coarse macho mode which must have been risible even at the time) alone with daughter Katy, allowing

---

[347] Interview to the *Christian Science Monitor*, 9 February 1976
[348] Tulard, op. cit. p.649
[349] Challen, op. cit. p.105; Devlin, op. cit. p.23; Geherin, op. cit. p.95.
[350] "Stick' in the Mud', Paul Attansio, *The Washington Post*, 4 May 1985, https://www.washingtonpost.com/archive/lifestyle/1985/05/04/stick-in-the-mud/e15535c5-27cd-4f00-abf8-1fd18a3d79bc/?utm_term=.b6c4d0fa1d2f (accessed 28 September 2021).
[351] Challen, op. cit. p.106; Devlin, op. cit. p.96.

her to become a hostage target for Chucky and Moke, so after Stick and Kyle shack up the script deviates from the book to turn into a tiresomely predictable shootout rescue/revenge thriller.

Stick the film was one of the sorest points in Leonard's career.[352] He hated the film so much his name was taken off the credits.[353] Asked of his reaction after seeing it he answered "I'm thinking maybe I should enter a Trappist monastery. It was just not what I wrote, not my book, not my screenplay".[354] On the plus side, this episode did make for free publicity, motivating Arbor House to anticipate a few months the publication of *La Brava*, Leonard's next novel.[355]

Leonard's biographers agree with him. Challen writes "Reynolds overplays every irritating millisecond. Reynolds did just about everything as wrong as he possibly could – the thing bears no resemblance to anything Leonard would ever dream of writing".[356] Devlin considers the film is neither hip nor cool, just heavy-handed action with a "cut-rate Ian Fleming conclusion".[357] Even Greg Sutter chipped in: "the film isn't even worthy of discussion. Reynolds took, and basically shat on, a really good character (...) if it hadn't been for that movie Leonard might have written another *Stick*".[358]

Leonard's biographers inevitably evaluate film adaptations of his work mostly on the basis of putative fidelity to the letter or spirit of the books, but the critical consensus didn't disagree: Paul Attanasio, in *The Washington Post*,

---

[352] Challen, op. cit. p.105.
[353] Devlin, op. cit. p.23.
[354] Geherin, op. cit. p.96 footnote 10.
[355] Geherin, op. et loc. cit.
[356] Challen, op. cit. p.105
[357] Devlin, op. cit. p.139
[358] Challen, op. cit. p.105

puts the blame on Reynolds: "Most of the time we watch Reynolds being cute with the girls, with the action added as an afterthought. And whenever the movie threatens to roll, Reynolds smothers it with long helicopter shots of yachts and limos coursing across Florida"[359]. *Variety* considered the film had a "plot of the convoluted kind beloved by exhibitors since patrons can wander out for popcorn and come back without missing anything", and Hallywell called it a "wearisome crime melodrama with too many pauses for the hero's self-examination".[360]

Apt judgements all, which, however, overlook one thing: *Stick* is really two films in one. The first half is effectively directed, with skillful use of understated elaborate long shots and occasional visual details that convey Leonardian coolness which the literary medium could not, as when Cornell (Richard Lawson, good) fixes Stick's necklace or when he casually sticks gum in the windshield of one of Barry's (George Seagal, overacting so much Attanasio called him a "one man CinemaScope") convertibles. The flamboyancy of the bad guys cast (George Dunning with fake red eyebrows as Chucky, José Perez as Rainy) is a legitimate interpretation of the Leonardian universe. And Leonardian dialogue delivery is not the best but is better than most.

Then something happened. According to Reynolds: "I wanted to make that movie as soon as I read the book. I respected Leonard's work. I felt I knew that Florida way of life, having been raised in the state. And I was that guy! (...) "I turned in my cut of the picture and truly thought I had made a good film. Word got back to me quickly that the people in the Black Tower [the head office for Universal

---

[359] *The Washington Post*, 4 May 1985.
[360] Hallywell, op. cit. p.961. That's also where the *Variety* quote comes from.

Pictures] wanted a few changes. (...) "I gave up on the film. I didn't fight them. (...) When I re-shot the film, I was just going through the motions. (...). All I can say, and this is not in way of a defense, is if you liked the first part of 'Stick,' that's what I was trying to achieve throughout".[361]

A classical Hollywood tragedy. Indeed, when the film departs from the novel it turns into a sort of humourless hour long *Three Dukes* episode with shoot outs and fighting scenes straight out of 70s Hong Kong action fillers, punctuated with insufferable love scenes between Stick and Kyle (Candice Bergen, miscast as Balzaquienne trophy wife). In sum, *Stick* starts like *Life of Crime* and ends like *Border Shootout*. It bombed at the box office, returning 8.4 million USD on a 22 million investment.

---

[361] *IMDb*, https://www.imdb.com/title/tt0090073/trivia/?ref_=tt_trv_trv (accessed 18 January 2022).

Glitz (1988)

> *Glitz*, 98 minutes, NBC 1988. Release date 28 October 1988. Directed by Sandor Stern. Written by Stephen Zito. Produced by Steve McGlothen.
>
> Cast: Jimmy Smits as Vincent Marra, Markie Post as Linda Moon, John Diel as Teddy Magyk, Madison Mason as Lt. Dixie Davis, Ken Foree as Moose, Geno Silva as Lorendo, James Purcell as Jackie Garbo, Robin Strasser as Nancy Donovan, Patrie Allen as LaDonna, Kathleen Freeman as Mrs Magyk.
>
> Cinematography: Richard Browen; Editing: Skip Schoolnik: Music: Dana Kaproff; Art Direction: Cindy Carr.

The Story

> *"Wonderful things can happen", Vincent said, "when you plant the seeds of distrust in a garden of assholes."* (*Glitz*, edition consulted: Harper Torch, New York 2002)

Glitz was the 23rd novel written by Elmore Leonard, published by Arbor House in 1985. Leonard got 450.000$ for the paperback rights novel with a 200.000$ advance and an equal amount for the film rights, as well as 165.000$ for a Book of the Month Club sale.[362]

Glitz started life as a draft screenplay initially tiled *Boardwalk*:[363] film producer Walter Mirisch commissioned Leonard to write a sequel to *In the Heat of the Night* (Norman Jewison, 1967), purported to be a Sidney

---

[362] Challen, op. cit. p.113.
[363] Challen, op. cit. p.112.

Poitier vehicle but, as writing progressed, Leonard came to see it more as a book than a script and he and Poitier were eventually estranged.[364]

Synopsis: Psycho serial killer mama's boy Teddy Magyk is trying to seek redress from police detective Vincent Mora, who put him behind bars for rape 7 years previous. In the hide-and-seek psycho way he goes about it, he murders inter alia a young and beautiful Puerto Rican "hostess" Vincent had taken under his platonic wing. Vincent, who happens to be on prolonged leave due to injuries suffered in the line of duty, makes it his business Teddy gets what he's looking for, grinding his axe long and cool, whilst seducing Atlantic City casino songstress Linda and turning the tables, or pretending to, on the whole local mafia/gambling/law enforcement establishment, till everything comes down in a - for Leonard - atypically cathartic showdown.

Glitz was the quantum leap in Leonard's sustained path to glory. He "hit the jackpot (...) at age 59, 34 years after publishing his first novel",[365] building up from the momentum of *Stick* and *LaBrava*, finally enabling H N Swanson to fulfil the promise he had made 3 decades before.[366] Leonard made the cover of *Newsweek* and became a national celebrity. Critical accolades showered, from the *Chicago Tribune* to *People* to the *New York Times*,[367] where Cristopher Lehmann-Haupt gushed: "you almost have to read it twice, the first time fast to find out what happens, the second time to savor it" (I agree, except for me it would be the

---

[364] Challen, op. cit. p.114.
[365] Geherin, op. cit. p.103.
[366] Geherin, op. cit. p.104.
[367] *Newsweek*, 25 April 1985.

cess was probably due more to timing than a sudden qualitative jump.[375] The novel is rather another step in Leonard's development of an individual voice that had started individually enough more than three decades earlier, if mostly unbeknownst to the general public. *Glitz* is very familiar Leonard territory, noteworthy variations being Teddy Magyk, Leonard's creepiest villain,[376] evincing an "eerie ability to get inside empty heads"[377] and to substitute "the real world for the realm of his own fantasies".[378] Rzepka further notes his name hints at his ability to appear and disappear.[379] Vincent Mora is not the usual Leonard divorcee but a widower and *Glitz*'s final showdown is dramatically closer to those of Leonard's early westerns than to the usual anticlimactic outcome of his later works. It is also Leonard's first and only whodunit, belying his claim to the effect that he never wrote one.[380]

As a commercial and critical success, *Glitz* is clearly a landmark in Leonard's work and in his stature as was a popular culture figure. Literarily, I don't think it quite compares to *The Big Bounce* or to *Swag*, and Leonard's talent for the catchy monosyllabical open ended title is for once wide off the mark. *Sleaze* would have been more appropriate.

The Director – Sandor Stern

Canada born (1936) Sandor Stern is a film and TV screenwriter, director and producer best known for his horror films. A University of Toronto Medical School graduate

---

[375] Geherin, op. cit. p.105.
[376] Geherin, op. cit. p.106, Sedato, op. cit. p.95.
[377] R Z Sheppard, 'Sleaze Factors', *Time*, 11 February 1985, quoted in Geherin, op. cit. p.107, footnote 30.
[378] Kris Mecholski, 'The Mozart of Motor City', in Rzepka, op. (ed) cit. p.82.
[379] Rzepka, op. (ed) cit. p.140. Amazingly, none of Leonard´s biographers seems to have noticed the similarity between "Magyck" and "Majestyk".
[380] Sedato, op. cit. p.94.

and former family doctor, Stern devotes himself full-time to the film and TV industry since the mid-60s. Beside prolific TV work, his foremost claim to fame may be the screenplay for *The Amityville Horror* (Stuart Rosenberg, 1979). His only non-TV feature film, *Pin* (1988) is a minor horror cult classic. *Glitz*, directed the same year, was his 10th feature film.

The Film

A low budget TV programmer (it was shown as an NBC "Movie of the Week"[381]), *Glitz* starts promisingly with a bank robbery shootout which cues to San Juan, Puerto Rico travelling shots with background salsa music, setting the tone for a late 80s neonoir with early 80s art direction and wardrobe. Camp gratification aside, the film quickly loses steam and goes the usual fair to middling Leonard adaptation way, namely pedestrian, borderline amateurish direction partially salvaged by cannibalizing as much Leonard dialogue as possible and sticking mostly to the plot (omitting some of the hardcore stuff, like Teddy Magyck's murder of an old lady).

On the plus side, the actors do their best to carry the dialogue and, uncooperative direction notwithstanding, mostly succeed, and Stern or his scriptwriter can claim 2 good ideas: (i) having Vincent (John Smiths just before shooting to fame with *LA Law*, likeable if occasionally irritatingly insolent) lean on a cane for the first half of the film, to underline his vulnerability, and (ii) Iris' murder scene, 6 shots in 17 seconds and no gore. Both Senator Hays and Eisenstein would have approved.

---

[381] Challen, op cit p.115.

other way around).³⁶⁸ It was also the occasion for Stephen King's famous review in the same newspaper: "(...) but it cost me money. After finishing *Glitz* I went to the bookstore at my local mall and bought everything by Elmore Leonard I could find" (the bookstore at the mall, there's a touch Leonard certainly appreciated).³⁶⁹

Glitz also signals a significant evolution in Greg Sutter's work as researcher, hitherto "largely confined (...) to the Detroit Public Library",³⁷⁰ but heretofore involving extensive field research.³⁷¹ As a result, "not in the least obtrusively, Leonard handles esoteric subjects such as psychic readings or the promotion of rock groups with the kind of detail found in extended *New Yorker*-like magazine articles".³⁷² Fun factoid: Sutter was assisted in his research by real life Ernesto "Chili" Palmer, whose name was to resurface in *Get Shorty* and *Be Cool* and who would also do a brief cameo in the film version of the former.³⁷³

Glitz got lots of attention from Leonard's biographers and Segato devotes the novel a full chapter ³⁷⁴ making much of the cop's ethical dilemma when faced with the necessity of shooting a suspect to preserve his own physical integrity (leading to the wounds Vincent is recovering from). I agree with Geherin when he writes that *Glitz's* suc-

---

[368] *New York Times,* 4 February 1985, C20. Quoted in Geherin op. cit. p.104 - footnote 19.
[369] Stephen King, 'What Went Down When Magyk Went Up', *New York Times,* February 1985. Available at: https://archive.nytimes.com/www.nytimes.com/books/98/02/08/home/leonard-glitz.html (accessed 8 January 2022).
[370] Challen, op. cit. p.113.
[371] 'The Sense of Place in Elmore Leonard's Crime Fiction', David Geherin, in Rzepka op. (ed) cit. pp.50-51.
[372] Devlin, op. cit. p.119 a propos Leonard's "naturalism".
[373] Challen, op. cit. p.115.
[374] Segato, '*Glitz o del detective inseguro*', op. cit. pp.91-101.

On the minus side, direction no better than it should be aside, (i) the heavy dose of Tinseltown tinsel required to accept the dramatic premise of Vincent's determination to sort out and avenge Iris beyond a reasonable doubt (ii) concurrently, the stretched limits of the Hollywood conventions that allow cops to throw the book away and perform police work in splatter video game mode and (iii), sadly not remotely an isolated case, the embarrassingly lame sex scenes between Vincent and Linda (Markie Post, going for Lana Turner but coming across as Doris Day).

There's no point in judging *Glitz* too harshly, as it fulfils its filler task passably - although the same could be argued for Poverty Row output, which didn't stop bits of it to soar. But it is only in the specific context of unfair comparison to works by Boetticher or Tarantino that *Glitz* appears to suck. In its natural ecosystem, it does OK-ish. Understandably, it is all but ignored by both Leonard scholars and film studies.

The Rosary Murders (1987)

> *The Rosary Murders*, 105 minutes, New Line Clnema, 1987. Release date: 4 September 1987. Directed by Fred Walton. Written by Elmore Leonard and Fred Walton. Produced by Robert G Laurel.
>
> Cast: Donald Sutherland as Father Robert Koesler, Charles Durning as Father Ted Nabors, Belinda Bauer as Pat Lennon, Josef Sommer as Lt. Koznicki, James Murtaugh as Robert Javison, Leila Danette as Mrs Washington, Addison Powell as Father Edward Killeen, Kathleen Tollan as Sister Ann Vania.
>
> Cinematography: David Golia; Editing: Sam Vitale: Music: Bobby Laurel and Don Sebesky; Art Direction: W Stuart Campbell.

The Story

> Father Edward Killeen: *"Break the seal of confession, and you destroy the Church."* Father Robert Koesler: *"People are going to die."* Father Edward Killeen: *"You're saving souls Bob, not lives."*

The Rosary Murders was published in 1978, the first of a series of 23 mildly successful whodunits written by Detroit born former Catholic priest and journalist William X Kienzle (1928-2021), featuring the thinly disguised alter ego Father Koestler, a late 20th Century version of CJ Chesterton's Father Brown (who merits a passing reference in the book).

Synopsis: Father Koesler, editor of a Detroit Catholic newspaper, assists the local PD in solving a case of serial killing of priests and nuns, next to whom the murderer always leaves a rosary – hence the title – as signature. Two-thirds through the book, the murderer confesses to Father Koesler, explaining that his killing urge was born of grief for his lost daughter, who committed suicide due to disgust from incest at the hands of her father, attempts by both to find solace and rehabilitation with members of the Catholic clergy having met with disbelief and dismissal. Like Father Michael Logan (Montgomery Clift) in Hitchcock's *I Confess* (1953) (except in this case the confessor didn't disclose his identity), Father Koestler is torn between the wish to stop the killing and the duty to keep the vow of the seal, reconciling both with the exercise of painstaking powers of deduction to give the police the crucial evidence needed to finally solve the case.

Considering his relative obscurity, at least to me, Kienzle is not a half bad writer. The portrait he paints of late 70s Detroit is an interesting complement to Leonard's, as it comments on many of the demographic and social developments which are the background of Leonard's fiction but that Leonard mostly leaves unwritten, namely the hollowing out of the inner city, the black/white conflict/dislocation and, of prominent interest for Kienzle, and the effect of post-Second Vatican Council practices and rituals in the local Irish, Italian and Polish communities, deadpan colourful dialogue assisting in carrying the narrative. It is as a whodunit that *The Rosary Murders* is to be found wanting, the intricate scholastics of the murder victim selection methodology incongruous with the stated motivation of the killer. Also, by revealing the murderer and the motive 2/3 through the book and revealing his identity a bit further on, introducing him as a previously unknown character, Kienzle breaks the spell of most effective whodunits (for those who generally respond to the format), which hangs on making the murderer one of the inner circle of main characters and to reveal his identity as late, surprisingly, and ingeniously as possible, the (dreaded) Agatha Christie's *Murder on the Orient Express* being a paradigmatic example.

As for Leonard's script for *The Rosary Murders*, it was written some 9 years after the novel's publication and at a time when Leonard's career had developed beyond the point where he might have needed to accept indifferent hack jobs, and it is the only instance of him adapting someone else's work to the screen, so it is tempting to speculate that the Detroit/Catholic connections might have played a role in interesting him in the project (however, there is nothing in the available literature to substantiate this assumption). *The Rosary Murders* does appear right in the middle of the "Catholic interlude" I refer to in my periodization attempt of Leonard's work, after the as-of-yet unfilmed novel *Bandits* (1987) which features an ex-nun as co-protagonist, and the subsequent *Touch* (1988), to be reviewed subsequently, but it bears reminding that the latter was written some 10 years previous to publication, precisely during the period Leonard was leaving the church for the AA.

The Director – Fred Walton

Fred Walton (1949) is an American film and TV director and screenwriter. Raised in Chevy Chase, Maryland in an upper-middle class family, Walton studied theatre in Denison University. Subsequently, with some family support he entered the film business, achieving early underground notoriety with *When a Stranger Calls* (1979), financed by shopping mall magnate Mel Simon.[382] Released shortly after John Carpenter's *Halloween* (1978), the film caused minor media buzz and for a short time Walton was hyped as an up and coming movie brat, which led to him being typecast as a horror film director.[383] Because he could afford to, he resisted industry entreaties in this direction, although he did direct *April Fool's Day* (1986), arguably his greatest hit. *The Rosary Murders* was his last theatrical release and Walton subsequently moved to TV, where he directed another dozen features before retiring from the industry and moving with his family to Oregon in 1996, where he lives to this day.

The Film

The Rosary Murders premiered in 1987, featuring Donald Sutherland as Father Koesler. Elmore Leonard's script was co-written with director Fred Walton.[384] The film, either due to Leonard or to Walton is unclear, departs from the novel in four main aspects: (i) it centres the plot and the investigation in Father Koesler instead of in police Lt. Koznicki, (ii) introduces a love interest in the person of journalist Pat Lennon (Belinda Bauer, fetching) whose confessed infatuation with Koesler merits the deadpan dopehead-trying-to-pass-as-having-achieved-enlightenment stare Donald Sutherland developed in this phase of his career and is an acquired taste, (iii) lets go of the coeval

---

[382] *Victoria Advocate*, 12 December 1978, p.29, https://www.newspapers.com/clip/34951339/victoria-advocate/ (accessed 28 September 2021).
[383] 'The Horror of Being a Hollywood Film Director', Lukas Gordon, 20 April 2016, *The Pidgeon Press*. Available at: https://web.archive.org/web/20160623180222/http://thepigeonpress.org/the-horror-of-being-a-hollywood-film-director/ (accessed 28 September 2021).
[384] Challen, op. cit. p.120; Geherin, op. cit. p.18.

politics to dwell on the doctrinal conflicts of the progressive (to which Koesler belongs) and conservative wings of the local Catholic clergy and (iv) finishes with an intendedly harrowing suicide letter from the murderer's daughter to seek to add gravitas to the proceedings.

Overbearing background music and chiaroscuro (with emphasis on the scuro) photography try and fail to ignite the film, which bounces between impossible love story, police procedural/psycho thriller and social drama, losing track of all three. Sedately watchable, if taking itself way too seriously, *The Rosary Murders*' best feature is Charles Durning, in his 3rd appearance in a "Leonard" film as the cynical conservative Father Nabors.

The Rosary Murders reportedly won the Audience Award and the screenplay and dialogue Special Mention at the defunct *Festival de Cognac du Film Policier* in 1988. It received minimal and indifferent critical attention and bombed at the box office.

Desperado (1987)

> *Desperado*, 93 minutes, NBC, 1987. Release date: 27 April 1987. Directed by Virgl W Vogel. Written by Elmore Leonard. Produced by Walter Mirisch and Charles E Sellier Jr.
>
> Cast: Alex McArthur as Dual McCall, David Warner as Police Chief Ballard, Yaphet Kotto as Bede, Donald Mophat as Malloy, Stephen Davies as Calvin, Lise Cutter as Nora Malloy, Sydney Walsh as Sally, Robert Vaughn as Sheriff John Whaley, Gladys Knight as Mona Lisa.
>
> Cinematography: Dick Bush; Editing: Mark W Rosembaum: Music: Michel Colombier; Sound: Anthony Milch; Direction: Bill Cornfold.

The Story

"Ballard, Company Police Chief: Marshal Dancey! I had no idea it's our time of the month to have you here!Marshal Dancey: You make it sound like a physical affliction."

Originally titled *Duell McCall* (for the protagonist's name)[385] and commissioned by Walter Mirisch to Elmore Leonard in 1985 as an attempt to jump on the coeval *Pale Rider/Silverado* (Clint Eastwood, 1985 / Lawrence Kasdan, 1985) Western revival bandwagon, *Desperado* was the last script Leonard wrote not based on one of his novels which was eventually adapted to the screen, and also his last piece of Western fiction (bar *Hurray for Captain Early!*, a short story published in 1994).

Synopsis: Dual McCall is a wandering maverick happening on a small town in which saloon he is called upon to

---

[385] Geherin, op. cit. p.118. In the film, the character is called Dual McCall.

prove his alpha male credentials with the local heavies, catching the eye of local magnate Ballard, whose entreaties to joint local private law enforcement he rejects, moving on to incidentally meet local beauty Nora Molloy, daughter of Shakespeare loving small rancher Malloy, who is resisting Ballard's heavies' offers to buy the ranch, resulting in an Oedipal transfer courtesy of the scriptwriters whereby heavies shoot Malloy, so McCall shoots two of them, causing the remaining heavies to flee and update Ballard on events, upon which Ballard decides to seek redress from McCall, enterprise which at a point includes taking Nora hostage, it all ending in a shootout and partially anticlimactic happy end.

This script is a lazy mishmash of early Leonard Western narrative devices and a few TV programmer clichés. The scarce available literature is mute on the point but one gets the feeling Leonard did this one just for the money (amount also undisclosed).

The Director – Virgil W Vogel

Peoria, Illinois, born (1919) Virgil William Vogel was an American television and film editor and director. His career began at Universal in 1940 as assistant editor, subsequently climbing up the editing ladder, notably editing Orson Welles' *Touch of Evil* (1958). His first shot at directing came in 1956, with the lo-budget sci-fi *The Mole People*, genre he revisited often in subsequent years with often pricelessly titled efforts, foremost the 1959 Swedish/US coproduction *Rymdinvasion i Lappland* (*Space Invasion of Lapland*), without the watching of which, I am now persuaded, one cannot consider oneself an accomplished film buff.

Vogel later moved to TV, where he directed dozens of episodes through the Golden Age of TV, including for *Bonanza*, *Mission: Impossible* and *Miami Vice*, up until his death in 1996.

The Film

Telecast on NBC in 1987, initially with a view to launch a new Western series in the vein of *Bonanza* or *Wagon Trail*, *Desperado* hit the small screen in a version that may have undergone substantial changes vis a vis the script Leonard wrote. The planned subsequent TV series didn't materialize, but Dual McCall's career continued with four sequels in the next two years: the delightfully titled T*he Return of Desperado*, *Desperado: Avalanche at Devil's Ridge* (both 1988), *Desperado: The Outlaw Wars* and *Desperado: Badlands Justice* (both 1989), none of which Elmore Leonard had anything to do with.

Other than the blog mentioned in the footnote on this page, there's exactly zero literature on this film, which is mentioned only cursorily by some Leonard biographers. The same source states that, other than having been aired in 1987, the only other release the film had was a UK VHS edition.[386]

Certainly hundreds of notches below *Pale Rider* or *Silverado*, *Desperado* is a medium-rare programmer which, due to the alleged subsequent script tampering or not, never gains traction as it goes through horse chase, love as great redeemer and final shootout scenes. Virgil Vogel reveals an elegant and assured hand directing the old classical Hollywood way, making the film seem a bit better than

---

[386] Indeed, this wasn't the easiest film in this book to unearth. I finally got it by purchasing a download from DVD Lady (dvd.lady.com), an online business with rather poor costumer reviews, but which in this case delivered.

it is, but otherwise the only half good thing in it is David Wagner, playing the evil magnate Ballard. In a rare emergence of Leonardian dialogue, when confronted with a townsfolk member reluctant to heed appeals to join a posse to hunt down McCall, Wagner says to one of his henchmen: "a free thinker. Shoot him!".

As entertainment value, that's little. Sparse and mostly poorly delivered instances of Leonard dialogue as the aforementioned apart, other Leonardianisms in *Desperado* might include, with an exegetical stretch, (i) Dual's prison escape, reminiscent of *3.10 to Yuma*, (ii) a shootout in the midst of a cowherd reminiscent of similar ones in the previous *High Noon II* and the subsequent *3.10 to Yuma* remake, and (iii) the unexpected open ended ending.

Touch (1997)

> *Touch*, 96 minutes, United Artists 1997. Release date 14 February 1997. Directed and written by Paul Shrader. Produced by Fida Attieh and Lila Cazès.
>
> Cast: LL Cool J as self, Gina Gershon as Debra Lusanne, Conchata Ferrell as Virginia Worrel, John Doe as Elwin Worrel, Christopher Walken as Bill Hill, Skeet Ulrich as Juvenal/Charlie Lawson, Maria Celedonio as Alisha, Bridget Fonda as Kathleen Freeman as Lynn Faulkner.
>
> Cinematography: Edward Lachman; Editing: Cara Silverman: Music: Dave Grohl; Art Direction: Daniel Bradford.
>
> Awards: Film Independent Spirits Award: Best screenplay and best director (nominated); SITGES Catalonian International Film Festival, Best Film (nominated)

The Story

> *"What´s the matter with her?" He was staring at Virginia on the sofa with the dishcloth folded over her eyes."He´s punched her in the face" Bil Hill said. "She´s got a big bruise, so I put a cold cloth on it". "No, I mean what else´s wrong with her?" the young guy said. "Something is, isn´t it? "Oh," Bill Hill said, "Well, yeah, she´s blind".* (*Touch*, edition consulted: Avon, New York, 1998, p.8).

Touch was the 25th Elmore Leonard novel, published by Arbor House in 1987, and the 14th adapted to the screen. It was written in 1977, making it, in chronological order or writing, the 15th novel by Leonard, and it was initially commissioned by Bantam as part of a two-novel deal with *Gold*

Coast,[387] but its publication was held back by lack of publisher interest due to unorthodox subject matter and unfortunate title selection (*Juvenal* to *The Juvenal Touch* to finally just *Touch*),[388] the post-*Glitz*" letters to my mother" period enabling Leonard to finally acquainting it with the general public ten years later. At this time, Leonard tried to sell the publishing rights back to Bantam but his new publisher, Arbor House, made a winning bid of 300.000$, or 10 times more what Bantam had paid upon commission in 1977.[389]

Synopsis: Juvenal is an ex-Franciscan monk who assists with counselling in a Christian alcoholic rehabilitation centre and concurrently presents stigmata and healing powers he himself is unable to explain and unwilling to categorically attribute to divine intervention, arousing the attention of the media, intent on either catapulting him to stardom (ex-evangelist turned RV salesman Bill Hill and his former associate Lynn Faulkner, who eventually falls for Juvenal) or exposing him as a hoax (TV talk show host Debra Lusanne). There is also pre-Vatican II Catholic traditionalist August Murray, who wants to turn Juvenal into an icon for the movement, role compromised by Juvenal's liaison with Lynn, who happens to also be an exotic dancer, profession August, uneducated in or insensitive to the whole Magdalene angle of Christianity, seems to deem inappropriate for

---

[387] Challen, op. cit. p.120.
[388] Challen, op. cit. p.120.
[389] For a detailed account of *Touch*'s pre-publishing history, see Challen, op. cit. pp.120-122. Devlin writes *Touch* was published "on the strength of *Glitz*". (Devlin, op. cit. p.24). Geherin contributes that Bantam had the novel already set into type in 1978 before deciding to suspend publication and that the novel was rejected a dozen times after that (op. cit. pp.15, 56 and 60).

the consort of a prophet, triggering the murder plot which is the book's thriller fig leaf.[390]

Supernatural undertones, at any rate underplayed, aside, this is familiar Leonard territory.[391] Juvenal's activity provides the opportunity for the longest and most detailed and perceptive descriptions of one Leonard'' recurrent themes, alcoholism and rehab, presumably drawn from personal experience.[392] Typically, once the situation is established the characters ramble along for about 170 of the book's 230 pages[393] until Juvenal finally decides to get in touch with his real feelings and turn Lynn into the - in unscrupulous TV talk show host Howard Hart's brilliant formulation - stigmata's inamorata.[394] The final action scenes that enabled the book to be marketed as a thriller don't stray too much from the formulas Leonard used back in his Western days and even incorporate one of his favourite devices, a defenestration, complemented by a supernatural caper virtuoso final twist before the loving couple finally drive west toward the sunset.

---

[390] Connotation which unsurprisingly did not escape Sedato (op. cit. p'148) who also points out Juvenal is an unusual Leonard protagonist, not being a cop, a criminal or an ex-convict, further and eloquently suggesting that his thaumaturgical abilities represent Leonard's hero's τέχνη at its utmost (p.149).

[391] Challen concurs (op. cit. p.122). Geherin (op. cit. p.56) notes that, unprecedented for Leonard, *Touch* doesn't contain a single killing.

[392] In Devlin's words: "A number of Leonard's personal experiences as a recovering alcoholic transform the book into an act of thanksgiving" (Devlin, op. cit. p.18).

[393] Edition consulted: Avon Books (Hearst Corporation) 105 Madison Ave, New York, NY 10016, First paperback printing, 1988.

[394] Rzepka points out that Juvenal's touch is supposed to heal but it is Lynn's touch that ultimately "saves" him (Rzepka, op cit p 191), a piece of analytical low hanging fruit which may mislead prospective readers into thinking redemption is a theme in the book. I don't see it. I see a *petit roman fleuve* commercial necessity drives into a thriller closure, whilst the characters talk to each other in a reflection of the author's ongoing catharsis and distancing from the tenets of the religious denomination he long embraced. But I might be wrong.

Rzepka includes *Touch* in a tetralogy of Catholic books which include also *Unknown Man #89*, *The Hunted* and the later *Pagan Babies*, and considers *Touch* Leonard's closest brush with magic realism, which, if "technically" correct, strikes me as farfetched, since the novel's tone and style are 100% Leonardian.[395] More pertinently, he recalls previous uses of Christian symbology in Leonard's work, citing *Valdez is Coming*'s "crucifixion".[396]

Juvenal is ultimately a typically Leonardian hero, a hemophilic Jack Ryan.[397] Lynn to Juvenal: "...do you believe God is doing this to you?"; Juvenal: "He could be. Or it could be psycho-physiological. I don't know (...)"; Lynn: "Which do you think it is?"; Juvenal: "I have no way of knowing. But when it comes right down to it, what difference does it make? It seems to do some good"; Lynn: "You're awfully cool about it"; Juvenal: "I accept it, that's all, do I have a choice?".

With hindsight, this may be the book Leonard needed to write to get alcohol and religion out of his system.[398] Written at the time Leonard switched from the church to the AA, it was finally published, probably coincidentally, around the time of the release of *The Rosary Murders*. An entertaining example is a paragraph long and dryly ironic

---

[395] Rzepka, op. cit. p.184..
[396] Rzepka, op. cit. p.190. Intriguingly, Sedato mentions *Touch* relatively briefly his book (pp.147-151) and excludes the novel from his four religious case studies (to wit: *City Primeval, Glitz, Freaky Deaky* and *Killshot*, op. cit. pp.77-136), although he does call it a "catholic" novel and also points out (p.150) the year Leonard wrote *Touch* was the year he stopped drinking. Challen (op. cit. p.122).and Devlin (op. cit. pp.11-12) recall Leonard worked on a recruiting film for the Franciscan order in the 60s, experience they claim served for inspiration for *Touch*. For a speculation on the influence of Leonard's personal background in putatively transcendent/immanent episodes in his work, see Devlin, op. cit. p.65.
[397] Devlin (op. cit. p.65) points out "the characterization of Juvenal draws on the (Christian) tradition of the Holy Fool".
[398] Although the author was reported baffled and frustrated by the initial difficulties in sealing the novel. Cf. Challen, op. cit. p.122.

recapitulation of Christian martyrs by August, who concludes St Augustine "...had died in a spirit of humility (and courage and penitence), but he was 76 years old and humility could be a wise move at that age, but not when the Church needed men who weren't afraid to stand up and defend their fate against the cowards within and the communists without (the sons of bitches)".

The Director – Paul Schrader

Paul Schrader (Michigan, 1946) is an American screenwriter, film director and film critic. Of German and Dutch descent, Schrader received a strict Calvinist education: he saw his first film when he was 18 years old.[399] After majoring in philosophy, with a minor in theology, from Calvin College, Schrader went on to study at UCLA Film school, upon recommendation of film critic suprema Pauline Kael.

If film came to Schrader relatively late in life, it came with a vengeance: he began his career as film critic in the college paper *Calvin College Chimes* in 1965, his first two reviews being of Luis Buñuel's *Los Olvidados* (1950) and Carl Dreyer's *Ordet* (1955),[400] early signs of the interests he would spend the next five plus decades pursuing, marked by a deep feeling of religiosity, particularly of the sacrificial/ascetic type, and a voracious curiosity for film, initially mostly of the European "arthouse" kind. Still under Kael's wing, Schrader started writing film criticism for the *Los Angeles Free Press* in 1969 and later the same year for *Cin-*

---

[399] 'Paul J. Schrader [1946]', *New Netherland Institute*, https://www.newnetherlandinstitute.org/history-and-heritage/dutch_americans/paul-j-schrader/ (accessed 18 January 2022).

[400] Paul Schrader's official website, paulschrader.org, has links to PDF files of all his critical writings.

ema magazine. His first book, published in 1972 was titled *Transcendental Style in Film: Ozu, Bresson, Dreyer*, and Bresson was to remain a latent and sometimes explicit influence in Schrader's films.[401] I happen to think Schrader is an interesting film director but his writing on film considerable more interesting (like Truffaut, except Truffaut's film are less interesting). Still, other than not being American and having a reputation for directing "deep", "spiritual" films, I don't see whatever Bresson, Dreyer and Ozu have in common (and I don't think I'd discern a transcendental style if it took to sharing my toothbrush). Back to Schrader, the same year he published his seminal *Notes on Film Noir*.

His screenwriting debut was *The Yakuza* (Sydney Polack, 1974), and the following year he wrote the script for *Obsession* (Brian de Palma, 1975). Once the movie brats found Schrader, they didn't let him go: in 1976 he wrote the script for *Taxi Driver* (Martin Scorsese, 1976) and went on to write or co-write some of Scorsese's best films, including *Raging Bull* (1980) and *The Last Temptation of Christ* (1988).

The notoriety provided by *Taxi Driver* allowed Schrader to direct his film debut, the crime drama *Blue Collar*, in 1978. He subsequently directed a further 19 films to date, the most renowned being *American Gigolo* (1980) and a remake of Jacques Tourneur's 1942 eponymous *Cat People* (1982). In the early to mid-80s Schrader seemed to be poised to become a household name, but his subsequent career was inconsistent, although with several interesting moments, and he drifted away from the limelight De Palma, Scorsese and others continued to enjoy. Still, his biopic of Yukyo Mishima (*Mishima: A Life in Four Chapters*, 1985) was nominated at the Cannes Film Festival for the Palme d'Or and his penultimate feature film, *First Reformed* (2017),

---

[401] For latent try *American Gigolo* (1980) and for explicit *First Reformed* (2018).

earned him his first Academy Award nomination (not that that means much). His last film to date, *The Card Counter* (2021) is one of his very best.

Schrader is an easy costumer for auteurists, because he has been a lifelong auteurist himself. Clearly, indeed ostensibly derived from his religious background, his films almost invariably follow a "man in a room" pattern: a protagonist haunted by guilt or remorse with a self-destructive behaviour pattern, who through sacrifice or catharsis painfully finds redemption. In a 2007 interview for *Newsweek* Paul Schrader was asked to pick the five most important films ever made. His choices reveal consistence in eclecticism: *La Régle du Jeu* (Jean Renoir, 1939), *Masculin-Féminin* (Jean-Luc Godard, 1966), *Persona* (Ingmar Bergman, 1966), *The Godfather* (Francis Ford Coppola, 1972) and *Tokyo Monogatari* (Yasujiro Ozu, 1953). Asked to which film he constantly returned, he answered *Pickpocket* (Robert Bresson, 1959), explaining: "It (...) made me realize there was a place for me in filmmaking - a type of film I could make. It's about a man, his room and the movement of a soul".[402]

The Film

Initially optioned for the screen by Bruce Willis, *Touch* hit the screens 20 years after writing and 10 after publishing of the eponymous novel, in the wake of *Get Shorty*'s success and at the height of the Golden Age of Leonard adaptations.[403] Bloody sacrificialism being right up his alley, Schrader wrote the script himself, following the book's

---

[402] 'Paul Schrader on Movies', *NewsWeek*, December 2007, https:www.newsweek.com/paul-schrader-movies-94571 (accessed 18 January 2022).
[403] Devlin op. cit. p.18.

plot and dialogue closely, a cameo of LL Cool J walking out of a TV interview being one of the few innovations.[404]

The film reportedly paid for itself, but critical reception was lukewarm at best. [405] *Time Magazine* pertinently pointed out *Touch* "was never meant to be *Get Shorty*, rather a wintry meditation on the difficulties of maintaining authentic faith in the age of tele-morality".[406] Most other reviewers concurred: Roger Ebert considered "the plot (…) sounds like a comedy. But the experience of seeing the film is subduing; the movie plays in a muted key", which he relates to Schrader's religious background, seeking to identify similarities with some of the director's earlier works such as *Hardcore* (1979) or *Mishima* (1985), and giving Skeet Ulrich, who plays a bemused Juvenal, the credit for whatever pathos the film has,[407] evaluation shared by Barbara Shulgasser, who gushed Ulrich was the only thing worth seeing in the film ("Johnny Depp, Tom Cruise and Tom Hanks all in one").[408] *Variety*'s Todd McCarthy considered *Touch* "a misfired adaptation of one of Elmore Leonard's most atypical novels" and noted Schrader, back behind the camera for the big screen after an unprecedented 5 year hiatus, "has never been suspected of being a closet comedy director, and this film will do nothing to change people's thinking".[409]

---

[404] Schrader originally wanted to adapt *Rum Punch*, but when Quentin Tarantino got the rights and turned it into *Jackie Brown* (1997), Schrader decided to use *Touch* as his next project (source: *IMDb*).
[405] Geherin, op. cit. p.142.
[406] Geherin, idem.
[407] Ebert, 'Touch', *Roger Ebert*, February 1997, https://www.rogerebert.com/reviews/touch-1997 (accessed 18 January 2022).
[408] Barbara Shulgasser, 'Newcomer Ulrich has star's "Touch"', *SFGate*, February 1997 https://www.sfgate.com/news/article/Newcomer-Ulrich-has-star-s-Touch-3135340.php (accessed 18 January 2022).
[409] Todd McCarthy, 'Touch', *Variety*, 9 February 1997, https://variety.com/1997/film/reviews/touch-3-1117436856/ (accessed 18 January 2022).

Leonard's biographers spend little time on the film and are slightly less dismissive than the critical consensus alluded to above. Challen calls it "a quirky movie"[410] and Geherin hyperbolically considers the film "firmed the acting reputations of (Bridget) Fonda, (Christopher) Walken, Skeet Ulrich and Tom Arnold".[411]

This consensus seems correct. *Touch* follows the recurrent Leonard adaptation predicament readers by now know by heart: faithful adaptation, transcribed dialogue often underserved by delivery and occasional glimpses of liveliness owed mostly to the actors, in this case foremost Bridget Fonda, as Ulrich's Juvenal, although not ineffective in the film's context, is overrated, and the rest of the excellent cast poorly directed and at best par for the course.

Schrader's signature "cold" style, evocative of Bresson or Sirk, reveals itself inadequate for either comedy or magic realism, and the films ends up in a limbo beyond both, leaving the viewers with the familiar uneasy feeling of watching a film to the end never having stopped waiting for it to really start. Actors aside, small mercies include entertaining American suburban interior decoration, a *contre-plongé* of a heart shaped ceiling mirror showing Fonda and Ulrich conversing in bed (the only "rhetorical" shot of the film), a newspaper headline stating "The Stigmata and his Inamorata" (thus 'cinematizing' one of the novel's best lines) and dodgy FX and film blood. For me, the film resonates of both *Ace in the Hole* (Billy Wilder, 1951) and *Bewitched* (1964-1972).

---

[410] Challen, op. cit. p.122.
[411] Geherin, idem, wrong on all counts as Walken and Allen's careers were already as established as they would ever be, Fonda retired from the film industry a few years later, and Ulrich never lived up to whatever promise he was supposed to be showing.

Freaky Deaky (2012)

> *Freaky Deaky*, 90 minutes, The Matthau Company 2012. Release date 22 April 2012. Directed. Written and produced by Charles Matthau.
>
> Cast: Billy Burke as Chris Mankowski, Christian Slater as Skip Gibbs, Crispin Glover as Woody Ricks, Michael Jay White as Donnell Lewis, Roger Bart as Jerry Baker, Breanne Racano as Robin Abbott, Sabina Gadecki as Greta Wyatt, Andy Dick as Mark Ricks, Gloria Hendry as Stg. Maureen Downey.
>
> Cinematography: John J Connor; Editing: William Steinkamp; Music: Joseph LoDuca; Art Direction: Jody Gaber.
>
> Budget: 6 M USD

The Story

Chris walked up to him, looking at the base of the chair. "Tell me what the woman said on the phone." "Was the bitch supposed to be in love with me." "What'd she tell you." "Say I get up I'm blown up." "That's all?" "Is that all? Man, that's final, that's all there is all, nothing else." Chris said, "Yeah, but do you believe it?" "Asshole, you expect me to stand up and find out?" (*Freaky Deaky*, edition consulted: Penguin, London, 1988 p 4)

Freaky Deaky was the 26th novel written by Elmore Leonard, published by Arbor House in 1988, part of a 3 million dollar two novel contract which included *Bandits*.[412] It

---

[412] Geherin, op. cit. p.16. Leonard got 1.5 million in advance, cf. Devlin, op. cit. p.25.

was Leonard's tenth novel of the 80s, the most prolific and one of the most profitable decades for the author. Like many a Leonard novel, it started life as a very different creature, a story about a female singer whose car is blown up by the Mafia, but Leonard felt that led to a dead end and changed course midway through.[413]

Synopsis: Detroit cop Chris Mankowski is trying to switch from the bomb squad to the less explosive sex crimes unit, his first case acquainting him with aspiring actress Greta Wyatt, who thinks she can just walk in a police station and report being raped two days after the fact, without evidence or witnesses, and pin it on a heavily addicted pillar of local society, film producer Woody, leading to mishaps leading to Chris being suspended.

Concurrently and apparently unrelatedly, over-the-hill former hippies Robin and Skip meet after a 20 year hiatus as Skip comes to Detroit to work as special effects technician, using explosives skills acquired in more revolutionary days, inspiring Robin to persuade Skip to extort money from Woody with a bomb threat, scheme that unexplainably but entertainingly has to be mediated through Woody right hand man former Black Panther Donnell, who prevents the worst from happening, but not before Woody's brother, Mark, is blown away in his stead.

Subsequently, all the aforementioned plot with and against each other to keep Woody's money, with plot convoluting till final detonation.

Freaky Deaky[414] is yet another milestone in Leonard's critical and commercial ascent, now firmly in big money

---

[413] Challen, op. cit. p.120.
[414] Slang for hanky panky, although it reportedly also denotes a risqué creole dance (Challen, op. cit. p.124). There is also an eponymous techno festival - see https://freakydeaky.com.

territory. It has lots of Leonard commonalities (Detroit, cops, caper structure, alcoholism, multiple viewpoints, circular structure, a sort of Nancy Hayes in Robin, a not quite Jack Ryan in Chris)[415] but also several novelties: a relatively coherent and conventional plot – including a suspended cop continuing to work on a case to clear his name – in a mixture of caper and comedy that future works would develop.[416] Leonard scholars devote considerable space to *Freaky Deaky*: Devlin 4 pages, Geherin 5 (although it was the last and latest Leonard novel at the time of his writing, which may have contributed to enhanced attention) and Sedato a whole 12 page chapter.[417] Devlin considers the novel " (...) measured by any standard, (...) a dazzler".[418] It was Leonard's own favourite novel and the Coen brothers are also avowed fans. [419]

Freaky Deaky starts with one of the best opening scenes in Leonard's work, reminiscent of his best early Western short stories, with a guy sitting on a bomb and the bomb squad speculating on the technicalities of the feasibility of

---

[415] Sedato, op. cit. p.112 & 114; Geherin op. cit. p.121. Other Leonard leitmotifs include the anecdote on the peplum set, originally from the unpublished short story *The Only Good Syrian Foot Soldier is a Dead One* (actually published in *Charlie Maltz and Other Stories – the Unpublished Stories*, Weidenfeld & Nicolson, London, 2018, which compiles Leonard's theretofore unpublished short fiction) which pops up recurrently in his work (p.255, Penguin Books, London, UK, 1988) the issues surrounding theatrical rights (p.262), and the masterful final plot twist whereby Chris' plans get short circuited because he has to pick up his dad at the airport.
[416] Devlin, op. cit. p.74; Geherin, op. cit. p.123.
[417] '*Freaky Deaky o del detective insicuro*', Segato, op. cit. pp.91-103. Even more than with Rzepka's aforementioned Catholic tetralogy, I totally fail to see the religious connection here.
[418] Devlin, op. cit. p.71.
[419] Challen, op. cit. p.23; Sedato, op. cit. p.104 - footnote 6. *IMDB*'s trivia page claims, however, that Leonard said this about all his novels upon release...

defusing it without blowing the sitting person up.[420] A further master stroke is Woody, a key character who, uncharacteristically for Leonard, doesn't say much, allowing the author to characterize him through the interactions and descriptions of others.[421]

But I must write my affection for this book is a little more qualified than that of the critical consensus. Uncharacteristic for Leonard (and to me perhaps the most salient aspect of the book) is the Shakesperean proliferation of characters and the absence of a distinct protagonist, Chris being a part time Jack Ryan at best. Also, the relative conventionality and linearity of plot are unfamiliar territory for Leonard, and the lightness of touch slightly artificial, as if Leonard was trying to do a Donald Westlake scherzo in the manner of Clint Eastwood's (delightful) Scorsese pastiche *Jersey Boys* (2014). Greg Sutter's research contributes (cool) allusions to Detroit landmarks like the Noguchi fountain, and abundant musical and literary name dropping leaves the impression Leonard was trying to endear himself with the critics by committing the uncoolest sin: trying to sound cool.[422]

Not only that, Leonard's allusions are rather dated for 1988. Like Sedato notes, Donnell and Robin are figures of the past.[423] As a Vietnam hippie hangover, *Freaky Deaky* comes at least 10 years too late and, slick and funny as it is, it doesn't match the edge and vibrancy of Leonard´s best work.

---

[420] Sedato, (op. cit. p.105) writes this scene was much appreciated by critics. Geherin (op. cit. p.131) reports that the first draft of the novel started with a scene of Skip and Robin reminiscing, but Leonard later changed it to the bomb squad scene. See also Geherin, op. cit. p.122.
[421] Geherin, op. cit. p.124.
[422] Edition cit. p.272. See also Geherin, *The Sense of Place in Leonard's Crime Fiction*, in Rzepka op. (ed) cit. p.46.
[423] Sedato, op. cit. p.107.

The Director – Charles Matthaw

Charles Matthaw was born into the film business in New York City in 1962, the son of actor Walter Matthau (1920-2000, whose screen persona wouldn't be out of place in many a Leonard novel) and the godson of none other than Charles Chaplin, after whom he was named. Charles appeared as a child actor alongside his father in such films as *Charley Varrick* (1973) or *House Calls* (1978), and joined his father's production company, Walcar Productions, in 1978.

After graduating from the University of Southern California Film School, he directed his first film, *Doin' Time on Planet Earth*, in 1988. His directing career has been sparse: 8 films in 33 years, including 2 television films and one in pre-production, mostly romantic comedies or dramas. In his first films, Charles often cast his father in main roles, as in *The Grass Harp* (1995), based on Truman Capote's 1952 eponymous play.

As a member of the Tinseltown aristocracy he can afford to be, or seem, detached from it. In an online interview he said: "My father enjoyed being a film star, but he also could see through the baloney of Hollywood". As for the ingredients for a good film: "A good script, creating a safe, collaborative and fun environment, and a lot of luck".[424]

The Film

Freaky Deaky was Matthau's 6th film and his last to date (although there are reportedly 2 further efforts currently in pre and post-production, respectively) and the most recent

---

[424] 'An Interview with Charles Matthaw', *The Original Van Goghs Ear Anthology*, April 8 2019, https://theoriginalvangoghsearanthology.com/2019/04/08/an-interview-with-charlie-matthau-2/ (accessed 8 January 2022).

Leonard film adaptation at the time of writing. Other than flashing the action back to 1974, which allows for more colourful wardrobe and art direction and annuls the sometimes anachronistic tone of the book, the film holds the record so far for carbon copy of plot and dialogue.

The result is mildly effective. The 70s camp, if entertaining, isn't exactly a novelty and verges often on the farcical. Woody (Crispin Glover, over the top), morphed from a fat slob to a slim hippie dopehead executive, mumbles along 2010s slang which would probably be unintelligible in the 70s. The director doesn't resist the occasional *clin d'oeil* to his father's career, with background shots of film theatres´ billboards announcing pops Matthau's vehicles, such as Billy Wilder's *The Front Page* (1974) or Joseph Sargent's *The Taking of Pelham 123* (ditto) in the background.

On the plus side, parallel edited storytelling of the Chris/Greta-Robin/Skip duets captures Leonard's rhythm and mood adequately, and Robin (mischievously played by Cindy Crawford lookalike Breanne Racano), may be the best Nancy Hayes type in the Leonard film canon.

On the minus, neonoir sax background music opening every scene Ms Gadecky (playing Greta) and/or Racano cavort in swimming pools or sashay in 70s attires, as well as unacceptably amateurish explosion FX, occasionally give the film an underproduced coating.

Finally, this film may break the record for (un)availability of critical references, on or offline. None of Leonard's biographers mention it even in passing and I found only one non-amateur review, through Rotten Tomatoes, from the *Cleveland Plain Dealer's*, which, whilst erring on the side of harshness, nails it: "loosey goosey crime thriller (...) has one thing going for it: The screenplay is based on a novel by (...) Elmore Leonard. But that just isn't enough. (...) it all feels like a bad Starsky and Hutch flashback".

Killshot (2008)

> *Killshot*, 95 minutes, The Weinstein Company 2008. Release date 23 January 2009. Directed by John Madden. Written by Hossein Amini. Produced by Lawrence Bender and Richard N Gladstein.
>
> Cast: Mickey Rourke as Blackbird, Brandon McGibbon as Blackbird's kid brother, Peter Kelly Godreault as Blackbird's brother, Michelle Arvizu as nurse, Richard Zeppieri as son-in-law/Mafia boss, Alexis Butler as girl in hotel room, Hal Holbrook as Papa, Diane Lane as Carmen, Robert Gow as prospective buyer.
>
> Cinematography: Caleb Deschanel; Editing: Mick Audsley and Lisa Gunning; Music: Klaus Badel; Art Direction: Brandt Gordon.
>
> Box Office: 2.9M USD (World)

The Story

The Bird said, "Don't call me Bird no more." That stopped Ritchie, confused him. "You said they call you the Blackbird." "Not anymore." "Well, what am I suppose to call you?" "My name, Armand" "Armand? You serious?" (*Killshot*, edition consulted: Warner Books, New York, 1990 p. 94)

Killshot was the 27th novel written by Elmore Leonard, and his 11th and last of the 80s, published by Arbor House in 1989.[425] It was his third bestselling novel of the decade,

---

[425] Challen (op. cit. p.124) mentions joint publishing by Arbor House and William Morrow. However, Elmore Leonard's official website does not corroborate this.

after *Glitz* and *Freaky Deaky*.[426] *Killshot* also marks the second change of agents in Leonard´s career, from H N Swanson, by then in his early 90s, to Michael Siegel.[427]

Synopsis: *Killshot* is "a frightening book about 'two fucking maniacs'",[428] namely psycho Richie Nix, who teams up with half Quebecois-half Ojibwe mob hitman Armand Degas (nicknamed the Blackbird on account of the putative zoo-metamorphic faculties of the womenfolk on his Ojibwe side) and concoct a plan to extort 10.000$ from ironworker Wayne Colson and his wife real estate saleswoman Carmen, by repeatedly threatening to kill them, resulting in a cat and mouse chase which includes the Colsons being enlisted in a federal witness protection program and culminating in a cliffhanger situation a la *Desperate Hours* (William Wyler, 1950).

It was *a propos Killshot* that *New York Times* literary critic Christopher Lehman-Haupt wrote his oft quoted description of Leonard's style: "(...) authentic dialogue built of sentences that no real person would utter (...) and absolute economy of language".[429] As previously noted [430], Leonard himself acknowledged the influence of Richard Bissell [431]. Challen quotes Leonard as saying, upon rereading Bissell at the time of *Killshot*'s writing: "My God! Here is the guy that influenced me more than everybody".[432]

Leonard's scholars devote significant attention to *Killshot*. Rzepka spends more than 20 pages in what has to be the most ambitious and comprehensive analysis of the

---

[426] Sedato, op. cit. p.115.
[427] Challen tells the story in some detail in op. cit. pp.127-128.
[428] Devlin, op. cit. p.75.
[429] *New York Times*, 13 April 1989.
[430] Cf. supra p. 19.
[431] 'Richard Pike Bissell', *Wikipedia*, https://en.wikipedia.org/wiki/Richard_Pike_Bissell (accessed 8 January 2022).
[432] Challen, op. cit. p.129.

novel available, and Sedato writes a full chapter about it (*Killshot o della famiglia,*).[433]

Killshot is the zenith of Leonard's art. It distills his recurrent themes and tropes and remodels them in a supremely crafted *roman fleuve*, seamlessly shifting from free indirect speech to interior monologues to multiple viewpoints,[434] the plot's egress revealed by dialogue, as if the characters are unable to prevent events, uncloaking the mindset of working class USA circa 1980.[435] The novel confirms the trends revealed by the previous year's *Freaky Deaky* towards a more linear plot structure and Shakespearean diffusion, revolving around two sets of characters whose story is told in parallel and intersections: (i) Wayne Colson, Jack-Ryan-on-duty, taking a backseat to his wife, Carmen,[436] who takes centre stage in the second part of the book, much like Karen in *Gold Coast* 9 years previous, consummating the emancipation of the female character in Leonard's fiction; (ii) Ritchie Nix, a psycho whose goal in life is to rob at least one bank in every single state of the USA (eventually leaving Alaska out)[437] and Armand "Bird" Degas, the psycho killer/half reluctant henchman duo we know from *City Primeval* and *Split Images*, here augmented into a *ménage a trois* by Donna, an ex-jail warden who tags

---

[433] Sedato, op. cit. pp 115-131.

[434] Rzepka writes *Killshot* " reveals a mastery of free indirect discourse and interior monologue unsurpassed in our time, and amongst the surest of all time, even if we include Jane Austen, Flaubert and Hemingway in the mix" (op. cit. p21).

[435] Another instance in Leonard's work of conjugal stress as plot driver, in the manner of the romantic comedy. Cf Michael Sinowitz, *Elmore Leonard and the Romantic Comedy or "Get Some Love into It"*, in Rzepka op. (ed) cit. p.33. Devlin writes *Killshot* offers a detailed picture of a blue collar marriage (op. cit. p.76).

[436] Challen maintains Carmen is the best female character in Leonard's work (op. cit. p.130).

[437] Sedato (op. cit. p.116) notes Leonard managed to create negative characters without ever repeating their traits whilst retaining credibility.

along, probably representing what Nancy Hayes would be like in her late 40s.[438]

Like the aforementioned *City Primeval*, *Killshot* is an "eastern-western" [439] and the final showdown comes straight from Leonard's 50s Westerns, [440] the expected match between Wayne and Richie never materializing, as Carmen and Armand take their places, Carmen recovering her husband's shotgun (no prizes for subtlety in phallic symbolism) and Armand losing his τέχνη.

Other aspects of the novel that stand out as either manifestations of recurrent Leonard themes or noteworthy innovations would include (i) the calligraphy leitmotif, Wayne and Carmen constantly seeking to guess personality traits from the way t's are crossed and i's are dotted: (ii) the frequent use of italic, often in individual syllables, to signify vocal emphasis in dialogue; (iii) the pressure exerted in Carmen by her nagging mother, a device similar to *Freaky Deaky*'s final change of plans due to Chris having to pick up his father at the airport, and (iv) scenes of stripping as humiliation, as in *The Moonshine War*.

I tried and failed to find a quote, by Stella Adler if memory serves, that goes something like "there are many actors who act well, but there aren't many actors who act as they should". I feel the same about *Killshot*. If books were to be ranked by order of perfection, this would be best Leonard novel. To me it ranks 3rd (no need repeating what 1 and 2 are).

---

[438] The latter a "halfbreed", also a recurrent character in Leonard's fiction, evocative of *Hombre*'s Russell. Cf. Karine Powers, *The Man with Five Names – Hombre on Race and the Cinematic Western*, in Rzepka, op. (ed) cit. p.110; also Rzepka, op. cit. p.169. Sedato calls Armand "*un killer disorientato*" (op. cit. p.122), and Rzepka notes he is "strangely moving" (op. cit. p.20).
[439] Rzepka, op. cit. p.5 and Sedato, op. cit. p.117.
[440] Specifically, *Last Stand at Saber River*, cf Sedato op. cit. p.130

The Director – John Madden

John Philip Madden (Portsmouth, 1949) is an English theatre, film, television, and radio director whose main claim to fame is the direction of *Shakespeare in Love*, a film which won the Academy Award for Best Picture in 1998, famously beating Steven Speilberg's *Saving Private Ryan* (Spielberg did get the award for best director). I didn't see *Shakespeare in Love* but on the basis of the only film by Madden I've seen (*The Second Best Exotic Marigold Hotel*, 2015), I would tend to agree with the general consensus that this award was just another one in a very, very long list of instances of questionable value judgements by the AMPAS.

Back to Madden, not all that much more to report. He began his career in British independent films, and in 1975 moved to the United States, where he worked in radio and the stage. In 1984 he began to work extensively in TV, on popular series like *The Return of Sherlock Holmes*, or *Inspector Morse*. He first garnered wide-scale notice with his feature *Mrs. Brown* (1997) featuring Judi Dench, and continued to direct films with A-class actors, e. g. *Captain Corelli's Mandolin* (2001) with Nicholas Cage and Penélope Cruz and *Proof* (2005) with Anthony Hopkins and Gwyneth Paltrow, beside the aforementioned.

The title list, secondary sources, and my single previous viewing suggest a directorial penchant for bland yucky feel good fare.

The Film

Killshot had a turbulent history before, during and after production. IMDb states the film rights were bought by Bruce Willis in 1989, who intended to play the role of

Wayne Colson.[441] This production never materialized and in 2000 Challen reports the rights had by then been acquired by Quentin Tarantino for Miramax, with a view to a production to be directed by Tony Scott, with Robert de Niro playing Wayne and Tarantino himself playing Richie Nix.[442] That production didn't come to be either and the film was finally released in 2008, some three years after principal photography and substantive reediting, with John Madden behind the camera and a script by Hossein Amini (with uncredited contributions by Anthony Minghella and Sydney Pollack, who both died before release and to whom the film is dedicated).[443]

The film had a lukewarm reception and is ignored by Leonardian literature (most of which was written before the film's release and otherwise concentrates on the writing, with film adaptations mostly an afterthought). I managed to find only one press of record review, by Joe Leydon in *Variety*, who discerningly points out that "*Killshot* earns points simply by not living down to expectations", considering it a "surprisingly solid and mostly satisfying crime drama" while acknowledging that "Scattered throughout *Killshot* are telltale signs — abrupt transitions, uneven pacing, sudden arrivals and inexplicable departures — that the pic underwent some serious re-stitching in the editing room".[444]

To its credit, *Killshot* soberly states in its opening credits that it is "based on" Elmore Leonard's book, thus disclaiming being a cinematic illustration of the novel. As most

---

[441] 'Killshot', *IMDb*, https://www.imdb.com/title/tt0443559/trivia/?ref_=tt_trv_trv (accessed 8 January 2022).
[442] Challen, op. cit. p.129.
[443] 'Killshot (film)', *Wikipedia*, https://en.wikipedia.org/wiki/Killshot_(film) (accessed 8 January 2022).
[444] Joe Leydon 'Killshot', *Variety*, 10 June 2009, https://variety.com/2009/film/markets-festivals/killshot-1200506973/ (accessed 8 January 2022).

Leonard adaptations, however, the film follows the book relatively closely and borrows dialogue abundantly, and mostly manages not to disservice it. The final showdown is significantly reworked, presumably to try to make the film more marketable, and unlike Leonard's fiction and most of its film adaptations, the tone is heavy and somber rather than ludic and tongue-in-cheek. Caleb Dechanel's gorgeous moody cinematography and Mike Rourke's performance as Armand/Bird (in Leydon's words, striking "an effective balance of purposeful menace and regretful melancholy") contribute to an effective slow burn drama with a very different feel from Leonard's work, but accomplished in its own right. *Killshot* is an underrated minor gem and an outlier in Leonard's filmography (I found no indication of the author's opinion of the film).

Get Shorty (1995)

Get Shorty, 105 minutes, MGM 1995. Release date 20 October 1995. Directed by Barry Sonnenfeld. Written by Scott Frank. Produced by Danny de Vito, Michael Shamberg and Stacey Sher.

Cast: John Travolta as Chili Palmer, Gene Hackman as Harry Zimm, Rene Russo as Karen Flores, Danny DeVIto as Martin Weir, Dennis Farin as Ray "Bones" Barboni, DelRoy Lindo as Bo Catlett, James Gandolfini as Bear, John Gries as Johnny Wingate, nee Propos as Nicky.

Cinematography: Donald Peterman; Editing: Jim Miller and Ted Woerner; Music: John Lurie; Art Direction: Steve Arnold.

Festivals: Berlinale 1995

The Story

"... Lovejoy *is about life, about universal feelings of sorrow and hope. It´s about redemption and retribution, the little guys´ triumph over the system...*" *Karen said, "Harry, you´re full of shit*" (*Get Shorty*, edition consulted: Delacorte Press, New York, 1990, p. 194)

Get Shorty was the 28th novel written by Elmore Leonard, published by Delacorte Press in 1990 (Leonard's previous publisher, Arbor House, ceased activity in 1988).

Synopsis: Loan shark film buff Chili Palmer embarks on an intricate odyssey involving indebted gambling film producer Harry Zimm, whom he both tries to shake down and advise on screenwriting, airline insurance company scam benefiter Leo, who eloped with 300 grand failing to notify his wife, who in turn hires Chili to retrieve whatever money maybe left and split it with her, and film star Martin Weir, who Harry is trying to hire for a production the script of which is doctored by Chili to resemble the shakedown on Leo he has been hired to undertake, and this only in the first 50 pages or so, before it gets complicated.

Get Shorty takes Leonard's fiction to another level, with a plot of rambling intricacy that's both Hawksian – about half of the book consists of dialogue irrelevant to the plot, including on Hawks' *Rio Bravo* (1959) and *El Dorado* (1966) – and Joycean, Chilly Palmer being a sort of Las Vegas Leopold Bloom. It is also Leonard's most explicit, and successful, flirt with postmodernism, the plot layer fudge and fiction/narrative "reality" blending in seamlessly and understatedly.

Critics caught on. Chip Rhodes writes the novel "explores postmodern concerns about identity and the inability to distinguished between the real and the fake".[445] Rzepka points out that *Get Shorty* is a "metafictional account of (Leonard's) own compositional process".[446] On another level, Geherin writes "*Get Shorty* is Leonard's revenge on Tinseltown, a satiric exposé of what he liked the least about the movie business".[447]

Innovative as it is, *Get Shorty* retains many recognizable Leonard fixtures, such as plot premises that are hinted at in the beginning but remain latent as characters ramble into

---

[445] Chip Rhodes, *Politics, Desire and the Hollywood Novel*, Iowa University Press, Iowa 2008. Quoted in Rzepka, op. (ed) cit. p.31. *Nolo contendere*, but the post-modern "fake" thing was at least 10 years passé by the mid-90s.
[446] Rzepka, op. cit. p.202.
[447] Geherin, *"The Sense of Place in Elmore Leonard's Fiction"*, in Rzepka op. (ed) cit. p.524.

an unexpected and unrelated conclusion, an ex-con or a signature defenestration.[448] Otherwise, it confirms the move away from the classical Leonard protagonist (man, woman or couple) structure, Jack Ryan being finally put to rest, Chili a distant reverberation. Indeed, as Phillip Derbsy observes in his essay on the novel, "we never identify with characters, even protagonists, because they are too individual".[449]

A further entertaining variation is Michael Weir, a spoiled feckless "7 million dollar a movie star" reportedly inspired on Dustin Hoffman, with whom Leonard, as previously indicated, had had an unproductive professional relationship.[450]

If Leonard's goal was to blend film with literature and succeed in both, *Get Shorty* was the zenith of his work.

The Director – Barry Sonnenfeld

Barry Sonnenfeld (1953) is an American film and television director, producer and actor. Like several other Leonard directors, Sonnenfeld was born and raised in New York City in a middle class Jewish family. He graduated from NYU (my alma mater, may I interject, if at an advanced

---

[448] Grella (*American Detective*, p.35) notes the theft of Chilli's leather jacket in Florida 12 years previous leads to Catlett's death in California 12 years later.
[449] "Pitching cinematic identification in *Get Shorty*", Philip Derbsy, in Rzepka, op. (ed) cit. p. 114. Derbsy adds: "the structure of happenstance and luck, the crazy pattern of change and coincident that leads his novels in apparently random and sometimes fantastic directions, as the people move about, scheme, collide, act and react (...) one thing always leads to another, but not necessarily in the most logical predictable or direct manner". Remark that applies to Leonard's oeuvre beyond *Get Shorty*.
[450] Grella, loc cit. p.43, Challen, in Rzepka, op. (ed) cit. p.53; Devlin, op. cit. p.25.

age and in film-unrelated German studies) Film School in 1978.

Having majored in cinematography at NYU, he began his career photographing porn films to make a buck before starting work as director of photography on the Oscar-nominated *In Our Water* (1982). Sonnenfeld met Joel Coen at a student party, which led to an invitation to photograph the Coen Bros' *Blood Simple* (1984) which then led to him photographing *Raising Arizona* (1987) and *Miller's Crossing* (1990).[451]

He got his first (reportedly unwanted, has he claimed he was happy as a cinematographer and had no interest in directing) shot at directing in *The Addams Family* (1991), a major – and unexpected – box office success, which was followed by the sequel *Addams Family Values* (1993) and the *Men in Black* franchise (three instalments, 1997–2012).[452] In between came *Get Shorty* (1995), which, as previously stated, started the main Leonard adaptation wave.

Sonnenfeld is an interesting costumer for the Leonard director roster. His track record and style, sometimes associated with Tim Burton and the Coen Bros, if in a lighter (and much lighter weight...) tone, seems to lend itself to the Dickens of Detroit caper. For an auteur theorist, he's an easy one. He said: "'*Get Shorty, Men in Black* and *The Addams Family* are autobiographical: they all are ultimately about my own sensibilities (...)."[453] Sonnenfeld cultivates a liberal urban Jewish image, a sort of Woody Allen-redux: his autobiography is titled *Call your Mother: Memoirs of a*

---

[451] Andrew Pulver, "I guess I'm a whore, a masochist and a whore", *The Guardian*, 12 August 1999, https://www.theguardian.com/film/1999/aug/13/5 (accessed 30th of January 2022).
[452] *The Guardian*, loc cit.
[453] *The Guardian*, loc cit.

Neurotic Fillmmaker[454] and in an interview to *The Guardian* he mused "I guess I'm a whore, a masochist and a whore".[455] However that may be, Sonnenfeld is an able entertainer whose neuroses and putative masochism and whoredom don't happen to catalyse in the inspiration a la Coen or Burton he perhaps wishes they would, but, as the aforementioned *Guardian* interviewer pertinently pointed out, "he gets bums in seats".[456]

The Film

Get Shorty's film rights were bought by Danny DeVito[457] for 1 million dollars[458] in 1992,[459] who turned it into a John Travolta vehicle, then at the height of his comeback after the success of Quentin Tarantino's *Pulp Fiction* the previous year.[460]

The film's narrative structure is a carbon copy of the novel's and the same goes for the dialogue, with three minor additions: (i) the initial sequence, that sets the stage for the Chili/Harry relationship, (ii) a brief Pablo Escobar "cameo" as Harry's business associate, to lend more flavour to the fiction/"reality" cocktail, and (iii) a final sequence providing a self-fulfilling epilogue to the script-within-a-caper plot. Otherwise, Travolta's Chili trumps the novel's in film geekiness, lip syncing whole chunks of dialogue while

---

[454] Published by Hachette Books, 2020; the first part of the title alludes to an episode when Sonnlefeld's mother embarrassed him by texting him during a ball game.
[455] *The Guardian,* loc cit.
[456] *The Guardian,* loc cit.
[457] Reportedly on Barry Sonnenfeld's advice, without even having read the book, cf. Challen, op. cit. p.134.
[458] Devlin, op. cit. p.26
[459] *Sight and Sound,* March 1996, p.43.
[460] Who turned the part down twice before being talked into accepting by Tarantino, cf. Challen op. cit. p.135.

watching *Touch of Evil* (Orson Welles, 1958), and Hollywood namedropping is even more pervasive.

Screenwriter Scott Frank stated he "messed" as little as possible with the novel's dialogue.[461] He asked Leonard what the books theme was and Leonard answered he didn't know, characteristically adding themes were a "Hollywood thing".[462] It was Travolta who insisted on the retention of the original Leonard dialogue instead of what he called a "functional Hollywood script".[463] Leonard himself told Barry Sonnenfeld "when someone delivers a funny line, I hope you don't cut to another actor to get a reaction, like a grin or a laugh or something, because these people are serious", advice Sonnenfeld mercifully followed.[464]

Get Shorty met with universal critical acclaim. *The Hollywood Reporter*'s David Hunter gushed rhetorically: "How cool can a mere movie be?".[465] In the same vein, Peter Travis wrote in *Rolling Stone*: "Do me a favor. If some jerk tells you that *Get Shorty* (...) is another ripoff of *Pulp Fiction*, clobber him with a stack of Leonard's 32 crime novels, preferably hardcovers. Leonard, now 70, was writing primo pulp before Quentin Tarantino gurgled his first 'fuck you'. What really hurts is that most films cut from Leonard's

---

[461] According to Challen, op cit p 134, a "huge Leonard fan"; also, Devlin, op. cit. p.141.
[462] Challen, op. cit. p.136.
[463] Travolta to Roger Egbert, quoted by Frankie Balye in *Visual Clues etc*, Rzepka op. (ed) cit. p.67.
[464] Orr, `The Elmore Leonard Paradox`, in *The Atlantic*, 2014, quoted in Rzepka, op. (ed) cit. p.3.
[465] *The Hollywood Reporter*, 6 October 1995. That "mere" speaks volumes, though. Available at: https://www.hollywoodreporter.com/review/get-shorty-review-movie-1995-1248374 (accessed 30 January 2022).

gorgeously terse prose (...) were bloated Hollywood hogwash."[466] In *Sight and Sound*, concurring with this last statement, John Wrathall perceptively and prophetically affirmed "Leonard's more lasting contribution to cinema has come indirectly, via his influence on Quentin Tarantino" pointing to common traits such as "intricate yet accident strewn plots, unheroic protagonists whose criminal ambitions never free them from mundane concerns, split second jumps from comedy to violence".[467] Roger Ebert considered "the plot moves effortlessly from crime to the movies - not a long distance, since both industries are based on fear, greed, creativity and intimidation".[468] *San Francisco Examiner*'s Barbara Schulgasser considered the film "a moving target. You're racing happily to keep up. Who cares if it makes sense?",[469] an enunciation of Hawksian ethos developed by Todd McCarthy in *Variety*: "(...) pic stays afloat thanks mainly to its scene-by-scene amusement quotient rather than because of any sustaining suspense or sense that anything's at stake". [470]

Get Shorty was the film that finally matched Leonard's novels' commercial success and effectively made Leonard a household name. Indeed, if this was the 20th Leonard film by the order of written material I confusingly chose for this book, by order of release it was "only" the 13th, and, for Leonard, most of the best was yet to come. Also, it was Leonard's favourite Leonard film.[471] It was one of Travolta's

---

[466] *Rolling Stone*, 20 October 1995. "Most" being the operative word. Available at: https://www.rollingstone.com/movies/movie-reviews/get-shorty-101122/ (accessed 30 January 2022).
[467] *Sight and Sound*, loc. cit.
[468] Roger Ebert, 'Get Shorty', *Roger Ebert*, 1995, https://www.rogerebert.com/reviews/get-shorty-1995 (accessed 20 January 2022).
[469] *San Francisco Examiner*, 20 October 1995. Available at: https://www.sfgate.com/news/article/Get-Shorty-is-long-charm-3125603.php (accessed 30 January 2022).
[470] *Variety*, 6 October 1995.
[471] Devlin, op. cit. p.141.

best ever performances, cool smile a shade short of irritating and funky walk to put a Motown choirman to shame. Gene Hackmann, as Harry Zimm and Danny DeVito as Martin Weir, are in the same campy league and one imagines the mood in the set must have been infectious, as everyone else from James Gandolfini as Bear and Rene Russo as Karen is in lockstep. Sonnenfeld's frequent use of elaborate long shots gives the film an occasional tinge of Scorsese lite, his take on Leonard's view of the tragicomedy of American enterprise campier and lighter than that of the book. Ultimately, this is the only Leonard adaptation so far that almost begs the question of whether it is at least as good as the book it's based on. The film won a Golden Globe for John Travolta (Best Actor in a Comedy or Musical)[472] and also entered the main competition selection of the 46th Berlinale.[473]

---

[472] 'John Travolta', *Golden Globe Awards*, https://www.goldenglobes.com/person/john-travolta (accessed 30 January 2022).

[473] Film Annual Archives, *Berlinale*. Available at: https://www.berlinale.de/en/archive/jahresarchive/1996/02_programm_1996/02_filmdatenblatt_1996_19960106.html (accessed 30 January 2022).

Jackie Brown (1997)

Jackie Brown, 154 minutes, Miramax 1997. Release date 25 December 1997. Directed and written by Quentin Tarantino. Produced by Lawrence Bender.

Cast: Pam Grier as Jackie Brown, Samuel L Jackson as Ordell Robbie, Robert Foster as Max Cherry, Bridget Fond as Melanie Ralston, Michael Keaton as Ray Nicolette, Robert de Niro as Louis Gara, Michale Bowen as Mark Dagus, Chris Tucker as Beaumont Livingston, LisaGay Hamilton as Sheronda.

Cinematography: Guillermo Navarro; Editing: Sally Menke; Art Direction: Daniel Bradford.

Festivals: Berlinale 1998

Awards: USA National Board of Review Top 10 Film 1998

Budget: 15 MUSD. Box Office: 39 MUSD (US and Canada)

The Story

"You look back,' Max said, 'you can't believe that much time went by. You look ahead and you think, shit, if it goes that fast I better do something with it" (*Rum Punch*, edition consulted: Dell Publishing, New York, 1993, p. 191)

Rum Punch was the 30th novel written by Elmore Leonard, published by Delacorte in 1992, the second part of a two-book deal.[474]

Synopsis: Ordell Robbie and Louis Gara, whom we know from *The Switch* (1978) are back,[475] this time selling illegal weapons and having Balzaquienne flight attendant Jackie Burke syphon the proceeds, the latter being caught red-handed by feds, who try to "turn" her, while concurrently bail bondsman Max Cherry.[476] falls for her and tries to rescue her, it all leading to triangular complications involving attempts to catch the weapons traffickers and/or elope with their money

Rum Punch is one of the "impossible-to-separate-from-the-movie" Leonard novels, and a final landmark in the consecration of the writer as both pop and literary landmark, mostly courtesy of the subsequent Tarantino adaptation.[477] It merited universal critical acclaim and is also one of a dozen or so Leonard novels to be object of an individual academic analysis (by Rossitsa Terzieva-Artemis: "*Moral Luck and Determination in* Rum Punch").[478]

We are back in Florida's Gold Coast, in Max's words "the arms capital of America (...) You can buy an assault rifle (...) in less time that it takes to get a library card". The themes and structure are very familiar Leonard territory, a money scam engendering several separate confidence dilemmas,

---

[474] Devlin op. cit. p.26. This was the 3rd Leonard novel published by Delacorte, which would also publish his six following novels up to 2000.
[475] A relative rarity for Leonard, whom as we have seen tended to prefer repeating character names in different contexts and less the characters themselves.
[476] Based in real life bail bondsman Max Sandy, subject of Sutter investigation, cf. Challen, op. cit. p.139 and Devlin, op. cit. p.94.
[477] Challen, op. cit. p.138
[478] Rzepka, op. (ed) cit. pp.146-163.

situations established in the first 50 or so pages, dragging along by false starts and dialogue exchanges until about page 300, at which time the situation resolves itself.[479]

Rum Punch is distilled Leonard, more "literary" than his usual style, somewhat more sexually explicit, with a comparatively more linear plot structure, the Max and Jackie romance "an inventive version of the meet cute" and also unusual as both sides are "mature" (Jackie in her 40s, Max in his 50s).[480] A Shakespearean cast of characters, all more or less illegally looking out for number one, manage to end up in an almost happy end, not unlike those of Leonard's early westerns, contrasting with the anticlimactic surprise final twist pervasive in Leonard's most other coeval capers.

Be all that as may, maybe I was not in the right mood but *Rum Punch* failed to impress me as much as the post-Tarantino adaptation hype would lead to expect. It's recognizably Leonard, perhaps too much so, and expertly crafted as it is it adds little to the Leonard one knows when one has read all his output up to this point. It is certainly enjoyable, but lacks, well, punch, and once again the frequent name dropping, this time of the Soul music/fashion brand variety, besides sometimes irritatingly bringing to mind Brett Easton Ellis, arouse the suspicion Leonard is again uncoolly trying to be cool.

The Director – Quentin Tarantino

Quentin Tarantino (Knoxville, Tennessee, 1963) is an American film director, screenwriter, producer, author, film

---

[479] As Devlin puts it (op. cit. p.95) "Living proof of Leonard dictum the right characters with the right names will make their own story".
[480] Michael Sinowicz, in Rzepka, op. (ed) cit. p.36.

critic, and actor, the only child of Connie McHugh and actor Tony Tarantino, who left the family before his son's birth. Tarantino's ancestry is reportedly Italian, Irish, and Cherokee (absent documentation on this last one, I wouldn't exclude a touch of phantasy/wannabe hippy/cool on the part of Ms McHugh). In 1966, the (remaining) Tarantinos moved to Los Angeles, where young Quentin became a Marvel Comics fan and an early film buff, who was allowed as a child to watch "mature" films such as *Carnal Knowledge* (Mike Nichols, 1971).[481] In what has to be one of the most sterling examples of life surpassing, if not art, at least film buff essays, Quentin was grounded by his mother at the age of 15 for shoplifting Elmore Leonard's *The Switch* from Kmart!

He started working in the film industry at a young age and the old-fashioned way, first as an usher at a porn film theatre and, in the 80s, in a five-year stint at a video store, experience which laid the groundwork for his encyclopedic film erudition. After a number of unremarkable jobs in various capacities in TV and video, Tarantino's big break came in 1992 with *Reservoir Dogs*.

The rest is film history. Every one of the 9 films directed by him (excluding sketches in sketch films, TV series' episodes and counting the two *Kill Bills* as one, as Quentin does) has been a major event, and Quentin Tarantino is currently, according to a recent study, the most-studied director in academia the UK, ahead of the likes of Alfred Hitchcock, Christopher Nolan, Martin Scorsese or Steven

---

[481] BBC Radio 1, '"It felt pretty good!" Quentin Tarantino on 'appearing 'in *The Avengers, Team America* and *Shrek*.' (2019), *YouTube*, available at https://www.youtube.com/watch?v=ix-ym3c736o (accessed 28th May 2022). To this day, Tarantino claims he is a fan of the Marvel Cinematic Universe (to each his own, like I always say).

Spielberg.[482] On the western shores of the Atlantic, none other than Peter Bodganovitch called him "the single most important director of his generation".[483]

Tarantino's style is characterized by non-linear storytelling, like Chris Nolan's, but whereas it could be said that non-linearity is the essence of Nolan's cinema [like, say, Alain Resnais' *L'Année dernière à Marienbad* (1959), Tarantino uses complex flashback/forward structures and repeated/alternative scenes instrumentally to conventional, if circumvolved, plot development and traditional narrative. His "glorification" of violence is also often pointed out and sometimes criticized, as if the flamboyant tongue-in-cheek meta tone – a sort of upscale Sam-Peckinpah-meets-70s-Hong-Kong-schlock treatment – weren't obvious. His eclectic gorgeous pop soundtracks and remake/remodel take on popular culture, as in substituting product placement by imaginary, if believable, consumer brands (.e.t *Big Kahuna* burgers or *Red Apple* cigarettes), complete the package. His self-confessed biggest influence is Sergio Leone and his favourite film *The Good, the Bad and the Ugly* (Leone, 1966).

21st Century culture vulture extraordinaire, Tarantino's film output portrays, mythologizes and embeds the fabric of contemporary life like few others'. He has been showered by recognition and praise. His second film, *Pulp Fic-*

---

[482] Mayer Nissim, 'Quentin Tarantino is most-studied director in the UK', *DigitalSpy* (2013), https://www.digitalspy.com/movies/a529084/quentin-tarantino-is-most-studied-director-in-the-uk/ (accessed 28th May 2022).

[483] Melena Ryzik, 'Tarantino Unveils 'Django, 'the Shortest Long Western', *The Carpet Bagger* (2012), https://carpetbagger.blogs.nytimes.com/2012/12/04/tarantino-unveils-django-the-shortest-long-western/ (accessed 28th May 2022).

tion (1994) won the *Palme d'Or* at Cannes and the Academy Award for Best Original Screenplay, besides receiving a nomination for Best Director.[484][485] In all, Tarantino's films have won 8 Academy Awards, 1 Palme d'Or, 7 BAFTA Awards and 8 Golden Globes.[486][487] In 2004, Tarantino was the President of the Jury of the Cannes Film Festival (one of a half dozen US directors to receive such a distinction in 75 years, along with Clint Eastwood, David Lynch, Martin Scorsese or Steven Spielberg).[488] Fittingly, in 2015 Tarantino received a star on the Hollywood Walk of Fame for his contributions to the film industry.[489] Revealingly, the French *Académie des arts et techniques du cinéma* awarded him in 2011 the Honorary César, reserved for the likes of Ingmar Bergman, Jean-Luc Godard or Walt Disney[490]. Perhaps more significantly, Tarantino is a self-confessed foot fetishist, and legitimately argues that in this respect he shares the podium with Luis Buñuel, Samuel Fuller and Alfred Hitchcock.

---

[484] 'Pulp Fiction', *Cannes Film Festival,* https://www.festival-cannes.com/fr/films/pulp-fiction-1 (accessed 28th May 2022)

[485] 'Pulp Fiction', *Oscars,* https://www.oscars.org/collection-highlights/pulp-fiction (accessed 28th May 2022).

[486] Available at *BAFTA,* https://www.bafta.org/search/bafta/Quentin%2520Tarantino (accessed 28th May 2022).

[487] Available at *Golden Globe Awards,* https://www.goldenglobes.com/search?keywords=quentin%20tarantino (accessed 28th May 2022).

[488] *'Liste des présidents du jury du Festival de Cannes', Wikipedia,* https://fr.wikipedia.org/wiki/Liste_des_pr%C3%A9sidents_du_jury_du_festival_de_Cannes (accessed 28th May 2022).

[489] 'Quentin Tarantino', *Hollywood Walk of Fame,* https://walkoffame.com/quentin-tarantino/ (accessed 28th May 2022).

[490] 'Quentin Tarantino', *César Académie des arts et techniques du cinéma,* https://www.academie-cinema.org/personnes/quentin-tarantino/ (accessed 28th May 2022).

59 at the time of writing, Tarantino is very much a Tinseltown senator, active as producer or exhibitor of independent or foreign films, labeled as "Presented by Quentin Tarantino" or "Quentin Tarantino Presents", often under his own Rolling Thunder Pictures company. In 2010, Tarantino bought the New Beverly Cinema in Los Angeles, keeping the theatre's management and allowing them to retain exhibition policy control, but contributing occasional programming suggestions, including his own films or prints from his personal collection. He is on record saying: "As long as I'm alive, and as long as I'm rich, the New Beverly will be there, showing films shot on 35 mm".[491] He has often alluded to retiring from film directing at 60, after his 10th film (that'd be one to go) and dedicating himself to writing. The reason is he feels the quality of most directors output decline as they grow old: "(...) I don't want to be an old-man filmmaker, making old-man movies who doesn't know when to leave the party. And I don't want to fuck up my filmography with a bunch of old-man stuff".[492]

---

[491] Jen Yamato, 'Quentin Tarantino's New Beverly Promises Double Features, Vintage Trailers, Tarantino Films & NO Digital. Ever', *Deadline* (2014), https://deadline.com/2014/09/quentin-tarantino-new-beverly-cinema-takes-over-theater-830233/ (accessed 28th May 2022).

[492] 'Quentin Tarantino: "It's a Corrupted Cinema"', *The Talks*, https://the-talks.com/interview/quentin-tarantino/ (accessed 28th May 2022). Tarantino is presumably thinking of Golden Era directors who finished their long careers in the 60s and 70s. Even in that case, he has only half a point: consider *Marnie* (Alfred Hitchcock, 1964), *Frenzy* (Hitchcock, 1972), *Seven Women* (John Ford, 1966) or *Sleuth* (Joseph L Mankiewicz, 1972), not to mention Fritz Lang's *Tiger* dyptich or Ingmar Bergman's *Fanny och Alexander* (1982) and *Saraband* (2003), I could go on and on. It is true that some major (Hollywood) directors either lost their mojo or were reduced to hack jobs from the 60s onwards (Anthony Mann, Nicholas Ray, Jacques Tourneur etc) but even they still did some good stuff (I love Mann's late Cinemascope big budget

The Film

Filmed five years after the publishing of *Rum Punch*, *Jackie Brown* was produced for 15 million USD and hit the screens on Christmas day 1997.[493]

Other than changing Jackie's family name and skin colour (casting 70s Blaxploitation actress Pam Grier in the main role), Tarantino uncharacteristically sticks very close to the novel's plot and dialogue. The setting changes from Florida to LA and the end is less happy than the one implied in the book, but that's it. Signature Tarantino moments are also few and far between, including a close-up of Gara moll Melanie's (played by Bridget Fonda, essentially repeating of her role as Lynn in *Touch*, which was also released in 1997) toes and a brief non-chronological sequence showing from two different perspectives the scene leading to Gara shooting Melanie. Tarantino follows the wise Leonard adaptation tradition of sticking to the written dialogue – although he does occasionally "enrich" it with profuse expletives – and characteristically stages long dialogue scenes, although this time with sparse editing and camera movement, the toned down style possibly a token of the director' respect for the writer.

Tarantino is an avowed longtime Leonard fan and reportedly (and implausibly) frequented an all-black school, hence his fluency in jive and licentiousness with the "n" word.[494] Tarantino's style, developed in his previous *Reservoir Dogs* (1992) and *Pulp Fiction* is as close as one can get to the cinematic equivalent of Leonard's universe, a quality

---

peplums) and were the exception rather than the rule. And anyway, all that was back in the day.

[493] Cf Challen op. cit. p.140; Cf Devlin op. cit. p.143.

[494] Cf Frankie Y Bailey: 'Visual Clues – Dress, Appearance and Protection in Elmore Leonard's Crime Fiction' in Rzepka op. (ed.) cit. p.66.

the writer himself recognized: upon seeing *True Romance* (Tony Scott, 1993, scripted by Tarantino) he said "this is what one of my books should be". Tarantino, in turn, later told Charlie Rose that he considered *True Romance* "basically like an Elmore Leonard movie that he didn't write."

Jackie Brown received generally positive reviews and Elmore Leonard claimed, again, it was his favourite screen adaptation of his novels.[495] Roger Ebert captured the empathy of Tarantino to Leonard's writing best when he observed the film was "about texture, not plot"[496] and "more revolutionary than it seems".[497]

I would agree. Before writing this book I hadn't seen the film since it's release in 1997, and then only once, and my recollection was of it being my least favourite Tarantino film. This changed with the benefit of hindsight. *Jackie Brown* foreshadows several of the director's later stylistic developments, the long shots of faces and walks, the Proustian Americana revisited in *Once Upon a Time in Hollywood* (2019), the biracial romance, this time bitter-sweet and "mature", as counterpoint to the action (or rather, and much like Leonard, the talk). Befitting the lead actress, the film has a 70s low-budget flavour and the frequent film quotes and background 70s funk and soul music serve the film better than they did the novel. Dialogue rendition,

---

[495] Exceptions, disparaging the film for the exact same reasons I and most everybody else liked it, include Mick LaSalle in the *San Francisco Chronicle* (available at: https://www.sfgate.com/movies/article/FILM-REVIEW-Tarantino-s-Latest-Caper-Funky-2788200.php - accessed 28th May 2022) and Janet Maslin in the *New York Times* (available at: https://archive.nytimes.com/www.nytimes.com/library/film/122497jackie-film-review.html - accessed 28th May 2022).
[496] Roger Ebert, 'Jackie Brown', *Roger Ebert* (1997), https://www.rogerebert.com/reviews/jackie-brown-1997 (accessed 28th May 2022).
[497] Quoted in Devlin, op. cit. p.144.

the major curse of the Leonard film adaptation, is here definitively exorcised, as if Leonard's lines had been written for Tarantino to film and for actors to speak for themselves. *Jackie Brown* is also a rarity inasmuch as it improved – at least for me – after having read the novel, and is maybe the only Leonard film adaptation which is clearly better than the book on which it is based.

Pronto (1997)

> *Pronto*, 100 minutes, Showtime Networks 1997. Release date 8 June 1997.
>
> Directed by Jim McBride. Written by Michael Butler. Produced by Richard Berg and Allan Marcil.
>
> Cast: Peter Falk as Harry Arno, Glenne Hadley as Joyce Patton, James LeGros as Deputy US Marshalll Rayland Givens, Sergio Castellito as Tommy "the Zip" Bucks, Walter Olkiewicz as Jimmy "the Cap" Capotorto, Luíz Guzman as Buck Torres, Bradford Tatum as Nick ""Joe Macho" Testa; Theresa Kablan as Gloria Ayers, Franco Treviso as Fabrizio.
>
> Cinematography: Alfonso Beato; Editing: Milton Ginsberg; Music: John Altman; Art Direction: J Patrick Coll and Dimitris Kakridas.

The Story

"I might ask you, since you seem to be the expert in these matters, when the last time was you shot anybody?' 'Yesterday,' Raylan said." (*Pronto*, edition consulted: Harper Torch 2002)

Pronto was the 31st novel written by Elmore Leonard, published in 1993 by Delacorte Press.

Synopsis: As ageing Miami bookie Harry Arno is planning to retire in Italy, where he served in World War II (and met none other than Ezra Pound), the Justice Dept sends Deputy Marshall Rayland Givens to enjoin him to join a witness protection program, while concurrently the Mob sends a crew to take him out. Once in Italy, a three party cat and mouse chase ensues, involving (i) Harry and his girlfriend, Joyce, (ii) Rayland and (iii) the mobsters, divided in parties of (a) Italian real deal tough guys and (b) American phonies who can't walk the talk, giving rise to numerous verbal duels and three firearm ones.

Pronto doesn't merit nearly the attention it deserves from Leonard's biographers. Challen confesses the book is one of his least favourites (although, this being Leonard, he still likes it very much) and he attributes this to his dislike of the character of Raylan Givens (which is baffling, as Rayland is an archetypal Leonard protagonist).[498] More perceptively, Devlin points out to the colourful use of bookie slang (example: "Gimme the Lions and the Forty-niners twenty times reverse, Bears a nickel, Chargers a nickel, Giants five times, New England ten times and the Browns twenty") [499] and reveals Leonard got it in research and included it in the book having no idea what it meant.[500] The press reviews were generally enthusiastic: "Speedy, exhilarating, and smooth. Nobody does it better", wrote the *Washington Post*;[501] " one of the best grabbers in years", proclaimed *Entertainment Weekly*.[502]

With good reason. *Pronto* is one of the very best Elmore Leonard books ever. The narrative structure is relatively straightforward for the author's standards, the caper plot again borrowing elements from Leonard's early Westerns.

---

[498] Challen, op. cit. p.141. Challlen further reports Greg Sutter almost got in trouble with the Mob while location scouting for the book in the wrong Italian neighbourhoods.
[499] Edition consulted: HarperTorch, paperback 2002, p.246.
[500] Devlin, op. cit. p.9.
[501] Jonathan Yardley, 'Book World' (1993), *The Washington Post*, https://www.washingtonpost.com/archive/lifestyle/1993/09/22/book-world/4c842877-fa5a-4587-a8b1-6cbfd99a0878/ (accessed 28th May 2022).
[502] Quoted in https://scw.overdrive.com/library/mysteries/media/35267 (accessed 28th May 2022).

The location is Italy, giving rise to numerous delightful accounts of American perceptions of European culture (carabinieri wearing swords that patently aren't meant to be used, nobody can make a Martini, there's Coca-Cola everywhere but Dr Pepper is unknown), and two running gags, one about Ezra Pound's poetry, the other a delayed gratification dare between a tough guy and a phoney about "taking down" the main character.

For me, *Pronto* ranks 3rd in Leonard's opus so far, after *Swag* and *The Big Bounce*, and features his most virtuoso prose, possibly excepting his best short fiction.

The Director – Jim McBride

Jim McBride (1941) is an American television and film director, producer and screenwriter with a long (1967-2009) if relatively sparse filmography (21 titles, including 6 TV series episodes, 4 documentaries and 4 TV films) whose main claims to fame are, in descending order of importance:

- Having had the courage, or foolhardiness, to direct a remake of Goddard's *A Bout de Souffle* (1960), titled *Breathless* (1983) remade as an American road movie featuring Richard Gere in the role originally played by Jean-Paul Belmondo, and who spends most of the film rambling about driving down to *Mejicoo*;
- Being named one of the twelve greatest living "narrative" filmmakers, on the sole evidence of his mockumentary debut "David Holzman's Diary"

(1967), by then New Yorker resident critic Richard Brody;[503]
- Being married to Tracy Tynan, the daughter of Kenneth Tynan.

Other than a vague recollection of having seen *Breathless* when it was first released and finding it mildly entertaining if somewhat overrated on account of all the *A Bout de Souffle* hype, that's all I have to offer on Jim McBride.

The Film

Released in the year of all Leonard adaptations (1997) with a screenplay from one Michael Butler, *Pronto* is a TV programmer that typically sticks close to the novel's plot and dialogue.

The film starts kind of nice with a long travelling of Miami's Art Deco district to set the tone and scene, and later moves to Corfu, which passes for Italy, for the Italian part, going through the Leonard motions in an easygoing TV film way. [504] Leonard dialogue is mostly spoiled by overdelivery, illustrating once again the author's complaint that he tried to avoid his writing to sound like writing only to suffer actors reading his dialogue and making it sound like acting. The focus shifts from Rayland (played by James LeGros, who might miss the distinction of being the worst Leonard protagonist ever – stone-faced, Stetson-wearing and with an incongruous mock-Texan drawl – only because the competition in that department happens to be stiff) to Harry (played by Peter Falk playing himself, arguably the

---

[503] Richard Brody, 'Who are the Twelve Greatest Living Narrative Filmmakers?' (2013), *The New Yorker* https://www.newyorker.com/culture/richard-brody/who-are-the-twelve-greatest-living-narrative-filmmakers (accessed 28th May 2022).
[504] Devlin, op. cit. p.142.

best thing in the film). Similarly, Glenne Hadley as Harry's trophy girl and subsequent Rayland love interest Joyce is spice-less – much unlike Therese Kablan, who, as main mobster moll Gloria, sets the TV screen ablaze every time she sashays in.

Unsurprisingly for a TV production of this kind, there's virtually zero literature on this work, even online. The only references to the film come from Leonard's biographers, Challen considering Peter Falk plays Rayland "well"[505] and Devlin writing the film is "intelligent" and "a story of the passing of the old order and the arrival of the new" (presumably a reference to Harry's retirement) before concluding mysteriously that the film, "good as it is, is not for all time".[506]

No, it's not. It is passable TV filler with a couple of cute ideas, sort of like *Big Bounce II* minus the production values and with indifferent actor's direction. I'd single out the scene where a gangster shoots his boss in the back and looks on both bemused and seemingly entertained, a curious illustration of Leonard's recurrent psycho killer theme of shooting a man, as Johnny Cash sang, just to watch him die, and the very last shootout showdown between Rayland and mobster Zip, the only scene in the film that might just measure to the novel and evokes Leonard's Western days.

---

[505] Challen, op. cit. p.141.
[506] Devlin, op. cit. p.143.

Out of Sight (1998)

Out of Sight, 123 minutes, Universal 1998. Release date 26 June 1997. Directed by Steven Soderbergh. Written by Scott Frank. Produced by Danny De Vito, Michael Shamberg and Stacey Sher.

Cast: George Clooney as Jack Foley, Samuel L Jackson as Hejira Hnry (uncredited), Viola Davis as Moselle Jennifer Lopez as Karen Cisco, Catherine Keener as Adele, Michael Kidman as Ray Nicolette, Steve Zahn as Glenn Michaels, Don Cheadle as Maurice Miller, Ving Rhames as Buddy Bragg.

Cinematography: Elliot Davis; Editing: Anne V Holmes; Music: David Holmes. Art Direction: Philip Messina.

Awards: OFCS Award Top Ten Films of the Year 1999 (10th place), Boston Society of Film Critics Award 1999.

Festivals. Deauville, Helsinki, London, Oldenburg, Venice 1998.

Budget: 48 MUSD. Box Office: 77 MUSD (USA and Canada 37

The Story

> *"Bless his heart. I´ll say one thing for Jack, he was never ugly or mean or drank too much. His idea of a normal life, though, was robbing banks."* (*Out of Sight*, edition consulted: Dell Publishing, 1997, p. 143)

Out of Sight was the 33rd novel written by Elmore Leonard, published in 1996 by Delacorte Press. *Out of Sight*, a title inspired by the lyrics of Stevie Wonder's 1965 *Uptight*, was to have been the title of *Riding the Rap*, but for an undisclosed reason Leonard decided to wait for his next novel to use it.[507]

Synopsis: Bank robber Jack Foley and fellow inmate Buddy escape from a Florida correctional facility through a tunnel dug in mud and run into young attractive US Marshall Karen Sisco, who happened to be at the mouth of the tunnel and with whom Foley gets to share the trunk of the getaway car, journey during which they get acquainted - he entreating and she declining, as the rules of elegant courtship prescribe – Foley's foul smell of gutter dejecta and the unorthodox circumstances of the encounter not preventing a conversation that includes an exchange on each other's favourite films.

Slapstick comedy romantic situation established, the usual rambling begins, involving an unfulfilled plan by former Foley co-inmates to rob a millionaire white collar criminal that supposedly has millions of dollars in cash stashed at home, plan which eventually downgrades to breaking into junkies houses for a mere couple of thou, all of which Foley tries to hide from Karen, while they often inadvertently bump into one another in Detroit, to where the action shifts, where Karen also meets Foley's ex Adele, in the course of which meeting she captures also co-inmate Chino, whom she delivers to the local PD in exchange for a transfer to the SWAT team, which eventually leads her to defuse final a job Foley – with whom in the meantime Karen had a one night stand – set up with heavies Glenn Michaels and psycho Snoopy Miller (predictably inspiring gags about his nickname), it all ending violently but very unexpectedly.

---

[507] Rzepka, op. cit. p. 127.

Out of Sight spent 7 weeks in the *New York Times* best seller list[508] and Leonard scholars praise it unanimously. Devlin considers it "may well be the best (Leonard's novel) to date"[509], "gently elegiac"[510] and featuring "dazzling shifts of points of view".[511] Challen considers it one of his favourites – a welcome respite after not having liked much the previous ones.[512] Rzepka writes a full essay on it, titled "`It's the way they're done´: style and legerdemain in Out of Sight", in the collection of essays he edited.[513] In the same work, Frankie Bailey, in his essay "*Visual Clues*" devotes a chapter to *Out of Sight*[514] which analyzes the detailed descriptions of what the novel's characters wear and, more importantly how they wear it, a sartorial manifestation of Leonardian τέχνη.

We're back to the to Florida/Detroit axis and to a classical Leonardian dramatic structure: a preposterous premise sets the stage, then life happens and plans drift, and finally, *commerce oblige*, there's closure, although characteristically unexpected and anticlimactic – indeed a Leonard twist on Noir conventions as the relationship between Karen and Foley despite of love could never be (ex-

---

[508] Devlin, op. cit. p. 2.
[509] Devlin, op. cit. p. 27.
[510] Devlin, op. cit. p. 98.
[511] Devlin, op. cit. p. 126. Quite so. The multidimensional dynamics between Karen and Foley, Karen and the cops, Foley and the gangsters, Karen and her dad, despite of the customary indecisiveness of action and changes of direction throughout the book, ~~it all~~ somehow works like a buildup to the final holdup.
[512] Challen, op. cit. p. 142.
[513] Rzepka, op. (ed) cit. p. 127-144.
[514] "Cops and cons in *Out of Sight*", Rzepka, op. (ed) cit. pp. 63-66.

cept they don't really love each other). Atypically for Leonard, the ending is both tragic and sad.[515] Rzepka entertainingly if farfetchedly considers Foley and Karen's one night stand "an erotic variation on Kant's mathematical sublime" (!). More to the point, he notes *Out of Sight* consists of a series of moments of "occlusion, disguise, vanishing, and invisibility". Indeed, Karen and Foley keep bumping into each other while trying to evade one another, the crime/thriller/suspense chase dynamics an allegory for the mating ritual. Rzepka further suggests Foley is Leonard's alter ego, having been born in the Big Easy etc.[516]

Out of Sight features several Leonardian τόπων: the fascination of women with the criminal element, the idea for Karen reportedly coming from a photo in Detroit News of "US Marshall Anna Garza guarding drug defendants in Florida with a pump shotgun resting on one hip and carrying a shoulder bag" [517] Karen is a synthesis of Leonard's two main female stereotypes, the Hawksian gal and the psycho-harlot, a "sexy tomboy, a daddy's girl who knows batting averages and boxing records".[518] Greg Sutter's research lends colour to Detroit, references to landmarks such as the RebCen resonating perhaps more strongly with the local readership. *Out of Sight* follows the trend initiated in the last few novels of increasing explicit sex scenes and expletive language. It is interesting to note that, in this, Leonard was a couple of decades behind the curve, and

---

[515] Along the same lines Rzepka, op. cit. p. 160. Michael Sinowitz (loc. cit. p. 36) considers Karen and Foley's one night stand "probably the most romantic" in Leonard's work. Also, the relationship revisits the age difference issue (Foley is 47) which occasionally surfaces in Leonard's couples, here maybe also a reflection on the authors own personal life. Devlin (op. cit. p. 88) hints in the same direction.

[516] Rzepka op. cit. pp. 127, 130.

[517] Devlin, op. cit. p. 22, Challen, op. cit. p. 143

[518] Devlin, op. cit. p. 27.

one wonders if, again, commercial considerations might not have played a part. After the trend of the last novels to a more structured plot, this one is lighter than air, people just chat and ramble after Karen and Foley get out of the trunk. Rzepka notes "(..) the flawless manner in which he intersects separate plot lines in scenes that, if they appeared in a book by nearly any other author, they would appear contrived".[519] Finally, and another novelty for Leonard, *Out of Sight* features lots of dialogue but at least as much description, and the description is at least as good as the dialogue.

The Director – Steven Soderbergh

Steven Soderbergh (Atlanta, 1963) is an American film director, producer, screenwriter, cinematographer, and editor. Born to a middle-class family with Swedish, Irish and Italian ascendance, Soderbergh spent his childhood and adolescence in the South (Charlottesville, Virginia, then Baton Rouge, Louisiana). As a teenager he developed a liking to filmmaking the coeval way, with Super 8 and 16 mm cameras, and enrolled in a film animation course at the local university, where he began making short films.

Soderbergh's pre-breakthrough came in 1986 when was he asked to develop a full-length promotional film for prog rock perennials Yes, entitled 9012Live, for which he received a Grammy Award nomination for Best Music Video, Long Form, [520](space) the profit thereof further al-

---

[519] Rxepka op. cit. p.138.
[520] Available at: *Grammy*, https://www.grammy.com/grammys/artists/steven-soderbergh/14277 (accessed 31st August 2022).

lowing him to go to Tinseltown to write and direct his milestone *sex, lies, and videotape* (1989) a modern melodrama which catapulted him to the public spotlight and won him inter alia a Palme d'Or at the Cannes Film Festival, making him the youngest solo director to receive this distinction.[521]

Sex, Lies, and Videotape became an icon of 1990s US independent cinema (Roger Ebert aptly called Soderbergh the "poster boy of the Sundance generation"). [522] In 2006 – coincidentally the year of Ebert's quip – the film was selected by the Library of Congress for preservation in the United States National Film Registry, being deemed "culturally, historically, or aesthetically significant".[523]

Whether by chance or design, Soderbergh subsequent career remained true to the "independent" ethos, as he directed pretty much what he fancied, from big to next-to-no budget films, from box office blockbusters to personal quirks, from biopics of *Kafka* (1991) and *Che Guevara* (2 parts, 2008) to call girl lifestyle mockumentaries *(The Girlfriend Experience*, 2009) or smartphone shot psycho-thrillers (*Unsane*, 2018). To balance his books, Soderbergh directed inter alia the *Ocean*'s franchise (2001–18). In total, his films have grossed over US$2.2 billion worldwide so far and garnered nine Oscar nominations, winning seven.

With thus acquired independence, Soderbergh has spent a part of his free time and spare cash experimenting with film as a mass cultural artefact, namely releasing a much abridged alternate cut of Michael Cimino's *Heaven's*

---

[521] Available at: *Festival Cannes*, https://www.festival-cannes.com/fr/films/sex-lies-videotape (accessed 31st August 2022).
[522] Ebert, 'Bubble', *Roger Ebert*, 2006, https://www.rogerebert.com/reviews/bubble-2006 (accessed 31st August 2022).
[523] Available at: https://www.loc.gov/programs/national-film-preservation-board/film-registry/complete-national-film-registry-listing/ (accessed 31st August 2022).

Gate (1980) in 2014, the same year he uploaded a black-and-white silent version of *Raiders of the Lost Ark* (Steven Spielberg, 1981), with *The Social Network*'s (David Fincher, 2010) score.

Also the indie way, Soderbergh prefers not to have his name at the start of a film's credits. "The fact that I'm not an identifiable brand is very freeing," he says, "because people get tired of brands and they switch brands".[524]

Soderbergh published a memoir, co-authored with Richard Lester,[525] entitled *Getting Away with It, or, The Further Adventures of the Luckiest Bastard You Ever Saw*, in 1999.[526]

As many others', Soderbergh's filmography leaves the impression of being a decades' long commentary on his debut's title, as his films often deal with shifting identities, sexuality and vengeance. Soderbergh makes much use of long close-ups, often coupled with jump cuts. A consummate cinematographer, Soderbergh photographed many of his own films under various aliases, *Solaris* (2002), a remake of the 1972 eponymous film by Andrei Tarkovsky (another quirky project) being in this regard a personal favourite of mine, reminiscent in style of Anton Corbijn's film work. Somewhat like Hitchcock, Soderbergh's signature sophisticated polish is a see-through veil for a universal sense of dislocation. In his films everything happens, and everyone lives, in the zone.

---

[524] Landon Palmer, '6 Filmmaking Tips from Steven Soderbergh', *Film School Rejects*, 2012, https://filmschoolrejects.com/6-filmmaking-tips-from-steven-soderbergh-5d503bc58a9b/ (accessed 31st August 2022).

[525] He of *inter alia* Beatles' films (*A Hard Day's Night*, 1964, and *Help!*, 1965) fame.

[526] *Faber & Faber*, London, UK, 1999.

The Film

Universal Studios paid 3 million dollars for the film rights of *Out of Sight*, at the zenith of successful Leonard film adaptations. The film was a major comeback for director Steven Soderbergh, whose career had been drifting since his debut *Sex, Lies and Videotape* some 10 years before.

The film had an all-star cast – marking the beginning of a long lasting association between Soderbergh and George Clooney, who was cast as Jack Foley – and a top technical crew, including production designer by Gary Frutkoff (*Devil in a Blue Dress*), editor Anne Coates (who won an Oscar for *Lawrence of Arabia*), costume designer Betsy Heimann (*Get Shorty, Reservoir Dogs, Pulp Fiction*),[527] scriptwriter Scott Frank (*Get Shorty*)[528] and perhaps most of all cinematographer Elliot Davis, a long-time Soderbergh companion. Produced by Jersey Films, at the time at the cutting edge (*Pulp Fiction, Get Shorty, Gattaca)*, for all the expectations the film fared relatively modestly at the box office.

Unsurprisingly, the film follows the novel plot and dialogue very closely, with easily identifiable exceptions: (i) a series of flashbacks between the Foley's prison times and

---

[527] In her review of the film in the *New York Times*, Janet Maslin offered "one of (Betsy Heinman´s) main contributions to posterity may be putting (Jennifer) Lopez in a black leather trench coat here". New York Times, 26 June 1998. Available at: https://archive.nytimes.com/www.nytimes.com/library/film/062698sight-film-review.html (accessed 31st of August 2022).

[528] "Who "knows exactly how to translate Leonard's narrative voice to the screen" (Janet Maslin, loc cit). Challen, while also praising the script, reports Frank told him he enjoyed the work but didn´t want to be "typecast" as "the Leonard scriptwriter". (Challen, op cit p 142).

the post-escape times (flashbacks were *de riguer* at the time, courtesy of Christopher Nolan, Quentin Tarantino etc), (ii) a brief sequence of Foley unsuccessfully trying to get a job,[529] (iii) the elimination of Foley and Karen's age difference (iv), a shift of the main focus from Karen to Foley,[530] (v) a significant sanitization of the murder and rape scenes during the burglaries and (vi) a final sequence added to hint at a possible happy end.

Out of Sight merits practically unanimous praise by both Leonard scholars and the critical establishment. Challen considers it the "all-time-best Leonard movie"[531], essentially due to George Clooney's role as Jack Foley. Devlin, noting the film's disappointing box office, suggested ""if only critics bought movie tickets, *Out of Sight* would have had a different story",[532] going on to note Soderbergh kept the novel's Detroit vistas "to great effect": a city "(...) wrapped in a blanket of snow that cannot conceal its festering corruption".[533]

Critics don't normally buy tickets, but they agreed with Devlin. And since *Out of Sight* closed the golden age of Leonard adaptations started the previous year, it lent itself to an exercise of comparisons, mostly favourable, with the other films, both in terms of their intrinsic value and of their putative fidelity to the spirit and tone of Elmore Leonard. Roger Ebert famously if somewhat hyperbolically compared the Lopez/Clooney duo with the Bacall/Bogart

---

[529] A scene which Leonard reportedly thought wouldn't work, but upon evidence of the final cut changed his mind. (Challen, op. cit. p. 143).
[530] "It's her book but it's his movie". (Challen, loc. cit.).
[531] Challen, op. cit. p. 142.
[532] Devlin, op. cit. p. 144.
[533] Devlin, op. cit. p. 147. I'd agree with the appraisal of Detroit's depiction in the film, but don't see corruption as a theme either in the book or the film.

combo, remarking the film was "is a crime movie less interested in crime than in how people talk, flirt, lie and get themselves into trouble. The characters mosey through scenes existing primarily to savour the dialogue". He considered *Out Of Sight* the most faithful to Leonard's style of the coeval batch of film adaptations, "the first film to build on the enormously influential *Pulp Fiction* instead of simply mimicking it", and pointed out to the complexity of the timeline: "The movie's constructed like hypertext, so that, in a way, we can start watching at any point".[534] Likewise, Stephen Hunter, in the *Washington Post*, writes "the film floats forward and backward in time" and manages to consider that Soderbergh does a better job at this than Tarantino, totally missing the point: "(Soderbergh) handles the shifts more adroitly, always keeping us on track".[535] Maslin, in the aforequoted review, wrote that Elliot Davis's photography made Detroit look like the most romantic city in the world,[536] and Scott Frank's script knew "(…) exactly how to translate Leonard's narrative voice to the screen."[537] Emanuel Levy, in *Variety*, risked it "should do reasonably well at the box office", but cautioned "an intricate format of flashbacks (…) enrich the tale but may prove too demanding for

---

[534] *Roger Ebert*, https://www.rogerebert.com/apps/pbcs.dll/article?AID=/19980619/REVIEWS/806190304/1023 (accessed 31st August 2022).

[535] *Washington Post*, 26 June 1998 https://www.washingtonpost.com/wp-srv/style/longterm/movies/videos/outofsighthunter.htm (accessed 31st August 2022).

[536] Thereby belying Leonard´s own verdict:" There are cities that get by on their good looks, offer climate and scenery, views of mountains or oceans, rockbound or with palm trees. And there are cities like Detroit that have to work for a living". https://www.brainyquote.com/authors/elmore-leonard-quotes.

[537] *New York Times*, loc cit. Available at: https://archive.nytimes.com/www.nytimes.com/library/film/062698sight-film-review.html (accessed 31st August 2022).

mainstream viewers" (actually just a half dozen flashbacks to prison times, it's not like we're talking *Marienbad* here...). He also agreed "tech credits are roundly impressive" and *Out of Sight* was "in many respects, (...) more satisfying and faithful to Leonard's spirit than *Jackie Brown*."[538]

Typically for Steven Soderbergh, *Out of Sight* is nothing if not polished. Cinematography, production design, art direction all shine like new money. And the critics are right to point out that Leonard dialogue delivery is among the very best and several of the novel's vignettes, e.g. Detroit landmarks, or the hotel bar pick up scene, are captured to perfection. But to shine is not to burn. Accomplished illustration that it is, *Out of Sight* is an uncharacteristic film for Soderbergh, who might have been attracted to the novel to portray the elusiveness of the relationship between Karen and Foley, but whose signature "cold" style is awkward for caper. Mick LaSalle, in the *San Francisco Chronicle*, wrote it best: *Out of Sight* is "if not a minor masterpiece, certainly an estimable achievement".[539]

---

[538] Emanuel Levy, 'Out of Sight', *Variety*, 22 June 1998, https://variety.com/1998/film/reviews/out-of-sight-2-1200453964/ (accessed 31st August 2022).

[539] Mick LaSalle, 'Clooney Breaks Out / `ER' star finally makes a show of it in crime caper `Out of Sigh', *San Francisco Chronicle*, 26 June 1998, https://www.sfgate.com/movies/article/Clooney-Breaks-Out-ER-star-finally-makes-a-3002432.php (accessed 31st August 2022).

Be Cool (1998)

> *Be Cool*, 123 minutes, Universal 1998. Release date 26 June 1997. Directed by Steven Soderbergh. Written by Peter Steinfield. Produced by Danny De Vito, Michael Shamberg and Stacey Sher.
>
> Cast: Dwayne Johnson as Elliott Wilhelm, John Travolta as Chili Palmer, Uma Thurman as Edie Athens, Ariel Kebbel as Robin, Vince Vaugh as Raji, Seth Green as Shotgun (uncredited), Debi Mazar as Marla, Danny De Vito as Martin Weir, Harvey Keitel as Nick Carr.
>
> Cinematography: Jeffrey L Kimball; Editing: Sheldon Kahn; Music: John Powell. Art Direction: Lauren E Polizzi and Dan Webster.
>
> Awards: Austin Film Critics Association (Worst Film 2006).
>
> Festivals. Deauville, Helsinki, London, Oldenburg, Venice 1998.

The Story

"(...) the guy saved my life. The least I can do is put him in a movie". Chili Palmer, *Be Cool,* p. 244 (edition consulted Weidenfeld & Nicholson, 2017)

Be Cool was the 35th novel written by Elmore Leonard, published by Delacorte Press in 1999. Leonard wrote it as a sequel to *Get Shorty* upon invitation by an MGM executive, with a view to turning it into a sequel to the eponymous film. [540]

Synopsis: Ten years after *Get Shorty*, Chili Palmer has moved up in life and is now a B-movie-producer with a hit under his belt (*Get Leo*, a thinly disguised allusion to *Get Shorty*) and is looking for another one. While discussing business opportunities during lunch with record company exec Tommy Athens, the latter unexpectedly gets whacked, triggering a sequence of events which include Chili meeting wannabe rock star Linda Moon, shaking off Linda's shark agent Raji, setting Linda up to open for Aerosmith, causing an enmity with Raji, who hires contract killer Joe "Loop" to take Chili out, but Joe mistakenly takes out instead a Russian mob operative, mob which, turns out, was behind Tommy's assassination, resulting in Russians going after Raji while he tries to use his gay Samoan bodyguard Elliot to go after Chili, except Elliot is an aspiring actor and Chili promised him an audition so in the final showdown, instead of taking out Chilli, Elliot throws Raij out a window. At the same time, or rather, much earlier, Chili meets Tommy widow Elaine, for whom he develops a shine. Understandably, all these events inspire Chili to use them as a script for a future hit movie, the novel ending with Chilli uttering the *nec plus ultra* of tongue-in-cheek: "*Look, we got all the material we need. Why don't we give it to the screenwriter? Instead of us fucking up the story (...)*".

A rare case of novel/film symbiosis, at least for a writer of Leonard's stature, *Get Shorty* was reissued as film tie-in

---

[540] Challen, op. cit. p. 146.

when the film adaptation premiered.[541] Atypically for Leonard, it received mixed reviews,[542] revealing that Leonard going mercenary and meta was hit-and-miss depending on the reviewers sensitivities.[543] The author himself confessed to losing interest in the novel, as he found it too plotty, but Greg Sutter's expertise in, and research of, the music business revived his interest.[544]

On the miss/hit debate, I'm hit. I fully understand and accept the reservations of the missing school, and it may help being a canonist reader of Elmore Leonard to appreciate *Be Cool*. It is evidently, indeed ostensibly, the most self-referential book Leonard wrote, flaunting the sequel/screen rights pitch throughout with the certainty (some might have thought arrogance) that these were sure to come.[545] However, Leonard τόπων (defenestrations, impromptu shootings, non-committal love affairs) abound and he portrays LA, the novel's setting – which he reportedly didn't much like – with the same eloquence and perceptiveness he portrayed Detroit, Florida and all other places and times he set novels in. Leonard's dialogue is at its zenith and is the real star of the book. Contrary to what the above synopsis may lead to expect, once the initial situation – Tommy's shooting – triggers the action, the characters spend a good 80% of the novel chatting about film quotes and the ins and outs of the music scene and business in ways that are mostly completely unrelated to plot development, here more than anywhere else in Leonard a MacGuffin contrived as afterthought.

---

[541] Frankie Y Bailie, *From Book to Screen: Visual Clues of Casting*, in Rzepka, op (ed) cit p. 69.
[542] Challen, op. cit. p. 146.
[543] "a meta-fictional account of his own writing process" (Rzepka, op. cit. p. 202).
[544] Devlin op. cit. p. 25. For a detailed account of the birth of *Be Cool*, see Challen, op. cit. pp. 146-150.
[545] One million dollars, Leonard's then going rate. Cf. Devlin, op cit p 26.

The Director – F Gary Gray

Felix Gary Gray (New York, 1969) is an American film director and producer, music video director, and actor. Gray moved to South LA as a child, where he lived and grew up in Reagan-era gangland, which was for him a defining experience. He started working as a cameraman for Fox News at age 20 and in that capacity covered the 1992 Rodney King riots, experience he put to use in his most personal film, the NWA biopic *Straight Outta Compton* (2015).[546]

Around the time of the riots, Gray began his career directing music videos, many of which critically acclaimed and award-winning, such as *It Was a Good Day* by Ice Cube (1992), *Waterfalls* by TLC (1995) or *Keep Their Heads Ringin'*, by Dr. Dre (1995), a song from his feature film directorial debut, the comedy *Friday* (1995, directed at age 26, same as Steven Soderbergh's debut).[547] With the exception of the aforementioned *Straight Outta Compton*, Gray has since mostly directed action films and/or capers, such as *The Negotiator* (1998), *The Italian Job* (2003), or the film that got him this entry in this book, *Be Cool* (2005). He also directed the eighth instalment of the *Fast & Furious* franchise, *The Fate of the Furious* (2017),

---

[546] Gray said in an interview to *Deadline*: "I was a news cameraman at Fox during those riots, and we watched the verdict on monitors and I had to go down there, for myself, to see it because this was where I grew up". He added:" There was always something, in every one of my pictures, that I wish I could go back and do differently. I don't feel that way here". Available at: https://deadline.com/2015/08/f-gary-gray-straight-outta-compton-q-and-a-1201498938/ (accessed 31st August 2022).

[547] F Gary Gray vastly beat his own goal of becoming a feature film director by the age of 45, an arbitrary benchmark he set himself in his youth because he thought that was about the age Steven Spielberg had when Gray became aware of him, with a grey beard an all (Spielberg was actually 25 when he first directed a feature film). Available at: https://deadline.com/2015/08/f-gary-gray-straight-outta-compton-q-and-a-1201498938/ (accessed 31st August 2022).

which is the 19th-highest-grossing film of all time, as well as the first film directed by an African-American to gross over $1 billion worldwide.[548]

I can't tell if a film is directed by an African-American, an Eskimo or an Albanian no matter how close I look but, in the US, race is a thing so a considerable part of Gray's rewards and accolades are related thereto, namely, the Best Director award at the 2004 Black American Film Festival for his work on *The Italian Job*, [549] the Ivan Dixon Award of Achievement from the Black Hollywood Education and Resource Center,[550] the African American Film Critics Association 2004 Special Achievement Award,[551] the Pioneer Director award from the Pan-African Film and Arts Festival in 2010, as well as being named one of the "50 Best and Brightest African Americans Under 40" by *Black Enterprise* magazine.

Gray says he prefers to direct next to the camera, an approach he said he learned from Kevin Spacey: "Actors feel safer, knowing you're with them and not just directing from afar and giving them adjustments out of nowhere (...) The other thing is, you don't have to swing for the fences with performances because you're right there and you can see all the nuances that they bring in the choices they make".[552]

---

[548] 'Box-Office Milestone: 'Fate of the Furious' Crosses $1B Globally', *The Hollywood Reporter*, 30 April 2017. https://www.hollywoodreporter.com/movies/movie-news/box-office-milestone-fate-furious-crosses-1b-globally-998794/ (accessed 31st August 2022).
[549] Available at: https://www.abff.com/miami/archives/history-of-winners/2004-winners/ (accessed 31st 2022)
[550] Available at: https://www.empireonline.com/people/f-gary-gray/ (accessed 31st August 2022).
[551] *Empire,* loc. cit.
[552] *Deadline*, loc. cit.

The Film

Be Cool was "vigorously marketed as a sequel" to *Get Shorty*,[553] reuniting the *Pulp Fiction* (Quentin Tarantino, 1995) team of Uma Thurman and John Travolta, the latter repeating his *Get Shorty* role as Chili Palmer.[554] The script, by Peter Steinfield, retains the novel's general narrative structure and much of the dialogue, while seeking to give it a more structured plot. Innovations are Raji (Vince Vaugh, strained) turning from black to white, but dressing, talking and acting gansta rap black, and violence generally tuned down or rendered farcically, e.g. the final defenestration becoming a slapstick accidental non-lethal self-immolation.

Healthy box office (95M$ on a 53M$ budget)[555] notwithstanding, *Be Cool* bombed with the critics, who generally - and more forcefully - aligned with the "it ain't funny" school of thought of some of the novel's reviewers. In *The Chicago Reader*, Jonathan Rosenbaum called it a "dumbass sequel", Roger Ebert considered it a "...classic species of bore: a self-referential movie with no self to refer to."[556] In *The New York Times*, Manohla Dargis wrote "like the characters, the scenes pile up but go nowhere". Unkindest, Joe Morgenstern wrote in *The Wall Street Journal* the film "...manages the dubious trick of being both execrable and boring". Few shared the condescension of Mick LaSalle in *The San Francisco Chronicle*: "it doesn't cut too deep, but

---

[553] Frankie Y Bailie, *From Book to Screen: Visual Clues of Casting*, in Rzepka, op (ed) cit p. 69.
[554] Travolta got paid to act 20 times more the Leonard did for the script rights. Cf Devlin, op cit p 26.
[555] *Box Office Mojo*, https://www.boxofficemojo.com/release/rl2101642753/ (accessed 31st August 2022).
[556] Ebert, 'Be Cool', *Roger Ebert*, 2005, https://www.rogerebert.com/reviews/be-cool-2005 (accessed August 31st 2022).

it's amusing". The director himself evaluated the film negatively. In an interview for *Deadline*, he said: "...when I walked into *Be Cool*, it was rated R and then at the last minute in preproduction I was told, 'Well, you have to make this PG-13´. I should have walked off the film. (...) Chili Palmer said the word f*ck 54 times in *Get Shorty*. To be able to say it once in the sequel? It robbed authenticity (...) We missed the mark with *Be Cool*. (...) You can't assume something is going to be good, just because."

No, you can't. But, being bad, *Be Cool* isn't that bad. It is not remotely at the level the best Leonard adaptations, it is guilty of lazy and formulaic planning and execution, The Rock, playing Elliot, excepted, all actor sleepwalking through the film in self-parody mode, but it remains a mildly enjoyable rant that scores enough undemanding laughs with very unPC farcical gags that would have caused the press to crucify the director weren't he black. A few good ideas include having Uma Thurman (playing Elaine) sport a black t-shirt with punk lettering reading "Widow" and a billboard in the background of the final shot announcing a film featuring Elliot and Nicole Kidman entitled *Samoan Rendez-vous*. *The Washington Post*'s Stephen Hunter summed it up best: "It's kind of -- hmmmm, less than good, a little better than not bad, almost all right, mediocre without being grating, sort of in the C-minus-to-C-minus-minus range." [557] Ultimately, and totally coincidentally, *Be Cool* is an appropriate coda and illustration of the mean qualities of the Leonard film canon.

---

[557] *The Washington Post*, March 4, 2005, https://www.washingtonpost.com/wp-dyn/content/article/2005/03/04/AR2005062900979.html (accessed 31st August 2022).

Conclusion

There's no point pretending one can come to the end of an exercise like this without an unhealthy dose of confirmation bias. Plus, I read each novel before seeing each film – except *Jackie Brown*, which I saw when it first came out, and *The Tall T*, which I had seen a few times in the past, but even these I saw again after reading the respective novels – and that very often works against the film. Plus, seeing this series of films in this manner inevitably creates a mindset different from that of the "pure" film viewer. Indeed, the body of work reviewed in this book isn't a body of work for any purpose other than that of this book, and it makes sense to analyse it commonly only in the context of its common literary source.

Still, some remarks are possible: (i) with only a few exceptions, the films don't diverge much from the novels, either because Leonard wrote the scripts himself, or contributed to them, or because the adapting writers wisely saw fit to mostly stick to plot and dialogue; (ii) with perhaps a few more exceptions, Leonard's signature dialogue is often poorly delivered and its effect spoiled, so general fidelity to letter seldom resulted in fidelity to the spirit, which is OK in the several cases in which some other spirit was extant, but still seems to reinforce the thesis that, pace Richard Corliss, the films were, sometimes for better and most times for worse, works mainly imputable to the director rather than to the writer(s), and finally (iii) the same goes for the absence of most recurrent themes of Leonard's writing, which are apparent only occasionally and only after looking hard.

Ultimately, and as indicated in the introduction, the main characteristic of these 31 films is its diversity, ranging from the seminal (*The Tall T, Jackie Brown*) to the dismal (*Border Shootout*). Let Leonard have the last word: "My characters are what the books are about: the plot just kind of comes along. But movies always want to concentrate on the action".[558] But he also once said "I've always seen my books as movies."[559]

Finally, I can´t honestly rob the reader of an attempt at a conclusive judgement of these films, which might go as follows: We could categorize the films as (i) good, but not "Leonardian" (maybe four or five) (ii) not very good but a fair evocation of Leonard´s universe (same), (iii) both (two or three) and (iv) neither (the rest). The previous chapters sought to leave an impression of where I feel the films stand, so I offer the following ranking:

Top 5 Novels:

- *Swag*
- *The Big Bounce*
- *Pronto*
- *Out of Sight*
- *Split Images*

Top 5 films:

- *Jackie Brown*
- *The Tall T*
- *Car Chaser*
- *Killshot*
- *The Big Bounce II*

---

[558] Interview to *The Guardian*, July 3, 2004.
[559] *The Elmore Leonard Paradox,* Christopher Orr, Jan/Feb 2014 Issue, *The Atlantic,* https://www.theatlantic.com/magazine/archive/2014/01/the-elmore-leonard-paradox/355734/ (accessed 28 September 2021).

Generally speaking, the books are better.

Sources and Bibliography

My first approach to online information was to use Ecosia, but that often proved insufficient so I had to frequently turn to the mainstream search engine monopolies. Else, the following individual sources seem worth mentioning:

On Elmore Leonard's life and work:

- Elmore Leonard has an official website (http://www.elmoreleonard.com/) with profuse information and illustrations;
- *Elmore Leonard's Criminal Records*, a documentary produced in 1991 for BBC Television is available at the independent video archive Media Burn (https://mediaburn.org/video/elmore-leonards-criminal-records);
- Charlie Rose's TV 1999 interview with Elmore Leonard and Martin Amis is widely available; see for instance: https://charlierose.com/videos/21702 ;
- Charles Rzekpa's extensive interviews with Leonard, carried out in 2009 and 2010, which constituted the basis for his later biography, are available at the *Crime Culture* website: https://www.crimeculture.com/?page_id=283 ;
- *Elmore Leonard – But Don't Try to Write*, a 2021 documentary directed by John Mulholland, which concentrates on Leonard's Westerns.

Regarding bibliographical sources, there are, to my knowledge, six books about Elmore Leonard, from all of which I have borrowed extensively:

- David Geherin's *Elmore Leonard*, published in 1989, has the merit of having inaugurated the field and set the standard, biographically, thematically and analytically, for Leonardian studies. It might be the overall best source for Elmore Leonard's life and work, if it didn't miss out on its final quarter century;
- James Devlin's *Elmore Leonard*, published 10 years later, covers the 90's and contributes several thematic insights into Leonard's work not fully addressed or developed by Geherin. Although certainly an interesting read for Leonard fans, it falls clearly short of the previous biography, occasionally reading more like a PhD thesis than a fully matured scholarly work;
- Paul Challen's *Get Dutch! A Biography of Elmore Leonard* was published shortly after Devlin's, a fact the author himself acknowledged but carried on regardless, persuaded there would be room in the market for more than one look at Leonard's life and work. He was right: unlike the previous authors, Challen is not an academic but a sports journalist and lifetime Leonard fan. His writing is comparatively unassuming and stays mostly clear of deep literary analysis, but it is an entertaining read and contributes to shed light on several aspects of Leonard's life and work other biographers missed.
- Charles Rzepka's *Being Cool: The Work of Elmore Leonard*, written shortly before Leonard's death, has the merit of encompassing the entirety of the writer's career and also benefits from all the previous literature. It is in several respects the most insightful of the scholarly works on Leonard's writing, if at

times verging on the speculative and somewhat unsparing with (what in the US is referred to as) post-structuralist jargon.
- Guilio Sedato's *Una commedia americana – Temi, innovazioni e religione nell'opera di Elmore Leonard*, published in 2018, is an interesting and insightful, if essentially monothematic, PhD thesis that somehow found its way to commercial publishing. To my knowledge it hasn't been translated into English. It remains the sole work on Elmore Leonard authored by an European, the present effort excepted.
- Charles Rzepka's edited *Critical Essays on Elmore Leonard: If It Sounds Like Writing*, published in 2020, brings together the editor, Geherin and several other scholars in a thematic survey of Leonard's work and presents 5 essays on 5 of his novels, of which 4 were brought to the screen. As always in works of this nature, quality varies. A number of the essays included seem to me to suffer from what I would diplomatically call academic overreach, but some, including David Geherin's *Sense of Place* and Kris Mechalski's piece on *Hombre*, are worth the book's price.

On the films, the online sources were mostly standard: *Box Office Mojo*, *IMDb*, *Metacritic* and *Rotten Tomatoes*. *IMDb* and *Metacritic* rankings of films based on Elmore Leonard's work, both incomplete, can be found here:

- https://www.imdb.com/filmosearch/?explore=title_type&role=nm0001465&ref_=filmo_ref_typ&sort=user_rating,desc&mode=detail&page=1&title_type=movie%20and%20here

- https://www.metacritic.com/person/elmore-leonard?filter-options=movies&sort_options=metascore&num_items=30

Several other "indie" rankings, equally incomplete, can be found here:

- https://www.indiewire.com/2013/05/from-best-to-worst-elmore-leonard-movie-adaptations-98187/
- https://theplaylist.net/from-best-to-worst-elmore-leonard-movie-adaptations-20130514/
- https://lebeauleblog.com/2015/10/23/worst-to-first-ranking-elmore-leonard-adaptations/
- https://www.ranker.com/list/movies-based-on-elmore-leonard-books/ranker-film

The first two are the more informative and entertaining.

Bibliographic sources are scattered throughout the book's footnotes and warrant no further listing. My personal auteurist prejudices are apparent in a relatively disproportionate number of references to "classic" *Cahiers du Cinema* or Andrew Sarris, which impact mostly the first half of the second part of the book. These may be frequent, but I dare think not dominant and do hope not overwhelming.

As for the films themselves, the vast majority are easily available, for free or a rental fee, in the usual mainstream streaming websites. The exceptions were (i) *The Moonshine War*, which, although from a major director (even if of limited commercial value today), was available only on DVD, (ii) *Desperado*, which, as previously mentioned (p.118, footnote 394), involved purchasing a download from a questionable online business I had the opportunity to describe at the appropriate moment, (iii) *Pronto,* which involved purchasing a VHS tape online and burning it into a DVD, and

(iv) the absolute winner: *Split Images*. Globally unavailable and an attempt to contact the director directly having proved unfruitful, I eventually managed to unearth an Australian VHS edition on Ebay Australia, have it shipped to the US, burned into a DVD and finally watch it. It took months.

Writers-on-Film Bodrum Lisbon London New York

www.ingramcontent.com/pod-product-compliance
Lightning Source LLC
Chambersburg PA
CBHW050241220526
45465CB00017B/99